THE
NORTH-WEST
FRONTIER

THE PROBLEM

of

THE NORTH-WEST FRONTIER

1890-1908

With a survey of policy
since 1849

by

C. COLLIN DAVIES

Ph.D. (Cantab.)

Late Captain 2/1st K.G.O. Gurkha Rifles
Lecturer in Indian History
School of Oriental Studies
University of London

CAMBRIDGE

AT THE UNIVERSITY PRESS

1932

CAMBRIDGE UNIVERSITY PRESS
Cambridge, New York, Melbourne, Madrid, Cape Town,
Singapore, São Paulo, Delhi, Mexico City

Cambridge University Press
The Edinburgh Building, Cambridge CB2 8RU, UK

Published in the United States of America by Cambridge University Press, New York

www.cambridge.org
Information on this title: www.cambridge.org/9781107662094

First published 1932
First paperback edition 2013

A catalogue record for this publication is available from the British Library

ISBN 978-1-107-66209-4 Paperback

To

PROFESSOR HAROLD TEMPERLEY

CONTENTS

MAPS

[1] From Colonel H. C. Wylly, *From the Black Mountain to Waziristan,* by permission of Messrs Macmillan and Co., Ltd.

PREFACE

This volume, which deals with one of the most complicated frontier problems in the world, opens with the search for the best possible strategic frontier upon the north-western borders of Hindustan, a frontier which at the same time would satisfy political, ethnological, and geographical requirements. It traces the growth of the Russian menace throughout the nineteenth century, until in 1907 the increasing danger from Germany forced England and Russia to compose their differences in Central Asia. The advantages and disadvantages of the four possible lines of resistance, the Indus, the old Sikh line, the Durand boundary, and the so-called scientific frontier, are dealt with in considerable detail. In the chapter on Anglo-Afghan relations an attempt is made to prove that Afghan intrigues amongst the Pathan and Baluch tribes have been a more potent cause of strife and unrest than has sometimes been supposed. An examination of the ethnological problem leads the writer to the conclusion that no single policy, operating from the snow-clad peaks of Chitral to the coasts of Mekran, could possibly be successful. The chapter on the frontier in the 'nineties shows how the forward policy pursued during those years produced its natural result, the tribal conflagration of 1897. Separate chapters are devoted to the problem of tribal control and the methods of coercion adopted by the British; the policy of Lord Curzon and its consummation, the formation of the Frontier Province; the fruitless efforts at finding a solution of the Mahsud question; and the depredations of the northern Afridi and Mohmand tribes leading to the expeditions of 1908. Other questions discussed are the arms traffic in the Persian Gulf, the causes of tribal unrest, and the baneful influence of English party politics upon important problems of imperial defence.

The student of the frontier must needs walk warily. Innumerable pamphlets have been written on this subject for the purpose of furthering party interests. No serious historical student is foolish enough to suppose that the papers presented to Parliament contain all the truth, but, although a judicious pruning of these official records must of necessity take place, there can be no excuse for the deliberate garbling of the Blue Books as was the case with the letters of Sir Alexander Burnes to the Government of India. Valuable as are the memoirs of generals and frontier administrators, in very many cases they lack, because of the official position of the writers, that fullness of revelation and freedom of discussion which a work of this kind demands.

In the following volume I have sketched the history of the Indian borderland almost entirely from official documents and original sources. Several years have been found necessary for the reading of these voluminous materials and, if it were only for this reason, I could not possibly claim to have made no mistakes. Nevertheless, in laying before the public the result of much anxious thought and often laborious investigation, I can conscientiously claim that I have above everything else taken great pains to be accurate.

To explain the manner in which I have dealt with the various sources at my disposal would require an elaborate introduction. My indebtedness, however, has been specifically acknowledged in footnotes and in the bibliography which I have thought fit to append to this volume. A glance at this bibliography will show the use that has been made of the Persian and Russian records deposited in the Public Record Office. The account of the proceedings of Russia in Central Asia, the history of Afghanistan, and of Anglo-Afghan relations are based upon an extremely valuable and conveniently arranged series (F.O. 65). Since the Foreign Office records cannot be consulted after the year 1885, the student, for events subsequent to this date, is forced to rely on administrative, intelligence, and military reports. The chief sources, however, for the history of the Indian frontier are the Secret Border Reports in the Political Department of the India Office. I wish to take this opportunity of thanking the India Office authorities for granting me permission to read these secret reports, and for their kindness in allowing me access to the confidential publications of the Government of India entitled *Frontier and Overseas Expeditions from India*.

In addition to many years of research in this country this history is the result of some years of residence and active service on the frontier itself. I was fortunate enough to serve through the Third Afghan War of 1919 and in the operations in Waziristan from 1921 to 1922. Part of my service was spent in the settled district of Peshawar, and I can therefore claim to have a certain amount of first-hand knowledge of the racial characteristics, customs, and religious beliefs of the tribesmen, and also of the topography of certain frontier districts.

Five of the chapters which follow have already seen the light of day and are included by the kind permission of Messrs William Clowes and Sons and Lieutenant-Colonel Cuthbert Headlam, D.S.O., M.P., the editor of the *Army Quarterly*.

In conclusion I desire to express my thanks for the valuable assistance which I have received in various forms from Sir Harcourt Butler, G.C.S.I., G.C.I.E.; Professor Dodwell of the School of Oriental Studies and the University of London; Sir Hugh Barnes, K.C.S.I., K.C.V.O.; Professor Holland Rose; Doctor A. C. Haddon; the late Mr G. P. Moriarty; the late Sir Valentine Chirol; and Miss Monckton Jones. I am indebted to Mr Douglas Donald, C.I.E., late D.I.G. of the Indian Police, for much valuable information about Tirah and Kurram, while the sympathetic interest of my wife has been a great encouragement throughout the preparation of this volume.

Formal acknowledgments are always inadequate, yet I would here express my indebtedness for his invaluable aid to Professor Harold Temperley, O.B.E., Professor of Modern History in the University of Cambridge, without whose inspiring guidance this book would never have been published.

C. C. D.

April 1932

Chapter I

FRONTIER POLICY: THE IMPERIAL PROBLEM

Frontiers are indeed the razor's edge on which hang suspended the modern issues of war or peace, of life or death to nations.

Lord Curzon, Romanes Lecture, 1907.

The importance of a frontier lies in the pressure behind it, the more populated a district the greater the pressure. So finely adjusted are European frontiers that no Power can annex a town or even the smallest village without disturbing the balance elsewhere. In South America, where boundaries are still very imperfect, there is no excitement about them normally; and, because the various districts are not over-populated, there is not the same intensity of atmosphere. Midway between these two extremes is the position occupied by the North-West Frontier of India lying between the Russians in Central Asia and the British in India. The advance of either Power has not been fatal in the European sense; there is really no balance of power here, only the struggle between these two great Powers. Nevertheless, it can be stated without any fear of contradiction that the most prolific cause of strife between nations has been this vexed question of frontiers.

All nations and great empires have continually striven to strengthen their boundaries, and to make their frontiers as strategically perfect as possible. In Asia, throughout the past century, two great Powers, separated by the mountains of Afghanistan and the deserts of Persia, were continually drawing closer and closer together, until, at one time, it seemed as if the whole of the debatable area which separated them would, sooner or later, be annexed by the stronger or be divided by agreement. At the root of our wars with Afghanistan, in 1839 and in 1878, was this desire to strengthen the existing bulwarks on India's only vulnerable frontier. Both in 1878 and in 1885, England and Russia were on the verge of war, owing to the former's dread of Russia's aggressive policy in Central Asia. That this fear of Russia, a fear at times amounting almost to a panic, was the real cause of the Second Afghan War (1878–80) is now generally recognized. The Panjdeh incident is too well known to need any description here.

Any great Power that fails adequately to protect its frontiers ceases to be great; any Empire that neglects this important duty of self-preservation is eventually overthrown. India, unguarded, with the mountain passes of the north-west unsecured, became the prey of Asiatic freebooters; Rome fell because her dykes were not strong enough to hold back the flood of barbarian inroads; and, in the eighteenth century, Poland, with no natural frontiers, had to submit to being partitioned.

From the earliest days of the British connection with India there have been two opposing forces at work, a forward tendency, and a policy which sought to restrict, or to prevent, expansion. Contrary to the wishes of the Directors of the East India Company and of fox-hunting politicians at home, British rule was extended in India, until the mountains of the north-west were reached. Governors-General, pledged to a policy of non-annexation and non-intervention, were sent out from England, but, in the majority of cases, they found themselves forced, like the Russians in Central Asia, to move forward and acquire fresh territories. Although it may be possible to overstate this theory, that the only alternative to retrogression is aggrandizement, still the fact remains that the Act of 1784, which declared schemes of conquest to be repugnant to the wish, honour and policy of the nation, was followed, after a short time, by the conquests of Wellesley, which, in importance, can be compared only with the annexations of Dalhousie. At first our conquests were forced upon us by French intrigues within India, and by a desire to blot out the Maratha pest. It was an external menace from the direction of Central Asia that forced us to garrison the gates of the north-west.

From the conquest of the Panjab, in 1849, frontier policy was in the hands of administrators of the Lawrence, or "non-intervention" school, but the arrival of Lord Lytton, in 1876, marked the end of what has been contemptuously termed "masterly inactivity". It was the Second Afghan War and the consequent occupation of Afghan territory that impressed upon statesmen the necessity for a scientific frontier. Military strategists became divided into two opposing camps, the Forward and the Stationary. Both these terms are unfortunate in that they can both be subdivided into the extremists and the moderates. The extreme section of the Forward School did not know where their advances would stop; the moderates desired the best possible strategical frontier with the least possible advance. On the other hand, the extreme advocates of non-intervention would have held the Indus line; the moderates were inclined to an advance, if it could have been proved to them that Russia constituted any real menace.

What then is the true frontier of India on her north-western borders, and what is our best line of defence? There are really four possible lines of resistance: the river Indus; the old Sikh line, which roughly corresponds to the administrative boundary; the Durand line, delimited in 1893 and demarcated, as far as possible, in the succeeding years; and the so-called scientific frontier stretching from Kabul through Ghazni to Kandahar.

The Duke of Wellington may be cited as an example of a famous general who advocated meeting an enemy on the banks of the Indus, but, it must be remembered, this was only proposed as a temporary expedient in 1808; no permanent occupation of this line was advocated. He qualified his views in the following words:

> The art of crossing rivers is now so well understood, and has been so frequently practised, and so invariably, I believe, with success, in the late wars in Europe, that we cannot hope to defend the Indus, as a barrier....I have no great reliance upon that river as the barrier to India.[1]

Early writers went astray in supposing that the Indus was once the north-west frontier of India. This is the origin of the "Back to the Indus" cry, which fortunately is seldom heard nowadays. One thing is certain: the Indus frontier, in the literal sense of the term, never existed. The British inherited their frontier from the Sikhs who never held the river line, but the foothills towards the independent Pathan country.

The greatest exponent of the Indus boundary was Lord Lawrence, who was strongly opposed to any forward move beyond the trans-Indus foothills. He advocated meeting any invader in the valley of the Indus; that it would be an act of folly and weakness to give battle at any great distance from our base; and, that the longer distance an invading army had to march through Afghanistan and the tribal country, the more harassed it would be.[2] He was of opinion that our true policy lay in attacking invading forces as they debouched from the mountain passes. Consequently, he objected to any extension of roads and railways towards Afghanistan and advocated that the territories of the amir should be left undeveloped, so as to render the passage of an army as difficult as possible. During the anxious period of the Mutiny, Lawrence proposed that Peshawar should be evacuated and the left bank of the Indus held in its stead. Fortunately the wiser counsels of Edwardes, James, Nicholson and Cotton prevailed with Lord Canning who was Governor-General at the time. It is now generally recognized that retirement would

[1] *Supplementary Despatches of Duke of Wellington*, IV, 592–601.
[2] *Parl. Papers*, 1878–9, LXXVII (73), 15.

have been a colossal blunder. Not only would it have meant loss of prestige, but it would have been followed by a deluge of Sikhs, Pathans and Afghans upon Delhi. Edwardes regarded Peshawar as "the anchor" of the Panjab, the removal of which would have caused the whole ship to drift to sea. On 7 August, 1857, Lord Canning telegraphed to Lawrence, "Hold on to Peshawar to the last". India was saved.

In his book entitled *Backwards or Forwards*, Colonel Hanna makes the somewhat startling statement that nature has rendered the Indus frontier so exceptionally strong as to merit the epithet invulnerable.[1] The greatest military authorities, however, are of opinion that a river is not a good line of defence, in that it can always be forced by an enterprising general. The history of invasions from Central Asia bears eloquent testimony to the fact that the Indus has never constituted a real barrier. The defensive capacity of a river depends very much upon whether the defenders' bank commands the other. This is not the case with the Indus, where the left bank is flat and is frequently commanded by the right. Although many of the defects of the old days have been remedied by improved communications in the rear, the natural defects still remain. The Indus is continually shifting its course, and, when in flood, overflows its banks for miles on either side. Even so recently as 1923 the Government of India approved of a scheme for checking the further erosion of this river, which was threatening to carry away the town of Dera Ismail Khan.[2] Again, the unhealthiness of the Indus valley renders it unsuitable as an area for the concentration of troops. Perhaps the weightiest argument that can be brought forward against meeting an enemy on the banks of the Indus is the disastrous moral effect such a course would have upon the inhabitants of the Indian peninsula.

These defects not only make the river a weak line of de-

---

[1] Hanna, *Indian Problems*, No. 3, p. 111.
[2] *North-West Frontier Province Administration Report*, 1922–3, p. vii.

fence, but they also render it a bad political boundary, if it were ever decided to evacuate the trans-Indus districts. As an example of the difficulties of a river as a permanent boundary, Lord Curzon mentions that: "The vagaries of the Helmund in Seistan, where it is the boundary between Persia and Afghanistan, have led to two Boundary Commissions in thirty years".[1]

Lastly, the "Back to the Indus" cry becomes absurd when it is examined from the point of view of the inhabitants of the modern North-West Frontier Province. Not only would withdrawal mean loss of prestige, but it would also be a gross betrayal of those peoples to whom we have extended our beneficent rule.

This disposes of the Indus, both as a line of defence and as a permanent boundary, and brings us to a consideration of the present administrative boundary, which we inherited, with all its strategical imperfections, from our predecessors the Sikhs. Lord Roberts, speaking on frontier defence in the House of Lords, on 7 March, 1898, stated that, when he was commander-in-chief in India, he had never contemplated defending this line. It might serve a useful purpose if we had to deal only with the local tribal problem, but as a line of resistance, to be manned against an invading foe, it was unthinkable.

A frontier more than one thousand miles in length, with a belt of huge mountains in its front, inhabited by thousands of warlike men,...seemed to me then, as it does now, an impossible frontier, and one on which no scheme for the defence of India could be safely based.[2]

Lord Roberts, a firm believer in the Forward Policy, laid great stress upon the necessity for good communications. The money that had been squandered upon useless fortifications should have been spent on the construction of roads and rail-

[1] Romanes Lecture, 1907, p. 21.
[2] Debate in the House of Lords, 7 March, 1898.

ways. In his opinion, all strategical points should be connected with the Indian rail system, so that, in the event of invasion, troops could be quickly despatched towards the scene of action. He was firmly convinced that this massing of troops would be the essential factor deciding the conflict.

"Those who attempt," wrote Napoleon, "to defend a frontier by an extended line or cordon of troops will find themselves weak at all points, for everything human has its limits; artillery, money, good officers, able generals, all are limited in action and quantity, and dissemination everywhere implies strength nowhere."[1]

The Durand line, which demarcates, where demarcation is possible, the respective spheres of influence of the amir and the Government of India over the frontier tribes, possesses no strategic value at all. The Khost salient between Kurram and Waziristan is but one of its many strategical imperfections. This disposes of three possible lines of resistance. The real frontier we are called upon to defend in India is the mountain barrier. There is an overwhelming consensus of opinion that, in order to do so, it is essential to cross the Indus and prevent the enemy from debouching on to the plains. To defend a mountain barrier, it is necessary to do more than this. The defenders must be in a position to see what is taking place on the other side. Nothing but disaster could result from a policy which forced us to remain in a state of passive defence while Russia consolidated her position in Afghanistan, which has ever served as a strategical base for the conquest of Hindustan.

Any great Power is ultimately forced to absorb barbaric states contiguous to its frontiers. This is the verdict of history: it is certainly a true account of what the British have been compelled to do in India. The greatest advance from the old red line of the maps was the result of Sir Robert Sandeman's work in Baluchistan. The strategical importance of Quetta must now be discussed.

[1] Quoted p. 109. Bird, Sir W. D., *The Direction of War*, 1925.

The proposal to occupy Quetta dates back to the days of General John Jacob of Sind fame, who, in 1856, urged Lord Canning to garrison this important point of vantage. To Jacob the British frontier system was that of an army without outposts. Thoroughly convinced 'of the importance of the Bolan route, he recommended that troops should be stationed at Quetta, for, as he pointed out, with Quetta in our hands we could threaten the flank of any army advancing upon the Khyber.[1] Sir John Elphinstone, the Governor of Bombay, warned Jacob that his proposal would fall on deaf ears, for the disasters of the First Afghan War, 1839–42, were not so easily forgotten by those who controlled the destinies of the Indian Empire. In his letter of 18 October, 1856, Lord Canning rejected the proposal on the grounds that, surrounded by hostile tribes and cut off from its true base, the isolated position of the garrison would be extremely precarious.

Unfortunately for those who desired an advance into Baluchistan, the next time the proposal was brought forward it had to face the united opposition of Lord Lawrence and his council. This time, in 1866, the proposal emanated from Lieutenant-Colonel Sir Henry Green, the Political Superintendent of Upper Sind. The political situation had altered considerably since the days of Jacob. Slowly but surely the Russian giant was advancing across the wastes of Central Asia. In 1865, Tashkent had fallen, and in the same year commenced that struggle which was to end in the subjugation of the khanate of Bokhara. Green pointed out that the British right to despatch troops into Kalat territory, whenever that step should become necessary, had been recognized by the Kalat Treaty of 1854.[2] The time for such a step had now arrived. Therefore, to improve the existing scheme of

---

[1] *Views and Opinions of General John Jacob* (ed. Pelly), p. 349. Lord Napier of Magdala, who objected to Jacob's original proposal, was in favour of the occupation of Quetta in 1877, *vide* F.O. 65, 1031, memo. dated May, 1877.   [2] For text see Aitchison, XI, 212–13.

frontier defence, he proposed that Quetta should be garrisoned and connected by rail with Karachi which would serve as an important base for operations. Green's recommendation was supported by Sir Bartle Frere, the Governor of Bombay, but the members of the Viceroy's council, as could only be expected of the champions of non-intervention, were unanimous in their opposition to any fresh advances. Lord Lawrence decided that the proposed advance was undesirable, in that it would create a feeling of unrest both in Persia and at Kabul. Concerning the best method of meeting any Russian advance, he wrote:

The winning side will be the one that refrains from entangling itself in the barren mountains which now separate the two Empires...the Afghans themselves, foreseeing this result, are likely in the end to throw their weight on the same side.[1]

Sir W. R. Mansfield, the commander-in-chief, was convinced that the Bolan route could be best defended by holding its eastern and not its western extremity. Lieutenant-Colonel Lumsden, the deputy quartermaster-general, pleaded that any advance beyond the existing frontier would mean an additional strain on an already overburdened exchequer. The fairest criticism of Green's proposal was that of Sir H. M. Durand, who advocated the improvement and completion of the Indus frontier group of railways. At the same time he recognized that an advance might be essential in the future.

Ten years passed. The exponents of "masterly inactivity" were no longer predominant in the Viceroy's council chamber; Khiva had fallen before Cossack hosts which were drawing nearer and nearer to the gates of India; and, more dangerous still, the estrangement of the amir, Sher Ali, had brought us to the brink of war. At last, in 1876, it was decided to occupy Quetta. It was not, however, until the following year that British troops actually took possession of this important position.

[1] *Parl. Papers*, 1878–9, LXXVII (73), 15.

The importance of Quetta, the "bastion of the frontier", is now almost universally recognized. Quetta, or Kwattar, which is the Pashtu word for a fort, occupies a position of extraordinary natural strength and of commanding strategical importance in the centre of the highland part of Baluchistan. Protected on the south-west by the lofty Chehiltan range and on the north-east by the Zarghun plateau, it dominates all the southern approaches to the Indus valley, for, as Sir Thomas Holdich has pointed out, "all roads south of Herat lead to Quetta".[1] Its strategical importance has been considerably enhanced by the construction of the Sind-Pishin railway, which owed its inception to the transport difficulties experienced in the Second Afghan War. An admirable account of the construction of this famous line and of the heroic efforts of General Sir James Browne is already in existence.[2]

In rapid succession to the occupation of Quetta came war with Afghanistan, from 1878 to 1880. During this struggle the question of the so-called scientific frontier was broached—should we hold on to the Kabul-Ghazni-Kandahar line? It was an extremely complicated problem that faced both military strategists and administrators. Some extremists advocated the retention of all our recent conquests in Afghanistan; others recommended a complete withdrawal, even to the banks of the Indus. But amongst the moderates the stumbling-block was the retention of, or withdrawal from, Kandahar. The question was further complicated by a discussion as to the relative merits and demerits of the Khyber, Kurram, and Bolan as channels of communication with Afghanistan. How many lines of communication were to be kept open; were we to hold both the western and eastern extremities; were they to be guarded by regulars or by tribal levies?

Lord Roberts was in favour of relinquishing all our con-

---

[1] Holdich, *The Indian Borderland*, p. 49.
[2] Innes, *The Life and Times of General Sir James Browne*, ch. xv and xvi.

quests with the exception of Kandahar. In his opinion our resources did not justify our keeping open more than one line of communications. Comparing the Kurram and Khyber routes, he pointed out that Kurram could be garrisoned by British troops stationed on the Peiwar; that the Turis were friendly; that the Shutargardan pass was closed only for about three months in the year, but could be crossed by an enterprising commander, even in the depth of winter. He was convinced that the Kurram was the best route for attacking Kabul, because the Sang-i-Nawishta defile, five miles from that city, was the only place at which any effective resistance could be expected. On the other hand, the only portion of the Khyber approach ever blocked by snow was the Lataband pass; and this only for about three days in the year. The great disadvantages of the Khyber route were the unhealthy climate during the intense heat of the summer months, and the fact that an army would be surrounded by extremely fanatical tribes. The advantages of the Khyber route in those days were chiefly political and commercial. If Afghanistan ever became a strongly united state, it was his opinion that we should hold either or both routes, since they afforded the quickest means of coercing Kabul. It is interesting to note that Lord Roberts was in favour of the withdrawal of the greater part of the European garrison from the fever-pit of Peshawar to some place on the left bank of the Indus, near Campbellpore. The important point to remember is that he was prepared to sacrifice both these routes, if only the Bolan and Kandahar were retained.[1]

The retention of Kandahar was advocated on military, political, and commercial grounds. Situated at the junction

[1] Those who agreed with Roberts as to the advisability of retaining Kandahar were Lord Lytton, Sir R. E. Egerton, Major-General Sir H. Green, Field-Marshal His Highness the Duke of Cambridge, Sir William Merewether, Sir Henry Rawlinson, and Lord Napier of Magdala.

The opposition included: Lord Wolseley, Sir John Adye, Chinese Gordon, Lord Lawrence, and Sir Erskine Perry.

of roads leading to Kabul and Herat, Kandahar dominated the whole of southern Afghanistan, and was a position of immense strategical importance. Easily defensible, with a good water supply, an essential factor in eastern warfare, its garrison would not be called upon to endure great hardships. In addition, the climate was salubrious; snow seldom fell, with the result that operations could be undertaken at all seasons. A strongly fortified Kandahar would serve as a menace to any troops advancing through Afghanistan by way of Kabul towards the Khyber, for, not only would the enemy's flank be threatened, but forces advancing simultaneously from Kabul and Herat would be isolated. In the opinion of Sir Henry Rawlinson, the greatest Central Asian expert of the time, it was most probable that an attacking force would advance directly upon Kandahar.

If a foreign army ever does descend upon the Indian frontier, it will be by way of Herat and Kandahar, where the roads are open and traverse districts that have been called "the granary of Asia", and not through the sterile and difficult passes between Kabul and Peshawar.[1]

It was argued that, in the event of war, the occupation of Kandahar would be of supreme importance, since, at that time, it was the first place between the Indus and Herat, at which supplies in any quantity could be obtained. Another argument put forward in favour of retention was that the Kandaharis would prefer British rule to that of the Amir of Kabul who had ever regarded Kandahar "as a sort of milch cow". Although Sir William Merewether was sure of his historical facts when he pointed out that in the past the bond between Kabul and Kandahar had not been of the strongest, yet it was not likely that an alien yoke supported by foreign bayonets would prove acceptable to the inhabitants of any country. Nevertheless government by the British would have meant the advance of civilization and the substitution of law

---

[1] Rawlinson, *England and Russia in the East*, p. 278.

and order for misrule and tyranny. There was also that ever important question of prestige, for in Asia the strong never retreat.

An attempt was even made to justify the retention of Kandahar on financial grounds, and it was argued that the wealth and riches of this fair city were so great that it would become a revenue-producing district, bearing the expenses of its own garrison. The majority of minutes written in support of retention entirely ignored the financial side of the question, and refused to acknowledge that permanent occupation would entail a drain of money and troops. When Lord Roberts stated that frontier service was unpopular with Indian regiments, Lord Napier blandly proposed, as a solution, increased rates of pay—to him extra expense was apparently immaterial.[1] The writer's own experience of both Indian and British troops is that they still strongly object to any prolonged service on the frontier, especially in such isolated posts as Chitral. In fact, all ranks regard frontier service as an exile.

To pass from the financial aspect to the military, would the occupation of Kandahar have been the end of our advance into Afghanistan? In order to save the garrison from starvation, it would have been necessary to protect the surrounding country, for to depend upon supplies from India would have been both a military and a financial blunder. The intervening country, between Kandahar and the Indus, was no granary. Kachhi, the easternmost portion of Kalat, was known as the *dasht-i-amwat* (the desert of death). Sibi and Dadhar were no better. It was predicted, therefore, that the defence of Kandahar would necessitate the occupation of Girishk and Kalat-i-Ghilzai, in which case the British would have been called upon to defend a frontier as unscientific as the one it was proposed to abandon, for both lines ran along the foothills of a wild, mountainous country. Some even went so far as to

---

[1] *Parl. Papers*, 1881 (C. 2811), p. 79.

assert that the British advance would not cease until Herat had been reached, for the greatest difficulty confronting the Forward School would be to know where to stop. That the Russians were faced with a similar problem becomes apparent by the following quotation from the diplomatic correspondence of the Baron de Staal.

Les circonstances qui ont motivé l'extension progressive de nos possessions en Asie Centrale ne sont que trop bien connues. Les difficultés, sans cesse renaissantes, qui résultent du contact entre une Puissance régulièrement constituée et des peuplades à demi sauvages nous ont plus d'une fois forcés de dépasser les limites que nous nous étions volontairement tracées et de nous imposer de lourds sacrifices dans le but d'assurer la sécurité de nos confins contre les instincts pillards de ces peuplades.[1]

Sir Henry Rawlinson offered a solution in the form of a compromise. He proposed that, whereas we should continue our military occupation of the city, the civil administration should be handed over to a local Governor appointed by Abdurrahman Khan, the new amir.[2] This might have proved a way out of the political difficulty; the financial problem would have remained unsolved.

Fortunately the counsels of the moderates prevailed. They realized that the recent acquisitions in Baluchistan would enable the British to occupy this position whenever it became necessary, for in their eyes the importance of Kandahar was a war-time importance only. Furthermore, the later extension of the railway to New Chaman advanced the British

---

[1] *Correspondance Diplomatique du Baron de Staal* (ed. Meyendorff, A.), I, 42–3. For Prince Gortchakoff's famous circular despatch of 1864 see *Parl. Papers*, 1873, LXXV (C. 407), appendix, 72–3. This circular explanatory of Russian policy in Central Asia was not officially communicated to the British Government. Gortchakoff read the circular to Sir A. Buchanan as "a personal and confidential communication". He also authorized Baron Brunnow to read the paper to Lord Russell. The text of the circular, however, almost immediately reached the Foreign Office in a roundabout way, from the British Chargé d'Affaires at Constantinople, to whom it was communicated by General Ignatieff (F.O. 65, 1150, memo. 8 February, 1882).

[2] *Parl. Papers*, 1881 (C. 2811), p. 63.

borders to the Khwaja Amran range, beyond which a broad desert stretched to the walls of Kandahar.

It is a deplorable fact that all questions connected with the rectification of the Indian frontier, especially the Kandahar problem, have tended to become party questions. While this heated controversy was being carried on in the East, a general election was taking place in the West, which resulted in the downfall of Lord Beaconsfield and the return of Mr Gladstone and the Liberals, in April, 1880. On 11 November of the same year the Secretary of State wrote to the Government of India expressing his strongest disapprobation of any permanent occupation of Kandahar. The new Government was opposed to its retention on financial grounds, and believed that, although some attempt had been made to prove that the inhabitants were friendly, the Kandaharis would strongly object to the imposition of a foreign yoke, alien in race and religion. To quote from the despatch under consideration:

It has been proved that there existed no organized military power in Afghanistan which could resist the advance of the British army, or prevent the occupation of any position in that country. But the difficulties of permanent occupation, or of supporting by a military force any Government imposed on the people by the British power, have been exemplified to the fullest extent. . . . The occupation of Kandahar, would, therefore, certainly involve the administration and the military occupation of Kalat-i-Ghilzai on the one side, Farah on the other, and an undefined territory in the direction of Herat.[1]

On 5 March, 1881, the question of retention was debated in the House of Lords, where it was carried by 165 votes to 76. On the 26th of the same month it was thrown out in the Commons by 336 votes to 216.

The year 1880, which witnessed the return of the Liberals to power, also saw the resignation of Lord Lytton and the arrival in India of his successor, Lord Ripon. The new Viceroy immediately commenced preparations for a retirement from all our recently acquired points of vantage in Balu-

[1] *Parl. Papers*, 1881 (C. 2776), p. 91.

chistan to Jacobabad, and even to the Indus. The railway, which had been constructed through the Bolan, was taken up and the materials sent to Bombay, but once more history repeated itself. A Viceroy sent out with implicit instructions to retire from the Bolan, a Viceroy whose earliest acts showed that he was fully determined to carry out these instructions, found that, in the face of the steady march of Cossack *sotnias* towards the oasis of Merv, retreat was impossible. Not only was Baluchistan retained and the railway reconstructed at considerable expense, but an extension of the line to Chaman also had to be undertaken.

Closely connected with the retention of Kandahar was the question of the so-called scientific frontier. Since the scientific or perfect frontier can scarcely be said to exist on the surface of the globe, the question naturally arises, what was meant by the term scientific frontier in this connection? The writer is firmly convinced that it would be impossible to demarcate on the north-west of our Indian Empire a frontier which would satisfy ethnological, political, and military requirements. To seek for a zone which traverses easily defensible topographical features; which does not violate ethnic considerations by cutting through the territories of closely related tribes; and which at the same time serves as a political boundary, is Utopian. What was meant by a scientific frontier in the 'seventies and 'eighties of the last century was the best strategical boundary which could be used as a line of defence against invasion from the direction of Central Asia. Even military strategists of the highest repute were at loggerheads as to the exact location of this line of resistance. Some would have included Herat, which they considered to be the "key to India"; others went so far as to suggest the occupation of such outlying places as Balkh; but it was generally agreed that the best line would be the Kabul-Ghazni-Kandahar front.

It was pointed out that this was shorter and could be more easily converted into a line of defence than any other frontier we had held, or that could be suggested. Neither the right nor the left flank could be turned, for the northern was protected by an almost impenetrable maze of mountains, the southern by an equally impassable desert. It was held that, if this line were connected with the main Indian railway system, troops could be rapidly concentrated on either flank. This rapid concentration of troops was an extremely, if not the most, important factor, for it was infinitely more important for us to be able to despatch troops to any part of the line than it was to construct immense and costly fortifications which the enemy might avoid by making a detour. The retirement already described necessitated the abandonment of the scientific frontier, but the question still remained open as to whether or not we ought to advance to this line to meet a projected invasion.

Our scheme of defence against Russia was settled not by military strategists but by diplomatists. The steady advance of Russia towards the northern frontiers of Afghanistan brought about a compromise between the Forward and Stationary Schools; and it was decided to build up a strong, friendly and united Afghanistan, which should serve as a buffer state between us and Russian aggrandizement. By means of an annual subsidy, together with gifts of arms and ammunition, an attempt was made to form a closer and more intimate alliance with the Amir of Afghanistan. Although there were times when the relations between the amir and the Indian Government were far from cordial, yet, during the reigns of Abdurrahman Khan and his successor, Habibullah, this scheme remained a successful solution of the imperial problem. At the same time the frontiers of Afghanistan were strictly defined by international agreement; and, as long as we controlled her foreign affairs, any violation of the amir's northern frontier by Russia would have been tantamount to a declaration of war.

Chapter II

FRONTIER POLICY: THE LOCAL PROBLEM

They (frontier wars) are but the surf that marks the edge and the advance of the wave of civilization.   Lord Salisbury, Guildhall Speech, 1892.

Closely interwoven with the problem of imperial defence is the local question of tribal policy. It is now proposed to describe and discuss the various methods by which the British have attempted to conciliate and coerce the wild caterans inhabiting the mountainous tract of country between India and Afghanistan. It cannot be said that the British have adopted a consistent or stereotyped policy towards these turbulent tribesmen. Not only have their methods varied from time to time, but, owing to geographical, ethnological, and political reasons, a policy, which was completely successful on one part of the frontier, was entirely unsuited to another area. It is hoped to prove in this chapter that any universal system of frontier policy, operating from the territories of the Mehtar of Chitral to the coast of Mekran, would have been an utter failure.

The conquest of Sind in 1843 and the annexation of the Panjab in 1849, by advancing the British administrative boundary across the Indus, made it coterminous with the territories of the Baluch and Pathan tribes, and eventually brought the Government of India into closer contact with the Khan of Kalat and the Amir of Afghanistan. Thus there grew up two distinct schools of frontier administration, the Sind and the Panjab. The policy adopted in Sind can be roughly described as an uncompromising repression of outrages by a strong military force; the success of the Panjab system depended to a very large extent upon an efficient political management of the tribes.

Sir Charles Napier, having crushed the power of the amirs, immediately set to work to place Sind under a military administration, selecting his subordinates not from the ranks of the civil service but from the soldiers who had helped him in the conquest of the country. This arrangement naturally had its disadvantages, and, like the conquest of Sind, became the subject of embittered controversy. The most exposed part of the Sind frontier stretched for a distance of about 150 miles from Kasmore to the northern slopes of the Hala mountains, but, at first, no troops were stationed there, neither was it thought necessary to place anyone in charge of it. This immediately led to marauding incursions by Bugtis from the Kachhi hills and Dombkis and Jakranis from the Kachhi plain, who entered Sind in bands of 500 or more, plundering and burning villages far inside the British borders. An attempt was therefore made to grapple with the problem by building forts and posting detachments of troops at certain points, and by appointing an officer to command this vulnerable part of the border. But these measures did not prove effective. Disorder reigned supreme. On several occasions British troops were signally defeated by these robber bands and once about sixty of the local inhabitants, who had turned out in a body to protect their homes, were mistaken for robbers and put to death by the 6th Bengal Irregular Cavalry, the very force which had been posted there for their protection.[1] Eventually, in 1845, Sir Charles Napier led an expedition against these disturbers of the peace, but it was only a qualified success. The Bugtis were by no means crushed, for, on 10 December, 1846, about 1500 of these freebooters marched into Sind, where they remained for twenty-four hours before returning to the hills, seventy-five miles away, with 15,000 head of cattle. It can be safely stated that, until

[1] *Records of Scinde Irregular Horse*, I, 275.

the arrival of Major John Jacob and the Scinde Irregular Horse, in January, 1847, no efficient protection had been afforded to British subjects along this exposed frontier.

According to Jacob, the fact that the inhabitants of the British border districts were allowed to carry arms was chiefly responsible for the prevailing unrest, for even our own subjects were in the habit of proceeding on predatory excursions. Some of the worst offenders were the Baluch tribes from the Kachhi side, who had been settled in Sind by Napier in 1845. Strange to relate, the marauders from across the border disposed of most of their loot in Sind where the banias supplied them with food and the necessary information to ensure the success of their raids. What was worse, the military detachments stationed at Shahpur and other places remained entirely on the defensive, prisoners within the walls of their own forts, for no attempt was made at patrolling the frontier. In 1848, Major, afterwards General, John Jacob was appointed to sole political power on the Upper Sind frontier where he completely revolutionized Napier's system. Under Jacob's vigorous and capable administration, lands which had lain waste for over half a century were cultivated once more, and the people, who had lived in constant dread of Baluch inroads, moved about everywhere unarmed and in perfect safety. All British subjects were disarmed in order to prevent them taking the law into their own hands, but, as the possession of arms in a man's own house was not forbidden, the people were not left so entirely defenceless as is sometimes supposed.[1] No new forts were built and existing ones were dismantled, for Jacob believed that the depredations of Baluch robbers could be best checked by vigilant patrolling, to which the desert fringe of Sind was admirably adapted. In other words, mobility was the system of defence. At first Jacob advocated that the political boundary should coincide with the geographical. His contention was based on the supposed per-

---

[1] *Records of Scinde Irregular Horse*, II, 243.

manency of the latter, but the gradual disappearance of the desert as a result of increased cultivation caused him to alter his opinion.[1] Although Jacob, in his military capacity, commanded all troops on this frontier and was responsible to no one but the commander-in-chief, his duties did not cease here. Not only was he the sole political agent, but he was in addition superintendent of police, chief magistrate, engineer, and revenue officer.

It is now generally accepted that Jacob's methods were inapplicable to the Panjab where frontier administrators were faced with a much more formidable problem. The first colossal mistake on the Panjab frontier was the initial step, the taking over of the frontier districts from the Sikhs, and the acceptance of an ill-defined administrative boundary. It will be remembered that the Sikhs, originally members of a reforming sect of Hinduism, gradually developed during the decay of the Mughal Empire into a strong military organization. By the second decade of the nineteenth century, the genius of Maharaja Ranjit Singh had led to the creation and consolidation of a powerful Sikh state in the Panjab, between the Sutlej and the Indus. It was not until after the death of this able and astute monarch that the Sikhs came into direct conflict with the British, who, after much stubborn fighting, annexed the Panjab in the year 1849.

It was extremely unfortunate for the British that the Sikhs had been their immediate predecessors in the Panjab, for Sikh frontier administration had been of the loosest type. They possessed but little influence in the trans-Indus tracts, and what influence they had was confined to the plains. Even here they were obeyed only in the immediate vicinity of their forts which studded the country. Peshawar was under the stern rule of General Avitable, a ferocious Italian, whose criminal code was blood for blood, whose object was the sacrifice of a victim rather than the punishment of a culprit.

[1] *Views and Opinions of General John Jacob* (ed. Pelly), p. 74.

Hazara groaned under the iron heel of General Hari Singh whose sole method of collecting revenue was that of annual incursions into the independent hills. Hence, on the Panjab frontier, the British succeeded to a heritage of anarchy, for the Sikhs had waged eternal war against the border tribes and even against the inhabitants of the so-called settled districts. The administration of the Panjab frontier was further complicated by geographical conditions which offered every inducement to a marauding life. Not only was the frontier longer and therefore more difficult to defend, but it was also extremely mountainous, whereas in Sind a strip of desert intervened between British territory and the haunts of the Baluch robbers, facilitating the employment of cavalry and the use of advanced posts. In the Panjab rich harvests waved in dangerous proximity to an intricate maze of nullahs and valleys which gave access to the plains.

The aims of the Panjab authorities were to protect their subjects from the attacks of marauding bands, to keep the trade routes open, and, as far as possible, to secure the tranquillity of the hitherto blood-stained border. It was imperative to put a stop to the state of affairs then in existence; and, in order to give the Pathans an impression of their strength, the British were forced to resort to reprisals. There could be no peace while raids were constantly taking place and individual acts of fanaticism rendered the life of any government servant unsafe. The evidence of Mr, afterwards Sir, Richard Temple, one of Lawrence's assistants in the Panjab, points to the fact that the tribes were absolutely incorrigible. He accuses them of giving asylum to fugitives from justice, of violating British territory, of blackmail and intrigue, of minor robberies, and of isolated murders of British subjects. Finally, he charges them with firing on British regular troops and even of killing British officers within the limits of the Panjab.[1] On the other

[1] Temple, *Report showing relations of the British Government with the tribes of the N.W.F.* pp. 63–4.

hand, the policy of Panjab administrators was one of forbearance, for, although British officials were prevented from
entering tribal territory, the tribesmen were allowed to trade
within the British borders. It seems clear that for over
twenty-five years no official of the Panjab Government
crossed the border: they were certainly discouraged from
doing so. Whatever the merits of this policy may have been,
it was evidently a concession to the susceptibilities of the
tribesmen, and intended in the interests of peace. The permission to trade and the provision of medical and other
assistance to tribesmen entering the Panjab were certainly
attempts to promote friendly relations. But the contumacious
attitude of the tribesmen themselves eventually drove the
British to resort to reprisals and resulted in a state of chronic
warfare for many years. Of course it could not be expected
that they would immediately cease from harassing the border:
the customs and habits of centuries are not so easily thrown
on one side. Thus the first step of the Panjab authorities was
a defensive measure; the next was an attempt at conciliation,
to show the tribesmen how they would benefit by becoming
friendly neighbours.

Various conciliatory methods were adopted. The hated
capitation tax of Sikh days and all frontier duties were
abolished; a system of complete freedom of trade was insti-
tuted, and commercial intercourse encouraged in every way.
Steps were taken to increase the Powindah[1] trade; fairs were
held for the exchange of commodities; roads were constructed
from the passes to the nearest bazaars; and steam communication was established on the upper Indus. Free medical
treatment was provided in the hospitals and dispensaries
established at various points along the frontier; tribal *maliks*
and *jirgas* were encouraged to enter British territory for the
settlement of their disputes; and attempts were made to
colonize waste lands with families from across the border.

[1] For Powindahs see ch. IV.

Lastly, the ranks of the army and police were thrown open to all those desirous of entering British service.[1]

Because the Panjab frontier was too long and too mountainous to admit of its being defended by the military alone, much depended upon the political management of the tribes. At first there was no special agency for dealing with the tribal tracts, and relations with the tribesmen were conducted by the deputy-commissioners of the six districts of Hazara, Peshawar, Kohat, Bannu, Dera Ismail Khan, and Dera Ghazi Khan. In 1876, the three northern districts formed the commissionership of Peshawar, the three southern ones that of the Derajat. The system of political agencies was not adopted until 1878, when a special officer was appointed for the Khyber during the Second Afghan War. Kurram became an agency in 1892, while the three remaining agencies of the Malakand, Tochi, and Wana were created between 1895 and 1896. The Malakand was placed under the direct control of the Government of India from the outset, all the other agencies remaining under the Panjab Government. This was the arrangement until the creation of the Frontier Province in 1901. To protect the frontier a chain of forts was erected along the British borders, parallel to which a good military road was constructed. A special force, the Panjab Frontier Force, was recruited from Sikhs, Pathans, Gurkhas, and Panjabi Musalmans, and was placed, not under the commander-in-chief, but under the Board of Administration.[2] It was not until 1886 that this force was amalgamated with the regular army. As an additional measure of defence, the inhabitants of the frontier districts were allowed to retain their arms, and were encouraged to defend their homes.

It is now proposed to examine the different methods of coercion applied on the Panjab frontier. Three methods of forcing the tribesmen to terms have been employed by the

[1] *Panjab Administration Report*, 1869–70, p. 21.
[2] *Idem*, 1892–3, pp. 32–3; *Confidential, Frontier and Overseas*, I, vi–vii.

British: fines, blockades, and expeditions. The idea of inflicting a fine was to get compensation for plundered property and "blood-money" for lives lost. If the territory of a tribe was exposed and could be easily entered by a punitive force, or, if certain clans of the tribe owned property or resided within the British borders, as a general rule the fine was promptly paid. If this did not happen, hostages were seized and detained until compensation had been paid. As a last resort the tribe was either blockaded or punitive operations were undertaken against it. A blockade consists in preventing a certain tribe from holding any intercourse with the inhabitants of British territory, and can only be successful under certain geographical and political conditions. Unfortunately, the cases in which a blockade can be successfully employed are extremely limited. To be completely successful the blockading forces must be in possession of the approaches to a country; they must be able to sever the arteries of trade and supplies; and must have the support or friendly co-operation of the surrounding tribes. From this it becomes apparent that the success of a blockade is largely determined by geographical conditions. This is the reason why the Adam Khel Afridis are so susceptible to this form of coercion. Surrounded by tribes with whom they have little in common, inhabiting hills within easy reach of the military stations of Kohat and Peshawar, and dependent upon their trade with British India for the necessaries of life, they are soon forced to come to terms.[1]

There can be no doubt that British policy was one of conciliation backed by force. Every endeavour was made to cultivate friendly relations, but, when kindness and conciliation failed, when the tribesmen continued to murder our subjects and to harass our borders, then the ultimate sanction was force. It was our bounden duty to protect our own; and for this reason, and this alone, can punitive expeditions be considered justifiable. The following opinion of General

[1] For fuller discussion of blockades see ch. VII.

Skobeleff illustrates the Russian military point of view. "In dealing with savage tribes the best plan is, to fight as rarely as possible; and when you do fight, to hit as hard as you can. By incessantly attacking them, you teach them the art of war." The Panjab system of punitive expeditions has been most unfavourably criticized, but chiefly by exponents of the Sind School, such as Sir Bartle Frere, who condemned it because it consisted of an indiscriminate slaughter and destruction of crops and villages. This meant that the whole tribe was punished for the offences of a few malcontents, and the real result was to make a desert and call it peace.[1] In defence of the Sind system he pointed out that the rules of ordinary civilized warfare were observed; that no wanton destruction of any kind took place; that plundering and laying waste were strictly forbidden; and that the punishment of the guilty alone was attempted. Frere, whose experience was confined to Sind, failed to recognize that the intensely democratic constitution of the majority of Pathan tribes rendered any distinction between the guilty and the innocent extremely difficult. Lord Lytton in his memorable minute of the 22 April, 1877, condemned the Panjab punitive system in the following words:

I object to it because it perpetuates a system of semi-barbarous reprisal, and because we lower ourselves to the ideas of right and might common to our barbarous neighbours, rather than endeavour to raise them to our own ideas, because it seldom touches the guilty, and generally falls most heavily on the innocent; because its natural tendency is to perpetuate animosity rather than lead up to good relations; because, as a rule, it leaves no permanent mark,...and it appears from the records of these expeditions, which are not always successes even in the most limited sense, that the losses suffered by ourselves often exceed the losses we inflict.[2]

Sir E. C. Bayley, a member of the Viceroy's council, in his

[1] Martineau, *Life of Sir Bartle Frere*, I, 363–8.
[2] *Parl. Papers*, 1878, LVIII (C. 1898), 142.

minute of dissent, pointed out that this attack was extremely unfair, for, in its inception, this policy had been forced upon the British as a natural consequence of Sikh misrule. To state that Panjab policy had not been successful was of course not in accordance with the truth, for, as Bayley pointed out, there were obvious good results. " It is not to be forgotten," he wrote, "that, under Sikh rule, some of what are now our frontier villages near Peshawar were actually held by a yearly tribute of so many human heads taken from their neighbours across the border."[1] Nevertheless, the impartial historian will find it difficult to agree with him that expeditions were never proposed by the local authorities, nor sanctioned by the supreme authority, until the list of unpunished offences was so great as to make an expedition absolutely essential for the preservation of British prestige. The student of frontier history is soon convinced that this policy of "butcher and bolt," as punitive expeditions have been contemptuously termed, will never produce any lasting effects. Amongst the democratically constituted Pathan tribes between the Khyber and the Gomal, there are always malcontents ready to stir up trouble on the slightest pretext; and it is the inability of these tribes to control and coerce their unruly members that has prevented punitive expeditions from having any permanent effects. It is therefore only in so far as they have had temporary effects that military reprisals can in any sense be considered successful. With the exception of the Ambela campaign of 1863, which was directed against a colony of Hindustani fanatics at Malka on the northern slopes of the Mahaban range, no formidable tribal risings occurred until the last decade of the nineteenth century. Nevertheless, between 1849 and 1890, no less than forty-two expeditions had been considered necessary to counteract the marauding proclivities of the turbulent tribesmen. The serious nature of the fighting in the Ambela campaign can be gauged from the fact that

[1] *Idem*, p. 145.

out of a total of 2173 British casualties for the forty-two expeditions, 908 were sustained in the year 1863.

Until the arrival of Lord Lytton, in 1876, the Panjab frontier was controlled by a system of non-intervention, varied by expeditions. The frontier zone became a sort of *terra incognita* which no man dared traverse, except under the protection of armed troops.[1] But in the 'seventies of the last century it became obvious that certain changes were necessary. The existence of two entirely different systems in two widely separated parts of the frontier, inhabited by tribes who differed considerably in characteristics and constitution, was a necessity, but, in the Dera Ghazi Khan district, an anomalous state of affairs had grown up in the meeting-place of Pathan and Baluch tribal areas. Certain tribes, such as the Marris and Bugtis, came into contact with both systems of frontier policy, for their territories were contiguous to the Dera Ghazi Khan district of the Panjab and also to the Upper Sind frontier. Under the former system they received allowances; under the latter this was not the case. In the Panjab they held possessions on both sides of the administrative boundary; in Sind this was not allowed. Under the Sind system, military posts had been pushed far into the neighbouring hills, with the result that the Panjab boundary was in the rear of the Sind posts. In the Panjab the tribesmen were dealt with by special regulations framed in accordance with their customary laws, tribal system, and blood-feuds. The reverse was the case in Sind where no notice was taken of tribal ties or of local custom. There, the prosecution of a blood-feud was considered as malice aforethought, and no allowances were made in passing sentences in such cases. To settle this difficulty, a conference between Panjab and Sind officials took place at Mittankot on 3 February, 1871.[2] The

---

[1] *Parl. Papers*, 1878, LVIII, 141.

[2] An unsuccessful conference had taken place in November, 1864; *vide Panjab Administration Report*, 1864–5, p. 107.

objects of this conference were to outline a uniform policy for the whole frontier; to arrange for the future management of the Marris and Bugtis; and to determine the exact relations between the Khan of Kalat and his sirdars. The Sind authorities considered that they alone were responsible for political relations and negotiations with the khan; and, acting in accordance with this belief, they had attempted to control the Marris and Bugtis through their legitimate chief. On the other hand, the Panjab Government had no direct relations with Kalat, and compensation for offences committed by these tribes had been obtained through Sind. In 1867 Captain Sandeman, the deputy-commissioner of Dera Ghazi Khan, soon to become famous for his pacification of Baluchistan, had entered into direct relations with these tribes. This action of Sandeman had been followed by a period of peace on the Panjab border. Far otherwise was the case on the Sind frontier, where the absence of any definite engagements was considered to be an excuse for marauding incursions. One flagrant case has been placed on record, where a tribe, which had been prohibited from entering Sind, still remained in receipt of allowances on the Panjab frontier.[1] The conference resulted in the following proposals being placed before the Government of India. In future, Marri and Bugti tribal affairs should be placed under the control of Sandeman who, for this purpose, should consider himself subordinate to the Sind authorities. The system of employing tribal horsemen to protect trade routes should be extended. All payments to Marri and Bugti chiefs should be made in the name of the Khan of Kalat, in order to strengthen his position in the eyes of his tribesmen. No decision was arrived at regarding the relations existing between the khan and his sirdars. These recommendations were sanctioned by the Government of India on 19 October, 1871.

During the years 1872–8 several important measures cal-

[1] *Parl. Papers*, 1877, LXIV (C. 1807), 77.

culated to improve the administration of the frontier districts were introduced.[1] To ensure a better understanding between Government officials and the tribesmen, civil officers were obliged to qualify themselves by passing an examination in either Pashtu or Baluchi. In the interests of peace the Nawab of Tank, a loyal but incompetent ally, was relieved of the police administration of his troublesome charge, for he had proved utterly incapable of preventing Mahsud robbers, who infested the district, from raiding both his own and the British borders. To increase its efficiency the militia of the Derajat, a local force acting as an auxiliary to the Panjab Frontier Force, was reorganized. Members of the militia, who had become too old for their strenuous duties, were discharged. No active member was to indulge in tribal blood-feuds under the pretence of being engaged on Government service.

In 1878, as a result of a Defence Committee which met at Peshawar in 1877, measures creating a Border Police and militia were sanctioned for parts of the Kohat and Peshawar districts. This meant that the procedure adopted at the annexation of the Panjab was reversed, for the militia now took the place of the military as a first line force. Lastly, with a view to their becoming industrious agriculturists, settlements or colonies of Afridis, Waziris, Gurchanis, Bhittannis, and Bugtis were formed in British territory. This has often been put forward as a solution of the frontier problem. As recently as 1920 Mr D. C. Boulger, a well-known writer on Central Asian affairs, advocated the deportation of the Mahsuds as the only solution to what is nowadays the most difficult problem on the frontier.[2] This scheme has been successful in some cases: in others it has proved an utter failure. It depends to a large extent for its success or failure upon two factors: the fierceness of the tribe, and the distance the recalcitrant tribesmen are removed from their original habitat. It has been

---

[1] *Parl. Papers*, 1878, LVIII (C. 1898), 68–76.
[2] *Contemporary Review*, 1920, p. 505.

tried with success in the Yusafzai country to the north-east of Peshawar.

Here whole villages of quondam outlaws are now disarmed and peaceably living on lands rented to them on favourable terms, and, as generation succeeds generation, are losing the martial instincts and war-like skill of their forefathers in the acquisition of the more civilized but equally absorbing attributes which bring wealth and prosperity.[1]

This cannot be said of the experiment in so far as the more turbulent Mahsuds are concerned. From this it will be seen that before the outbreak of the Second Afghan War, in 1878, a more or less uniform system of border defence had been adopted for the whole of the Panjab frontier. While this system of defence was being evolved in the north, great changes had been taking place on the southern frontier.

Relations between Kalat and the Government of India were regulated by the treaty of 14 May, 1854, which pledged the khan to abstain from negotiations with any other power, without first consulting the British; to receive British troops in Kalat whenever such a step should be thought necessary; to protect merchants passing through his territories; and to prevent his subjects from harassing the British borders. In return for this he received an annual subsidy of Rs. 50,000.[2]

The authorities in Sind sought to control the trans-border population through the Khan of Kalat. There was, however, a great difference of opinion in frontier circles as to the correct relationship existing between the khan and his sirdars. Some authorities regarded the efforts of the sirdars to rid themselves of the khan's control as the inevitable disintegration of the feudal system caused by advancing civilization. Others believed that the system of government was federal, not feudal. In reality the khan was the head of a confederacy of tribal chiefs, who, at the same time, in so far as they held fiefs

---

[1] *Nineteenth Century Magazine and Afterwards*, February, 1898, p. 252.
[2] For text see Aitchison, XI, 212–14.

in Kalat in return for which they furnished troops, were quasi-feudal vassals of the khan.[1] About the year 1869 it became apparent that Khudadad Khan, who had used his subsidy to raise a standing army, was attempting to increase his authority at the expense of his confederated chiefs; and, it was obvious that, if British support were withdrawn, Kalat would become the scene of internecine struggles. "It is surely time for our Government", wrote Sandeman, in 1869, "to interfere when we find that the Khan of Khelat's mismanagement of his khanate has led to the peace and administration of that part of the Punjab border being placed in much jeopardy; for such truly is the case."[2] Sandeman therefore urged that immediate steps should be taken to reconcile the contending factions, for he considered that the sirdars were too powerful and had too much influence in the country to admit of either the British or the khan ignoring their grievances. Within the khan's territories affairs steadily grew from bad to worse, and the unsettled state of Kalat was reflected in the wave of unrest which spread along the British borders. By the end of 1871 it became apparent that the sirdars were in open revolt against the khan's authority. The climax was reached in 1873, when Major Harrison, the British agent, was recalled, and the khan's subsidy withheld, because he had failed to comply with the terms laid down in the treaty of 1854. Instead of sanctioning an expedition, the Government of India decided to despatch Sandeman on a mission of reconciliation to the khan's territories. It was Sandeman's second mission, in 1876, that led to the Mastung agreement and the treaty of 1876, which marked the death of non-intervention on the southern frontier.[3] By the Mastung agreement the khan and his Brahui sirdars were formally

---

[1] *Confidential, Frontier and Overseas*, III, 33–6.

[2] *Parl. Papers*, 1877, LXIV (C. 1807), 6.

[3] *Idem*, 1877, LXIV (C. 1808): (*a*) Mastung Agreement, 13 July, 1876, pp. 255–7; (*b*) Treaty of Jacobabad, 8 December, 1876, pp. 314–16.

reconciled. The Treaty of Jacobabad, signed on 8 December
of the same year, renewed and supplemented the treaty of
1854. In return for an increased subsidy the khan granted
permission for the location of troops in, and the construction of railway and telegraph lines through, Kalat territory.
The importance of the treaty lies in the fact that it was the
foundation of the Baluchistan Agency, for on 21 February,
1877, Major Sandeman was appointed Agent to the Governor-
General, with his headquarters at Quetta. Lord Lytton
justified this advance on the ground that it was impossible
to remain inert spectators of the anarchy in Kalat, when the
connection between Kalat and Sind was so intimate that any
disturbance in the one was immediately reflected in the other.

Sir Robert Sandeman's tribal policy was one of friendly
and conciliatory intervention. Casting all fear on one side
he boldly advanced into their mountain retreats and made
friends with the tribal chiefs or *tumandars*. Recognizing that
the British side of the question was not the only side, he never
condemned the action of a tribe until he had fully investigated its grievances. This had been impossible under a system
of non-intervention which prohibited officers from entering
the independent hills. The weakest part of his system was
that it depended too much upon the personal influence of one
man. There have not been wanting critics who have regarded
his system of granting allowances as blackmail. This charge
falls to the ground when it is remembered that those in receipt
of allowances had strenuous duties to perform in the guarding
of trade routes and passes, and in the carrying out of *jirga*
decrees. Allowances may be termed blackmail when they are
granted solely to induce the tribesmen to abstain from raiding,
but Sandeman never withheld allowances because of offences
committed by individual members of a tribe. This, in his
opinion, was tantamount to punishing the loyal section of a
tribe for the offences of its unruly members. For this reason
he always demanded that the actual offenders should be

brought to justice, that the guilty alone should be punished. But even a system of allowances, granted for the purpose of inducing the tribesmen to keep the peace, is not, in its early stages, to be deplored. When it is remembered that plundering has been the profession of these wild freebooters throughout the ages, it is useless to expect them to reform, unless some powerful inducement is offered. Allowances may be expensive; they may savour of blackmail to the fastidious, yet they are infinitely preferable to the still more expensive system of punitive expeditions. The Sandeman system was quite successful amongst Baluch tribes where there were tribal chiefs powerful enough to control the tribes for which they were responsible. Its introduction by Mr R. I. Bruce, the Commissioner of the Derajat, into Waziristan among the more democratic Mahsuds, where no such authority existed, ended in complete failure.[1] Bruce, who had previously served under Sandeman, hoped that Mahsud *maliks*, chosen by him, would, in return for allowances, be able to control the *ulus*, the name given to the body of the Mahsud tribe. But Bruce made a fatal mistake. He introduced his *maliki* system without first having occupied a commanding and central position in the Mahsud country. Sandeman, on the contrary, realized that the first essential was to dominate the Baluch country with troops; and an extremely important part of his scheme for the pacification of Baluchistan was the holding of dominant positions between the tribes and the safe retreat afforded by Afghanistan. This he accomplished by the occupation of the Bori and Zhob valleys. The conquest of Baluchistan was practically bloodless, for fortunately it was rarely necessary to resort to force. It must not, however, be forgotten that his system, like all other frontier policies, ultimately rested on force. The policy of Sir Robert Warburton in the Khyber was similar to that of Sandeman, in that an attempt was made to gain the confidence of the surrounding tribes. But, in reality,

[1] See ch. VII.

the two systems were fundamentally different, for, in the Khyber, the object aimed at was the control of the pass. To this everything else was subordinated. It was not considered necessary to extend British control over the neighbouring tribes, though friendly intercourse was not forbidden. For this reason the British never interfered with the internal feuds of the Khyber Afridis, who were allowed to wage war, even within sight of the walls of Jamrud, so long as their struggles did not affect the protection of the pass.

It will be convenient at this stage to summarize the later history of Baluchistan, for, after 1890, interest chiefly centres in the Pathan frontier. By the Treaty of Gandamak, May, 1879, Pishin and Sibi were handed over to the Government of India by Yakub Khan as "assigned districts", which meant that any surplus of revenue over expenditure had to be handed back to the amir.[1] Although this treaty was abrogated by the massacre of Cavagnari and his escort, these areas were retained by the British, but were not declared British territory until 1887, when the Agent to the Governor-General was appointed Chief Commissioner for them. The ten years preceding Sandeman's death, in 1892, were marked by tremendous administrative activity. Communications were opened out in every direction; irrigation schemes were taken in hand; forests were developed; and arrangements made for the collection of land revenue. In the administration of justice the indigenous system of *jirgas*, or councils of tribal elders, was adopted and developed. This method still holds the field. Local cases are referred to local *jirgas*, while more important disputes are placed before inter-district *jirgas*, or before the *Shahi Jirga*, which meets twice a year, once at Sibi and once at Quetta. The province as now administered can be divided into British Baluchistan, consisting of the tracts assigned by the Treaty of Gandamak; agency territories, which have been acquired by lease or otherwise brought under the

[1] Aitchison, XI, 346.

control of the Government of India; and the native states of Kalat and Las Bela.[1]

This brief survey of frontier policy brings us to the year 1890, but, before proceeding to discuss the events of the 'nineties, some account of the frontier tribesmen is essential.

[1] *Indian Statutory Commission*, 1930, v, pt ii, 1280–90.

Chapter III

ETHNIC CONSIDERATIONS

Now, these tribes are savages, noble savages perhaps, and not without some tincture of virtue and generosity, but still absolutely barbarians nevertheless.   R. C. Temple, 1856.

No ethnological problem is more complicated and intricate than that which is presented by the North-West Frontier of India. Hidden away in dark, inhospitable nullahs and still darker ravines, in lonely mountain passes and on barren, wind-swept plains, dwell a people, the human flotsam and jetsam of the past. The first migration of which we have evidence is that of the Aryan-speaking peoples who established themselves on the Panjab plains in prehistoric times. Centuries later, within historical times, successive waves of invaders swept like devastating torrents through the mountain passes of the north-west. Persian, Greek, and Afghan, the forces of Alexander and the armies of Mahmud of Ghazni, the hosts of Timur, Babur, and Nadir Shah, and the troops of Ahmad Shah Durrani, all advanced by these routes to lay waste the fair and smiling plains of Hindustan. All these migrations and invasions added to the heterogeneity of the existing population on the Indian borderland.

With the exception of the exploits of Alexander the Great, we know little of the history of this area prior to the era of Muhammadan conquest. That the modern Peshawar district once formed part of the ancient Buddhist kingdom of Gandhara, authorities are now agreed, for, from the Khyber pass to the Swat valley, the country is studded with crumbling Buddhist stupas. Here, too, have been unearthed the best specimens of Graeco-Buddhist sculpture in existence. Apart from archaeological remains the only historical evidence we possess is that of certain Chinese pilgrims: of Fa-hien, who, in the opening years of the fifth century A.D., visited the upper part of the Kurram valley, then known as Loi; and of Hiuen Tsiang, who, in the seventh century A.D., found the inhabitants still professing Buddhism. Through centuries of almost unbroken silence we arrive at the era of Muhammadan conquest, when, between the thirteenth and sixteenth centuries, numerous Pathan tribes from Afghanistan spread over and conquered the country roughly corresponding to the modern North-West Frontier Province.[1] The inhabitants of this province and of the eastern part of Afghanistan, to the west of the Durand line, are essentially Pathan in origin. North of Dera Ismail Khan the Indus constitutes a rough ethnic boundary, for, with the exception of the cis-Indus tract of Hazara and scattered families in the Panjab, the Pathan advance ceased when the banks of this river were reached.

The population of the frontier zone can be divided into Baluch, Pathan, and non-Pathan. The Baluch inhabit the greater part of Baluchistan; the Pathan is found both in the North-West Frontier Province and in Baluchistan; while the non-Pathan element, with certain exceptions to be noted hereafter, must be sought for in the mountain fastnesses of Chitral and in the Swat Kohistan. We shall first examine the non-Pathan section of the population.

Even folklore, traditions and legends are singularly silent about the races who inhabited the frontier prior to the Pathan invasions. According to tradition the Kohat valley was once occupied by Gabris, Safis, and Maujaris. The names alone have been handed down to us; of the original stock not the slightest trace remains.[2] Similarly, of the gigantic Belemas

[1] Plowden, *Kalid-i-Afghani*, chs. I–V. Selections from the *Tarikh-i-Murass'a*.

[2] Tucker, *Settlement Report*, Kohat, p. 41.

who once dwelt in Mianwali, and of the Pothi of the Marwat plain, not a vestige can be discovered.[1] Thus a study of these legendary aborigines, though interesting, is barren of useful results and need not detain us. From traditional aborigines we turn to existing races. The Khands of the Peshawar district, of whom very little is known, are supposed by some to be very early settlers.[2] Amongst the Orakzais of Tirah are to be found several aboriginal sections known as Tirahi. Again, the origin of the Afridis of Tirah and the Khyber has always puzzled ethnologists. Sir Aurel Stein is of opinion that "physical type, local habitation, and name all uniformly point to the present Afridis in essential racial character being the descendants of a stock established in the region of Tirah since very early times".[3] Furthermore, amongst the wild and almost inaccessible hills of the Dir, Swat, and Panjkora Kohistan are to be found remnants of the population which existed in Buddhist times. All these non-Pathan tribes, who have embraced Islam and dwell in these remote parts of the Hindu Kush, are called Kohistanis by the Pathans themselves. Chitral too is the habitat of non-Pathan tribes, but a detailed examination of its inhabitants has been reserved for the next chapter.

It is now proposed to deal with those colonies of Hindus which are to be found scattered throughout the independent tribal zone. In Afghanistan, Baluchistan, and the Frontier Province are to be found colonies of Sikhs and Hindus living in the midst of an alien population. Practically all the trade of the Indian borderland, with the exception of that carried on by the migratory Powindahs, is in the hands of these Hindus. In fact, they constitute an economic necessity. They are the bankers, pawnbrokers, and goldsmiths. Everywhere they are to be found as shopkeepers, grain dealers, and cloth

---

[1] Thorburn, *Bannu or Our Afghan Frontier*, p. 14.
[2] *Punjab Glossary*, ii, 491–3.
[3] *Journ. Roy. Asiatic Soc.* July, 1925, p. 404.

merchants. Except for fanatical outbreaks they are in no great danger. In Baluchistan their position in this respect has improved considerably since the British occupation of the country. That they were considered as inferiors by their proud and more warlike overlords can be gauged from the fact that an unwritten law existed which provided for the protection of women, children, and Hindus from blood-feuds. Lax and unorthodox in their religious observances, they will even drink water from skins that have been filled by Muhammadans. Some Hindus have even adopted the Pashtu suffix *zai* (son of), as is the case with the Sawarezai of Duki.[1] In many cases Hindu women and children can only speak Pashtu, while the Ramzais of Loralai have adopted Baluch dress and customs.[2] In the majority of cases Hindus are under the protection of Muhammadan overlords, for which they have to pay certain dues and taxes. As a rule these are trivial. In several Pathan communities a distinctive dress has to be worn by Hindus; and it has been stated that Hindus living amongst the Mohmands are forced to wear striped trousers. For several months during the year 1919 I was in close proximity to the Mohmand village of Lalpura, but I cannot recollect ever having noticed this peculiarity. The very presence of these Hindus and the religious toleration they enjoy is a proof that we often over-estimate the fanatical propensities of Muhammadans and fail to realize that on the subject of Islam and Toleration much biased history has been written.

With these exceptions the frontier tribesmen are either Pathans or Baluch. The boundary between Baluchistan and the Frontier Province is political, not ethnic. In fact the expression Baluchistan is a misnomer, for within its political boundaries are included large numbers of Pathan tribes and a block of territory, known as the Brahui country. What

[1] *Baluchistan District Gazetteer*, 1907, II, 107.
[2] *Imperial Gazetteer India*, Baluchistan, 1908, p. 112.

approximates more nearly to an ethnic boundary between Pathan and Baluch runs from near the town of Chaudhwan in the Dera Ismail Khan district, through Thal-Chotiali and Sibi to Chaman. North of this line dwell the Pathan tribes of Baluchistan, namely the Kakars, Tarins, Panis and Shiranis, who are to be found in Quetta, Harnai, Pishin, Thal-Chotiali, Bori and Zhob. Roughly speaking the Pathans, that is the Pashtu and Pakhtu-speaking peoples, inhabit southern and eastern Afghanistan, the northern portion of Baluchistan, and the trans-Indus country from Dera Ismail Khan to the Swat Kohistan.

It is hardly necessary to mention that no hard and fast ethnic or linguistic boundaries can be drawn in India, for, unless separated by some stupendous mountain barrier or by some natural obstacle like a wide river, Indian races and languages gradually merge into each other. On account of the migratory and nomadic habits of the border tribes the same limitation is encountered when an attempt is made to define tribal areas and boundaries. South of Dera Ismail Khan, the Indus no longer serves as an ethnic line, for a strong Baluch element is present in the population of Sind and the south-west Panjab.[1] Neither is affinity of race any criterion of language, for all Pathans do not speak Pashtu. To give but one example, many of the Panis around Sibi speak Jatki or Siraiki. Brahui is not the sole medium of conversation amongst the Brahuis, for one section of a tribe may speak Brahui while another may be found using Baluchi. If affinity of race is no criterion of language, the converse is still more true. Language is not by any means a test of race, for, in the mountain fastnesses to the north and north-east of Peshawar, Pashtu serves as a convenient *lingua franca* and is used in many cases by the supposed aboriginal population. The Pathan language is a branch of the Eastern Iranian group. There are two principal dialects, the north-eastern with its

[1] Longworth Dames, *The Baluch Race*, p. 53.

centre at Peshawar, and the south-western which radiates from Kandahar. The former, the Pakhtu, is harsh and guttural, whereas the Kandahari dialect, the Pashtu, is soft and sibilant. Variations of the latter are to be found in Bannu, Dawar and Waziristan.

Numerous theories have been put forward to explain the origin of the Afghans and Pathans. They have been traced to Copts, Jews, Armenians, Albanians, Turks, Arabs, and Rajputs. Most of these theories are those of writers living in a prescientific age, before the examination of anthropometric data revolutionized the study of ethnological problems. They may therefore be dismissed as fanciful. The Hebraic descent theory has been a long time dying and cannot therefore be dismissed without a brief criticism of the arguments with which its supporters have attempted to uphold it.

In the first place, this claim is strongly advocated by the Afghans themselves, who believe, or wish others to believe, that they are the direct descendants of Saul, the first king of Israel. The traditions of any people are useful in that they throw light on national characteristics, and often on their origin, but the Afghan claim to Hebraic descent is supported only by wild, fictitious genealogies. It is the outcome of a widespread practice amongst Muhammadans, by which they claim or invent some connection with the Prophet or with noted personages whose names occur in the Koran or other sacred writings. Travellers and explorers have been almost unanimous in declaring that the Afghan has pronounced Semitic features. It is true that, as a rule, the Afghan nose is long and curved, but this Jewish or, rather, Hittite nose is very widespread, and is a characteristic of races in no way connected with the Children of Israel. Ujfalvy noticed it on the coins of the Kushan kings of the first century A.D., and drew attention to the fact that this was also a characteristic of the so-called Dard tribes of the Hindu Kush:

Le type du premier des rois Yué-tchi à l'apparence sémitique, se trouve encore de nos jours chez les Dardous des vallées himalayennes.[1]

Lastly, the prevalence of Biblical names, such as Yusaf, Israel and Uriah, together with the existence of Jewish customs, have been brought forward in support of this theory. To ward off the Angel of Death, certain tribes have a custom resembling the Passover, in which they sprinkle the blood of an animal over the doorposts of a house where a sick person resides. Another ceremony is the placing of the sins of the people upon a heifer, which is driven out into the wilderness in the same manner as the Biblical scapegoat. In addition to these, the offering up of sacrifices, the stoning to death of blasphemers, and a periodical redistribution of lands have been cited in support of this theory. Mention has also been made of a sort of Levitical clan amongst the Pathans, in which priestly functions are invested. The use of Biblical names and customs is common to all Muhammadans; the Prophet himself adopted them from the Jews around him. In any case it would not be correct to trace customs, such as the use of a scapegoat, to Israelites alone. We trust we shall hear no more of this conjecture, for which there exists scarcely a shred of evidence. Before proceeding to the conclusions arrived at from the examination of anthropometric data, it is necessary briefly to explain the meaning of the terms Afghan and Pathan. Are all Pathans Afghans, or are the latter a special race who in later times have acquired the title of Pathan?

There is no satisfactory explanation of the original meaning of the term Afghan. On the other hand, the word Pathan is probably an Indian corruption of *Pakhtana*, the Pakhtu-speakers. Of one thing we can be certain: the term Pathan, as applied in Dir and Swat, has no racial significance. Here it denotes status and is restricted in application to those who

[1] "Mémoire sur les Huns blancs", *L'Anthropologie*, 1898, ix, 407.

possess a share (*daftar*) in the tribal lands and a voice in the tribal councils. A person who has lost this status is no longer a Pathan; instead of being a *daftari*, he becomes a *fakir*.[1] In the past writers, who have accepted Bellew as an authority, have attempted to restrict the term Afghan to the Abdali and kindred tribes. Mr Longworth Dames, a well-known authority, objects to this distinction on the ground of insufficient evidence. He points out that the first historical mention of the Afghans finds them, in the eleventh century A.D., inhabiting the mountain fastnesses of the Sulaiman range, "now occupied by their descendants, the very tribes which the advocates of the exclusive claims of the Durranis will not admit to be true Afghans".[2] It will be sufficient for our purpose to remember that the word Afghan is used nowadays in its widest sense to denote any inhabitant of the modern kingdom of Afghanistan, while the term Pathan is loosely applied to any tribe speaking the Pashtu (Pakhtu) language. In this sense the word Afghan is by no means a racial term, for within the borders of Afghanistan are to be found, not only Pathans, but a heterogeneous population composed of Turks, Tajiks, Dehgans, and Usbegs, who belong to very different races. Even to-day it would be difficult to discover any common bond, whether of blood, traditions or language. Islam itself is split up into the Sunni and Shiah sects. The term Pathan, on the other hand, includes the Pashtu and Pakhtu-speaking peoples of southern and eastern Afghanistan and the Indian borderland. In the frontier zone it is used in contradistinction to the Hindki element, the name given to the subject Indian races inhabiting the Pathan country. It should also be borne in mind that many of those who return themselves as Pathans during census operations do so in order to increase their social status, or to gain the protection which the name affords.

[1] *N.W.F.P. Administration Report*, 1901–3, pp. 19–20.
[2] *Encyclopaedia of Islam*, s.v. Afghanistan.

We now come to the results deduced by Sir Herbert Risley from an examination of anthropometric data. According to him the vast bulk of the population of the frontier is of the so-called Turko-Iranian type, in which the Turki element predominates. More recently, Dr Haddon has termed the main racial element of this area Indo-Afghan. The members of all tribes included in this category appear to possess the following main characteristics: stature above the mean; complexion fair; eyes generally dark, but occasionally grey; hair on face plentiful; head broad; nose moderately narrow, prominent, and very long. This seems to be a fairly homogeneous group and can hardly be regarded as a fusion of Turki and Persian elements. If we are to believe Risley, the inhabitants of Hunza and Nagar; the Kafirs of the Hindu Kush; the Pathans, Baluch and Brahui; the Hazaras of Afghanistan; and even the Med fishermen of the Mekran coast can be included within this group. Unfortunately Risley's classification was based upon absurdly small data and has not escaped adverse criticism. The Pathans of Baluchistan were definitely classified as Turko-Iranian, but Bray points out that the measurements were taken haphazardly and without sufficient caution and discrimination.[1] Both Pathan and Baluch elements are supposed to be present in the Marri and Bugti tribes; therefore it is quite possible that the actual men measured may not have been pure Baluch. According to Bray it is impossible to take a tribesman haphazardly and assume that he is of Baluch origin: measurements should be restricted to families of known pedigree. Again, there can be no greater difference physically than that which exists between the Hazaras of Afghanistan and the Med fishermen of the Mekran coast, both of whom Risley classified as Turko-Iranian. To anyone who has had an opportunity of examining Hazaras in one of the Pioneer battalions of the Indian Army, it is obvious that there are abundant signs of that depression

[1] *Census Report*, Baluchistan, 1913, pp. 179–80.

at the root of the nose and corresponding flatness of the cheek bones peculiar to the Mongoloid type. The origin of the Brahui tribes living around Kalat has always constituted one of the most perplexing of Indian ethnological problems. Speaking a Dravidian language in the midst of Eastern Iranian dialects, the Brahui are definitely Turko-Iranian in physical characteristics. Dr Haddon considers their presence to be a case of "cultural drift", but whether they are an advance guard from the south-east or a rear-guard from the north-west remains to be proved.[1]

We must now pass on to compare and contrast the Pathans of the north with the Baluch of the south. Both are Muhammadans, as a rule of the orthodox Sunni sect, recognizing one God, Allah, and one true Prophet, Muhammad; both are warlike and predatory in the extreme, possessing most of the vices and virtues of semi-barbarous races; and both abide by a peculiar code of honour, the most sacred duties of which are to recognize as inviolable the person of one's guest, to exact an eye for an eye and a tooth for a tooth, and to wipe out dishonour by the shedding of blood. In addition, both are organized on a tribal basis. Though their points of resemblance are many, the Pathan presents in many respects a strange and strong contrast to his more southerly neighbour. The Pathan tribal system is ethnic; the Baluch and Brahui political. All tribes, whether Pathan or Baluch, are divided into clans, septs, and families, the important point of difference being that all Pathans trace their descent from one eponymous ancestor. Other uniting forces are common vendetta, common pasture, and common inheritance, but the true bond of union in the Pathan tribe is the fact or fiction of kinship. In other words, the Pathan tribe consists of kindred groups of agnates reckoning descent through the father. In the Baluch and Brahui tribal systems the fact of common vendetta takes the place of common descent. It is the active participation of

[1] Haddon, *The Wanderings of Peoples*, p. 26.

aliens in any blood-feuds the tribe may have on hand which paves the way for admission to tribal membership. As a reward the stranger receives a share of the tribal lands, and eventually he may be allowed to intermarry. On the other hand, the Pathan tribal system is far more homogeneous. These alien groups do not intermarry: they are associated but not intermingled. Be this as it may, "the tendency is continually to merge the fact of common vendetta in the fiction of common blood".

The Pathan is intensely democratic and refuses to obey even his tribal chiefs or *maliks*, unless they are great warriors or bloodthirsty, fearless desperadoes. The Baluch, however, swears fealty to and obeys the dictates of his hereditary chief or *tumandar*. Though both are extremely ignorant of the commonest tenets of their religion, the Baluch is free from that bigoted fanaticism which characterizes his priest-ridden neighbour. Of the Baluch it has been truly said, "An oath by the head of his Sardar is considered more binding than an oath on the Koran". Less turbulent, less fanatical, and less bloodthirsty, he is far easier to control than the Pathan. According to Hughes-Buller, to whom I am indebted for the above contrast, there are three other points of difference.[1] Baluch tribes, because they are politically organized under hereditary chiefs, are more easily recognized and localized than Pathan tribes whose sections, united only by the fact or fiction of kinship, may be scattered over a very wide area. The Baluch method of fighting is a bold frontal attack, for the tribe is organized expressly for offensive action; the Pathan prefers to shoot his enemy from behind, and, as a rule, adopts a more defensive attitude. This does not prevent the Pathan from being continually on the war-path, for descriptions of his treacherous ambuscades are a feature of the history of every frontier campaign. Lastly, a difference has been noticed in their annual migrations. The Baluch and Brahui periodi-

[1] *Census India*, Baluchistan, 1901, v, 27, 40, 128, 129.

cally migrate to fresh pasture lands; the Pathan migrations are largely commercial in character.[1]

Few writers have dealt fairly with the Pathan. With rare exceptions all have depicted him as a villain of the deepest dye. Treacherous, pitiless, vindictive, and bloodthirsty—these are the epithets with which their pages abound. It is quite true that his anger is like a slumbering volcano, or, as the frontier proverb has it: "A Pathan's enmity smoulders like a dung-fire". Equally true are the accounts of his insatiable avarice, for the tenets of his faith are conveniently forgotten when they conflict with his business, his desires or his passions. *Afghan be iman*, the faithless Afghan, was constantly on the lips of the Gurkhas with whom I served on the frontier. Yet, it was the faithless Afridi, who, in 1897, held the Khyber forts against their own kith and kin, while British troops remained inactive at Peshawar. In passing judgment on this barbarous and semi-civilized highlander one should remember that his character is a bewildering mixture of virtues and vices, in which, unfortunately, the latter predominate. Reckless courage and touching fidelity go hand in hand with the basest treachery, and intense cupidity is blended with open-handed hospitality. Temple, Ibbetson, Macgregor, and Elsmie, to mention only a few, judged him by nineteenth-century standards, and forgot that the outlook of this primitive barbarian was still medieval. A rude, perfidious savage he may be, yet one cannot but admire his proud bearing and resolute step, his martial instincts and independent spirit, his frank, open manners and festive temperament, his hatred of control, his love of country, and his wonderful powers of endurance.

General descriptions are apt to be misleading, for the tribes are so numerous, and the physical features of the frontier zone so diverse, that manners and customs necessarily differ from the fever-infested Swat valley to the healthy slopes of the

[1] For a description of tribal migrations see the next chapter.

Takht-i-Sulaiman. Many writers have erred in this respect. According to Ibbetson, "his hair, plentifully oiled, hangs long and straight to his shoulders" and "his favourite colour is dark blue". But the northern tribes shave their heads and often their beards, while the colour and cut of their clothes vary in different localities.

The Pathan code of honour, known as *Pakhtunwali*, imposes upon the tribesmen three obligations, the non-observance of which is regarded as the deadliest of sins, and is followed by lasting dishonour and ostracism. He must grant to all fugitives the right of asylum (*nanawatai*), he must proffer open-handed hospitality (*melmastia*) even to his deadliest enemy, and he must wipe out insult with insult (*badal*). This leads to blood-feuds, which, as a general rule, have their origin in *zar*, *zan*, and *zamin*, in other words, gold, women, and land. Hence the tribes are perpetually at feud, tribe with tribe, clan with clan, and family with family. There is hardly a Pathan whose hands are not stained with the blood of his hereditary enemies. The fury of the Pathan vendetta finds its European counterpart in the modern Albanian blood-feud.[1] No blood-feud can exist between members of the same family, for, within this sacred circle, it would be nothing less than murder. As a general rule women, children, and mullahs are exempt from its operations. Another case of exemption is that of the *rahzan* or war-leader of the Marri Baluch, who incurs no liability for blood-feuds on account of persons killed during the discharge of his duties.[2] Feuds are naturally more numerous in the independent hills than within the British borders. They are of rare occurrence amongst the law-abiding Marwats, but are almost domestic incidents in the Afridi country where it is not uncommon to

[1] (a) Peacock, W., *Albania*, 1914, ch. x. (b) Durham, M. E., *High Albania*, 1909. (c) For another interesting parallel see Temple, R. C., "The Afghans and Mainotes", *Journal United Services Institute of India*, April, 1880, IX, No. 42.

[2] Bray, *Ethnographical Survey*, Baluchistan, 1913, I, 8.

find one half of a village at deadly feud with the other. Indeed, the Afridis are so distracted by intestine quarrels that they have little time for carrying on feuds with the neighbouring tribes. Among the Kafirs of the Hindu Kush there are no blood-feuds, for, as Robertson has pointed out, the Kafir custom of avenging murders prevents their taking place. Not only is the offender's property confiscated, but he is at once forced to leave his native village and become an outcast. According to the customary law of the Mahsud and Shirani, only the actual murderer should be punished, but theory is one thing, practice another. There is, however, a growing tendency in some quarters to blot out the remembrance of former wrongs by means of a payment known as blood-money. A temporary cessation of feuds may occur during harvest operations, or in the face of a common danger, such as the advance of a British punitive force. The Maidan Jagis had been for years at deadly feud with the Turis of Kurram, but, in the spring of 1907, the leading men of both factions concluded a two years' truce, which was faithfully kept on both sides. Again, Pathans, who are hereditary enemies, may serve together for years in the Indian Army, but, once across the border, revenge is again uppermost in their minds. Under this system of bloody vengeance, murder begets murder, and the greater the bloodshed the greater the probability of the duration of the feud. Unfortunately, the unruly tribesmen fail to realize that, under the disastrous influence of this barbarous custom, many of their noblest families are being brought to the verge of extinction. Until this civil warfare, for it is nothing less, dies out, there can be no united people and no reign of peace.

Blood-feuds are not the sole cause of internecine warfare, for the tribes are also split up into several political and religious factions. The most important of the former are the Gar and Samil, which appear to have originated in the Bangash country, whence they spread to the Afridis, Orakzais, and Mohmands. Bellew, with his usual adroitness, fabricated a theory according to which these factions represented the religious differences amongst the Bangash, prior to their conversion to Islam.[1] A more probable explanation is to be found in the Bangash tradition that Gar and Samil were the names of two of their ancestors. Whatever their origin may have been, their existence has undoubtedly complicated the frontier problem, in that it has served to aggravate an already chronic state of internal warfare. West of the Gar and Samil, the Spin (White) and Tor (Black) political factions prevail.

With few exceptions all the tribesmen are Muhammadans of the orthodox Sunni sect, which means that they recognize all the successors of Muhammad and accept not only the Koran but also the Hadis, or traditional sayings, not embodied in the Koran. The Turis of Kurram, many of the Orakzais of Tirah, and certain Bangash clans are Shiahs, that is, they regard Ali, Muhammad's son-in-law, as his first true successor. But the frontier tribesmen are often ignorant of even the fundamental tenets of their faith, and the Waziris are not infrequently uncircumcized. The important point to remember is that the religious creed of the Pathans does not affect their political convictions, for a tribe or clan may be Samil and Sunni, or Samil and Shiah: the combination varies.

No description of these tribes would be complete without some account of their internal administration and of their method of negotiating with the British Raj. Even the most lawless community is compelled to recognize the necessity for some sort of government; even the rudest form of customary law needs enforcing. From Chitral to the Kabul river the British are able to deal with important chiefs and rulers, such as the Mehtar of Chitral and the hereditary chiefs of the numerous khanates into which Dir and Bajaur are divided. In these khanates a form of feudalism exists, for in many cases

---

[1] Bellew, *Enquiry into the Ethnography of Afghanistan*, p. 106.

these petty khans hold their lands as nominees of the great feudal chiefs of Dir and Nawagai. The khan has two kinds of retainers: the *tiakhor* or personal servants, and the *mulatirs* or fighting men. The latter are granted land and houses in the vicinity of the positions they are employed to guard. Yet, even in the midst of this, the communal system of government by *jirga* is to be found.[1]

In the valleys of the Hindu Kush, the Kafir tribes on the borders of the Frontier Province are ruled by headmen, called *jast*. To obtain this distinction a man must be possessed of great wealth, and be head and shoulders above his fellow-tribesmen. For the management of affairs of secondary importance a body of thirteen persons is elected annually. The head of this tribal council is known as the *Ur Jast*.

Farther south, between the Kabul and the Gomal, there are no powerful chiefs corresponding to the northern khans. Here the controlling power is a Council of Elders or tribal *maliks*, known as the *jirga*, through which agency all negotiations between the tribesmen and British frontier officials are carried out. The more democratic a tribe the larger the *jirga*. For this reason a full *jirga* often means nothing less than a gathering of every adult male. Sir Dennis Fitzpatrick, after the conclusion of the Durand Agreement of 1893, had, in his capacity of Lieutenant-Governor of the Panjab, to conclude an arrangement with those Mohmands who had fallen within the British sphere of influence. These Mohmands stated that there were no *maliks* in their country and 900 of them came to discuss the new political situation. "When they arrived they absolutely refused to put forward any men to represent them, even to the extent of being allowed to sit in front at the meeting. Almost the whole number sat down before us just as they managed to find room, and such of them as got near enough all tried to talk together."[2] This will serve to

[1] *Confidential, Frontier and Overseas*, I, 520.
[2] *Parl. Papers*, 1901 (Cd. 496), p. 156.

illustrate the difficulties with which British administrators are faced. Rarely, if ever, does any *jirga* represent the whole tribe, for there are always unruly members who refuse to recognize any control save their own interests and desires. The tribal council is usually composed of a certain number of influential *maliks* and mullahs who attempt to enforce their decrees by meting out punishment in the form of outlawry, heavy fines, or the destruction of property. For the enforcement of *jirga* decrees, the Mahsuds of Waziristan have an institution known as the *chalweshtis*, or tribal police. No blood-feud can arise because of any death caused by them in the execution of their duties. In ordinary times the *jirga* deals with questions of inter-tribal politics, and, since its functions are political rather than social, it cannot be compared to a caste *panchayat*.

Because of the close connection between the semi-independent hills and the settled districts of the Frontier Province, a modified form of the *jirga* system has been introduced into the administered area. This system is in accordance with the Frontier Crimes Regulation of 1901, which superseded the Panjab Frontier Crimes Regulation of 1887. This Regulation empowers the Deputy-Commissioner to make both civil and criminal references to Councils of Elders, that is, to *jirgas* of three or more persons convened according to tribal custom. Where the Deputy-Commissioner is convinced that a civil dispute is likely to lead to a blood-feud or to a breach of the peace, especially where a frontier tribesman is a party to the dispute, he is at liberty to refer the case, for investigation and report, to a Council of Elders of his own nomination. When the decision of the *jirga* is received, he may remand the case for further investigation, refer the enquiry to another *jirga*, or pass a decree in accordance with the finding, provided that not less than three-quarters of the members of the *jirga* have agreed to this decision. Similarly, criminal references may be made to a Council of Elders, if it is inexpedient that the question of the guilt or innocence of an accused person should be tried in the ordinary law courts. Here the Deputy-Commissioner's power to nominate the *jirga* is limited by the accused person's right to object to any member. The maximum punishment for an offence investigated in this manner is fourteen years' rigorous imprisonment. Under this Regulation members of hostile tribes may be debarred from entering British India. Again, where a blood-feud is likely to arise between two families or factions in British territory, the Deputy-Commissioner may, on the recommendation of a *jirga*, order the parties concerned to execute a bond for their good behaviour, for a period not exceeding three years.

An attempt was made in certain parts of the province to modify this system of trial by *jirga*, and to assimilate it to that in use in the Baluchistan Agency. Instead of appointing small *jirgas* for each case, periodical "*jirga* sessions" were held to which all cases awaiting trial were referred. It was hoped that this arrangement would do away with the corruption inherent in small councils and avoid constant summonses to the members of the *jirga*. But even this system had its drawbacks, for, on account of its size and the large number of cases which came before this *jirga*, the members were precluded from proceeding to the scene of each offence for the purpose of supplementing by their own investigations the facts which had already been brought to their notice.

It was not only in the administration of justice that difficulties were experienced. To-day the land tenures of the settled areas resemble those of the adjoining Panjab districts, but this generalization is not true of the early days of Panjab rule. When the Pathans overran the frontier zone they divided the land amongst their various tribes, clans, and septs. Their intensely democratic constitution resulted, with rare exceptions, in a periodical redistribution of lands, known as *vesh* or *khasanne*. The land of each tribal sept was termed a *tappa*, and there was a time when redistribution even of these *tappas* took place. When this ceased, *vesh* continued within the *tappa*, and involved the transfer of whole villages, not merely of individual holdings within the village itself. This was the state of affairs when the British took over the frontier tracts from the Sikhs, and *vesh* was recognized in the early settlements. This system gradually disappeared in the settled districts, because it was opposed to the spirit of British revenue procedure, and because the Pathan began to realize the advantages of fixity of tenure. With the exception of one village, there never seems to have been any system of *vesh* amongst the Bannuchis. This was most probably due to the fact that irrigated country was unsuitable for communal tenure. When the Frontier Province was formed in 1901, *vesh*, with few exceptions, was to be found only across the administrative border. The most important exception was the system of *khulla* (mouth) *vesh*, which prevailed, as late as 1904, in certain unirrigated tracts of the Marwat *tahsil* of Bannu. Under *khulla vesh* fresh shares were allotted to every man, woman, and child. The probable explanation of the survival of *vesh* in the unirrigated tracts of Marwat is that the careful agriculturist has realized the impossibility of effecting any improvements in his sandy holdings, and has therefore been less opposed to such an exchange than would have been the case in a more fertile, irrigated region. The custom of *vesh* still prevails in the independent hills, especially in Buner, Dir, Swat, Bajaur, and Utman Khel. The Waziris, however, have never practised it, and amongst the Mohmands it has entirely disappeared. In Dir, Swat, and Bajaur certain lands, known as Seri, owned by powerful khans or mullahs, are exempted from its operation. The bad effects of this system are patent. Land remains unirrigated, substantial houses are not built, and no improvements are effected. Not until the Pathan realizes the advantages of fixity of tenure will the custom of *vesh* become extinct.

One often hears or reads that the true solution of the

frontier problem, as far as the Pathans are concerned, is to introduce into their country that system which has proved so successful in Baluchistan, namely the Sandeman system. This chapter will have served its purpose if, at the outset, it proves the impossibility of that suggestion. Characteristics, customs, and constitution differ from tribe to tribe. The influence of physical features and many other factors only add to the extreme complexity of the problem. Of necessity we have been forced to adopt different policies, with innumerable local variations, from the snow-clad peaks of the Hindu Kush to the shores of the Arabian Sea.

Chapter IV

TRIBAL DISTRIBUTION AND CHARACTERISTICS

The population contains several ethnological strata, representing the deposits formed by different streams of immigration or invasion.

Imperial Gazetteer of India, 1908.

In this chapter an attempt will be made to describe, as briefly as possible, the tribes of the Frontier Province, with special reference to those inhabiting the area lying between the Durand and the administrative boundaries, for it is these Pathan tribes who are the chief actors on the frontier stage between 1890 and 1908. Reference has already been made to the fact that no rigid or fixed tribal limits exist. Both the Durand and administrative lines violate ethnic considerations. Indeed, no true ethnic lines could possibly be constructed, for the border tribes, because of their migratory and nomadic habits, live for part of the year on one side and for the remainder on the other side of these political boundaries.

In the extreme north of the province dwell the non-Pathan Chitralis. Chitral forms part of a larger tract of country to which the name Dardistan has been given by certain writers, but Leitner's contention that it should be applied to the whole of the area lying between the Hindu Kush and Kashmir has not been accepted by subsequent writers on the ground that there is no country so called by its inhabitants.[1] According to Grierson it is convenient to give the name Dardic to all the Aryan languages spoken in this tract; but, of these, Khowar, the *lingua franca* of Chitral, is the one most nearly related to the Iranian Ghalchah languages spoken north of the Hindu

[1] *Asiatic Quart. Rev.* 1893, v, 167.

Kush.[1] For our purpose it will be sufficient to remember that Chitral is bounded on the north by the Hindu Kush; on the east by the Gilgit Agency, Mastuj, and Yasin; on the west by Badakhshan and Kafiristan; and on the south by Dir.

The mists of obscurity hang thickly over the origin of the Chitralis, and, in all probability, like most of the inhabitants of the borderland, they are a very mixed race. Evidence exists of immigration from Wakhan and the Pamirs, and also of some admixture of Mongolian blood attributed to Chinese invaders. Sir Aurel Stein failed to see any great difference between the Chitralis and the Ghalchah-speaking peoples of the Pamirs and the Oxus, but noticed a distinct difference in physical features between them and their Dard brethren of Astor and Gurez.[2] The latest enquirer points to the existence of some strain of Indo-Afghan blood in their composition.[3]

The Chitralis call their country Kho and their language Khowar, hence the divisions of Chitral are known as Turikho, Mulkho, and Ludkho. The population is divided into three classes, the Adamzadas, Arbabzadas, and Faqir Miskin, which represent social, not racial distinctions. The occupational form of caste is to be found in the *dartoche* (carpenters), *kulale* (potters), and *doms* (musicians). In fact the caste system is stronger and more prevalent in Chitral than in any other part of the province, but, even here, it is slowly disappearing under the influence of that levelling creed, Islam. In religion the Chitralis are converts to Islam and are of the Sunni persuasion, but idolatry and many primitive beliefs still survive. In the Ludkho valley the inhabitants are Maulais, that is, they pay special attention to the Shiah doctrine of *Taqqiah* or concealment in times of danger, according to which they can disguise their real religious convictions to avoid persecution.

---

[1] *Linguistic Survey of India*, VIII, pt ii, 1–3.
[2] Stein, *Serindia*, I, 26–7.
[3] *Journ. Roy. Anthrop. Inst.* XLII, 466–7.

The head of this sect is the Agha Khan, the leader of the Khoja community in Bombay. The people of Hunza are also members of this strange sect.

In martial qualities the Chitralis compare very unfavourably with their more warlike neighbours, the Pathans, and may be said to be dangerous only when they have the advantage of overwhelming numbers. Neither is the Chitrali subject to those fanatical outbursts which characterize the more bigoted Pathan. The women of the Hindu Kush may be described as female Don Juans. Robertson observed that most Kafir women had their *affaires* to which their husbands did not object, owing to the fact that it meant an increase in wealth, for the ordinary punishment for adultery was a fine of cows.[1] In Chitral, however, the injured husband can slay both the seducer and his wife, if caught *flagrante delicto*. Sir George Robertson described the Chitralis as treacherous and prone to acts of cold-blooded cruelty, but observed that revolting excesses and revengeful murders went hand in hand with pleasant manners and engaging light-heartedness. If his description be true, then Chitral well deserves its name, the land of mirth and murder. Leitner in all his works holds a brief for the "laughter and song-loving" Chitralis, and vehemently attacks Robertson for his unfavourable verdict. In fact, the accounts of Robertson and Durand could be more properly applied to the ruling class, for many of the Mehtars (rulers) of Chitral have waded to their thrones through stream of blood.

South of Chitral, between the western borders of Hazara and the Mohmand tribal area, lie the independent tracts of Dir, Swat, Bajaur, and Buner. Any attempt at an accurate description of the tribal distribution of this area would result in a perplexing mass of detail which would render the narrative almost unreadable. It has therefore been thought sufficient to treat this intricate problem in a very general manner.

[1] Robertson, *Kafirs of the Hindu Kush*, p. 444.

Towards the end of the fifteenth century, according to local tradition, two large branches of Pathan tribes, the Khakhai and the Ghoria Khel, migrated from their homes in the hilly country around Kabul to the Jalalabad valley and the northern slopes of the Safed Koh. The most important divisions of the Khakhai were the Yusafzai, Gugiani, and Tarkanri: the Ghoria Khel were divided into five tribes, the Mohmands, Khalils, Daudzais, Chamkannis, and Zeranis. The Yusafzais, advancing into the modern Peshawar district, expelled the inhabitants, known as Dilazaks, and finally conquered the country north of the Kabul river and west of Hoti Mardan. By the opening years of the sixteenth century the Ghoria Khel had also reached the Khyber area. According to Ibbetson, who took Bellew for his authority, these tribes were only returning to their original homes whence they had been expelled in the fifth and sixth centuries of the Christian era. There is, however, not a shred of evidence for this assertion. Eventually, these powerful tribes displaced the original inhabitants, driving some to the Swat Kohistan and forcing the Dilazaks across the Indus. Later the Ghoria Khel attempted to oust the Khakhai branch, but were signally defeated by the Yusafzais.

The Yusafzais and their kinsmen, the Mandanr Pathans, form the bulk of the population in the area we are now describing. The Mandanr are to be found in the so-called Yusafzai plain of Peshawar, while the Yusafzai proper dwell in the hilly country to the north, where they have lost their original designation and are known by the names of their various sections and sub-sections.[1] Conflicting accounts are extant of the virtues and vices of the Yusafzai tribes. Frugal and abstemious, yet extremely hospitable, even the smallest village possesses its *hujra* or guest-house. Patriotic and proud of their descent, of which they eternally boast, there are few

[1] The Akozais of the Swat valley and Dir; the Malizais of Buner; the Isazais of the Black Mountain and the Indus; and the Iliaszais of Buner.

finer specimens of Pathans than the Yusafzais of Buner, although the physique of those inhabiting the fever-infested Swat valley and the low-lying Yusafzai plain suffers in consequence. But there is a darker side to the picture, for these sons of Joseph are extremely priest-ridden, and most of the disturbances in this area have been fomented by Sayyids and religious fanatics.

The Swati tribes driven across the Indus by the invading Yusafzais are now to be found in Allai, Nandihar, Tikari, Deshi, and the adjoining Hazara district. For this reason the term Swati is misleading, for nowadays it has no connection with the Swat valley. In accordance with border custom all Swatis claim Pathan descent, but in reality they are very heterogeneous in origin. Bigoted Sunnis and untrustworthy, eternally at feud with one another, they have been depicted as villains of the deepest dye by the writers of the old gazetteers, yet it would be a mistake to look upon them as cowards, for they have been known to fight with a fury akin to that of the Dervishes of the Sudan.

The Ghoria Khel, who followed in the wake of the Yusafzai invaders, are represented in the Frontier Province by the Mohmands, Daudzais, Khalils, and Chamkannis. The Mohmands alone need detain us.

Like many other frontier tribes, such as the Mamands, Bangash, and Darwesh Khel Waziris, the Mohmand tribes are to be found both in Afghanistan and in British territory. Those within the British sphere of influence can be divided into the *Kuz* (plain) Mohmands, whose lands lie to the south of Peshawar within the British administrative border, and the *Bar* (hill) Mohmands of the independent hills to the northwest. The Mohmands of the settled districts represent one of the many cases of fission, where a branch or section of a tribe has broken off from the parent stock and lost all connection with it. The trans-border Mohmands can be divided into three chief clans, the Tarakzai, Baezai, and Khwaezai. In addition there are affiliated and vassal clans, while those in receipt of government allowances are known as the "assured" clans.[1]

The Mohmand hills are wild, rugged and desolate. In many parts water is so scarce that cultivation can be carried on only with the aid of artificial wells. Fierce, treacherous, and ruthlessly cruel, these tribes do not scruple to mutilate the dead and wounded left behind by their enemies. According to Paget and Mason[2] they are inclined to be cowardly, but, taking into account their later struggles with the British and my own experiences in 1919, I do not by any means consider them lacking in courage. Their domestic customs are very similar to those of the Yusafzais, except that they have no *hujras*. As is the case in nearly all Pathan communities, the women are mere drudges, little better than beasts of burden, for they are the hewers of wood and drawers of water, and, as the wells are few and far between, this is most laborious work.

Around the Khyber and to the south in Tirah dwell the Afridis, whose origin lies hidden in the mists of obscurity. Some authorities have identified them with the Aparytae of Herodotus; others believe them to be of Pathan origin, the descendants of one Karlarnaey. The latest opinion, that of Sir Aurel Stein, is well worth recording: "The Afridi tribes, though at present speaking Pashto, contain a large, if not predominant racial element, which was established in Tirah long before the advent of those Afghan invaders, who during Muhammadan times gradually pushed their way into the belt of hills and alluvial plains west of the Indus".[3]

Many and lurid are the descriptions of the poor savage Afridi, who has been forced by his geographical position to

[1] The affiliated clans are divided into the *Kuchi* (nomad) and the *Udredunkai* (settled). The vassal clans are the Mullagoris, Safis, and Shilmanis.

[2] *Record of Expeditions*, pp. 228–9.

[3] *Journ. Roy. Asiatic Soc.* July, 1925, pp. 402–3.

play a political part in the drama of Anglo-Afghan relations. Elphinstone described him as the greatest of robbers amongst robber hordes. Mackeson painted him with an avarice so great that he would not scruple to sell even his own kith and kin. A truer and more sympathetic account is that of Sir Robert Warburton, who for eighteen years was Warden of the Khyber, and was himself of Afghan extraction. According to Warburton the Afridi is forced from his earliest childhood to look upon his nearest relative as his deadliest enemy. Distrust of all mankind is, therefore, almost a religion to the Afridi. Once this distrust is removed, he is capable of the greatest devotion, and may turn out to be your staunchest friend. But, treat him unfairly or abuse him, interfere with his customs or his women, and he will cut your throat without the slightest compunction. In appearance lean and wiry, his eagle eye, proud bearing, and light step speak of a freedom born of his wind-swept mountain glens. In religion an orthodox Sunni, he is, nevertheless, ignorant of the commonest tenets of the Koran, and superstitious in the extreme. His never-ending blood-feuds, confined to the various clans and septs of the Afridi tribe, and his intensely democratic nature, render tribal cohesion and united action well-nigh impossible.

The southern valleys of Tirah are inhabited by heterogeneous tribes, known collectively as Orakzais, or lost tribes.[1] Many clans of foreign extraction, such as Yusafzais, Waziris, and Ghilzais, are to be found amongst the Orakzais. In fact, the aboriginal element appears to exist only in the Tirahi sections. The most warlike and courageous of the Orakzai tribes are the Lashkarzais, concerning one of whose sections, the Mamuzais, it has been written: "There is perhaps no other tribe between the Kabul and Kurram rivers which is so much under the influence of the mullas and so fanatical as

[1] Ismailzais, Massuzais, Lashkarzais, Daulatzais, Muhammad Khels, Sturi Khels, and *hamsaya* (vassal) clans.

are these people".[1] The Mamizais have the unenviable distinction of being known as the *kichan* or dirty clan. The heterogeneous character of the Orakzai tribes however renders any general description difficult.

To the west of Tirah stretches the Kurram valley, of whose inhabitants the most important are the Turis. According to Ibbetson they are probably relics of the invasions of Chengiz Khan and Timur, but Edwardes considered them to be of Indian extraction and believed their original home to be at Nilab on the Indus.[2] Unfortunately for Edwardes, his theory is at variance with both Turi traditions and the history of tribal immigrations into the Frontier Province, for the Turis themselves claim to have come originally from Persia, which claim would quite probably account for their being Shiahs, while the history of Pathan migrations definitely shows that the pressure has been invariably exerted from the Afghan and not from the Indian entrances to the great mountain passes. The fact that the Turis are Shiahs may have resulted from the efforts of wandering Sayyids and other religious teachers.[3] When it is remembered that the Turis are intensely democratic and are divided into both religious and political factions, it is not to be wondered at that before the arrival of the British, in 1892, Kurram was a seething hotbed of intrigues. There is now a political agent in the valley, who is assisted in his duties by a council of tribal elders whose proceedings are regulated by the *Turizuna* or Turi customary law.

Between Kurram and the Gomal lies Waziristan, the frontier Switzerland, an intricate maze of mountains and valleys bounded on the west by the Afghan province of Khost and the Birmal hills, and on the east by the British settled districts. It is inhabited by four tribes: the Darwesh Khels,

[1] *Confidential, Frontier and Overseas*, ii, 196.

[2] (a) Ibbetson, *Punjab Castes*, p. 69. (b) Edwardes, *Some Notes on the Valley of Kurram and its Peoples*, 1857.

[3] In this connection it should be remembered that Sind was once a Shiah stronghold.

the Mahsuds, the Dawaris, and the Bhittannis. In the heart of Waziristan around Kaniguram dwell the Mahsuds, between whom and British territory is interposed the Bhittanni country. On all other sides they are flanked by Darwesh Khels who are astride the Durand boundary. To the north, in the Tochi valley, is the area occupied by the Daurs or Dawaris. According to their own traditions both the Mahsuds and Darwesh Khels are Pathans, though Bellew, without any adequate explanation, supposed them to be of Rajput extraction.[1] It is now generally agreed that these two tribes, collectively known as Waziris, left their original homes in the Birmal hills of modern Afghanistan sometime towards the close of the fourteenth century, and gradually extending eastwards occupied the country in which they now reside. The Darwesh Khels can be divided into two main sections, the Utmanzai, who are chiefly confined to southern Waziristan, and the Ahmadzai, who are to be found scattered throughout the country. The Mahsuds, the scourge of the Derajat borders, have three branches: the Bahlolzai, Shaman Khel, and the Alizai.

To no border tribes does the generalization, that their geographical position has forced them to play the robber part, more aptly apply than to the inhabitants of Waziristan. Though ignorant, illiterate and superstitious, the Waziri is so vain and obstinate that he can never imagine himself to be in the wrong. Intensely democratic he knows no law but his own passions and desires. Treacherous and dogged in the pursuit of vengeance he will not scruple to kill even a woman or a child.

In Kaniguram and surrounded by Mahsuds dwell a people calling themselves Baraki, but known to their neighbours as Ormurs. Little is known of their origin, except that they differ considerably in customs and characteristics from their

---

[1] (a) Bellew, *Races of Afghanistan*, ch. IX. (b) Raverty, H. G., "The Waziri Afghans and their Country", *Asiatic Quart. Rev.* 1895.

Mahsud neighbours. Their language, Ormuri or Bargista, is akin to the Ghalchah languages of the Pamirs and therefore, like Pashtu, Eastern Iranian.

In the Tochi valley of northern Waziristan dwell the Pashtu-speaking Dawaris, who are not considered to be of Pathan descent. Notoriously unwarlike they form a strong contrast to their Waziri neighbours, and, with the exception of the Bannuchis, to be noted later, they are in many respects the worst of the border tribes. Their unnatural vices and outbursts of frenzied excitement are to a considerable degree the result of an extremely unhealthy climate added to the pernicious habit of opium-smoking and drug-taking. Oliver described the Dawari in the following words:

> An object of supreme contempt to his warlike neighbours the Waziris, he is even looked upon as a bad character by a Bannuchi. Worse probably could not be said of him. To call him dirty would be a compliment; his clothes, usually black cotton to start with, are worn till they would be considered malodorous by a Ghilzai.... His unnatural licentiousness would have made him conspicuous in Sodom or Gomorrah.[1]

This evidence has been corroborated by later observers. About the only thing that can be said in favour of the Dawaris is that they are diligent, hard-working and patient cultivators.

The Bhittannis, whose territory stretches along the eastern borders of Waziristan from the Gomal to Marwat, are a Pathan tribe holding lands on both sides of the administrative boundary. They have a long-standing feud with the Mahsuds who have to pass through their limits in order to raid the Tank and Bannu borders. During part of 1921 and 1922 I was able to visit their country and observed that in many cases they lived in miserable brushwood hovels or in caves on the hill-side.

From Bannu through Kohat, and along the Indus as far north as Akora in the Peshawar district stretch the lands of

[1] Oliver, *Across the Border*, p. 121.

the Khattaks, the most favourable specimens of Pathans on the whole frontier.[1] Hard-working and industrious, they are engaged in agricultural pursuits or find employment as carriers in the salt trade. Brave, active, and trustworthy they make good soldiers. That they are industrious and loyal is to a large extent the result of nearly eighty years' contact with the benefits of British administration in the settled districts.

In Bannu dwell the Bannuchis and Marwats. The history of tribal immigrations into Bannu is yet another proof of the truth of the assertion that all frontier invasions have been caused by pressure exerted from the Afghan side. The Bannuchis claim to be of Pathan origin, but in reality they are the most mixed and hybrid of all the border tribes. Intermarriage with low-caste Hindus, Sayyids, *hamsaya* clans, and other foreign elements has produced a mongrel race who represent "the ebb and flow of might, right, possession and spoliation". Of the heterogeneous elements which go to make up the Bannuchi people, Edwardes has written:

> Every stature, from that of the weak Indian to that of the tall Dooranee; every complexion, from the ebony of Bengal to the rosy cheek of Cabul; every dress, from the linen garments of the south, to the heavy goat-skin of the eternal snows, is to be seen promiscuously among them, reduced only to a harmonious whole by the neutral tint of universal dirt.[2]

Of poor physique, cowardly, untruthful and bigoted, according to the official description in the gazetteers, their only redeeming features are those which make them good agriculturists, and prompt revenue payers. Notwithstanding their filthy habits and degraded character the women of their Isakhi clan are renowned for their beauty. "Who marries not an Isakhi woman deserves an ass for a bride." Even the smallest Bannuchi village has its *chauk*, a sort of mud platform near the village mosque, where, under the shadow of gigantic pipal or

[1] For Khattak history see *Kalid-i-Afghani*, 1875, ch. v.
[2] Edwardes, *Year on the Punjab Frontier*, I, 70–1.

shisham trees, every idle fellow airs his complaints. The Marwats, a branch of the Lohani Pathans, are a strong contrast to their degraded neighbours, and are a fine and law-abiding race.

The flat and dreary wastes of Dera Ismail Khan are peopled chiefly by Jats, the Pathan element forming only about one-third of the total population. The district appears to have been colonized by two simultaneous streams of invaders, the Jats and Baluch from the south, and the Pathans from the north-west. The most important Pathan tribes within the settled areas are the Khasor, Baluch (an unfortunate name for a Pathan tribe), Kundi, Gandapur, Mian Khel, and Babar. Across the administrative border, around the Takht-i-Sulaiman, dwell the Shirani tribes. The Shiranis, or, as they prefer to style themselves, the Maranis, live on both sides of the Sulaiman range, those on the eastern slopes being known as the Largha, those on the western as the Bargha. It is interesting to note that Shirani marriage customs differ from those prevailing elsewhere on the border, for the father of the bride gives a dowry instead of receiving a price for his daughter.[1]

It is proposed to conclude this chapter with a short description of the nomadic tribes who periodically migrate into the Frontier Province. The climate and physical features of every country profoundly affect the habits of the people who live there. Prosperous cities cannot arise in the midst of desert wastes, small oases cannot provide for the herds and flocks of large tribes. Nomadism is the chief characteristic of the tribes of Baluchistan, who are for ever wandering off in search of fresh water supplies. In the same way a large proportion of the population of the Frontier Province is essentially nomadic in character. Extremes of heat and cold force certain tribes to migrate periodically from summer to winter

[1] For Shirani customs see (a) *Baluchistan District Gazetteer*, Zhob, 1907, I, 74–5; (b) *Punjab Glossary*, III, 407–16.

quarters; a scarcity of water and the absence of suitable grazing grounds compel them to move continually from old to new pastures.

Migrations into the North-West Frontier Province are of three kinds: trading caravans, groups of men seeking temporary employment, and this continual movement backwards and forwards between the hills and the lowlands. During the last twenty years there has been a considerable decrease in the number of immigrants from Afghanistan. Three reasons have been assigned for this: the difficulty of obtaining permission to leave the amir's territories; the contraction of the available grazing areas in India; and the fact that caravans are more liable to be plundered now that the border tribesmen are better armed. Of all the nomadic tribes entering the Province by far the most important are the Powindahs, or warrior traders, in whose hands lies the bulk of the carrying trade between Central Asia and the bazaars of Hindustan.[1] They are the frontier gypsies for whom the road and a roving life have an irresistible attraction. In the autumn they collect together on the plains of Ghazni, and, laden with merchandize from Bokhara, Herat, and Kandahar, they commence their march towards India. In the cold weather they are to be found in all the large cities throughout the length and breadth of India, while some of the more venturesome go as far afield as Australia. The spring finds them once more trekking towards Ghazni. Large numbers of these Powindahs, when they reach the Derajat, form fixed camping grounds or *kirris* on the *Daman*, where they live with their families, flocks, and herds. Using these *kirris* as headquarters they spread over the plains to engage in trade. The members of this class form a valuable source of income to the Derajat authorities, to whom they pay taxes in the form of *tirni* or grazing dues. Then there are those Powindahs who accompany the *kafilas*, but do not bring their families with them. Lastly, there are people known as

[1] *Hayat-i-Afghani* (tr. Priestley), p. 19.

the *charra* folk, who come in small groups and wander through the towns and villages of the Derajat in search of employment as labourers.

In this chapter an attempt has been made to show how intricate and complicated the local problem of tribal control really is. To understand it, some knowledge of the tribes, of their characteristics, customs, and geographical distribution is essential. The history of tribal migrations proves that practically all the available evidence points to a series of immigrations from the west, that is, from the direction of the Sulaiman range and Afghanistan. Perhaps the most important lesson of all, and one that should profoundly affect our future frontier policy, is that savage and bloodthirsty tribes become less barbarous and more reconciled to peaceful pursuits under a settled administration.

Chapter V

THE FORWARD POLICY IN THE 'NINETIES

It appears to the Government of India that the time has arrived when it becomes of extreme importance that an effort be made to bring under our control, and, if possible, to organize, for purposes of defence against external aggression, the great belt of independent tribal territory which lies along our north-western frontier, and which has hitherto been allowed to remain a formidable barrier against ourselves.

Government of India to Panjab Government, 17 August, 1887.

At this time it appears to the Commander-in-Chief that there are strong reasons for a fresh departure in our policy towards the frontier tribes, in order that, when the time arrives, they may identify themselves with us and assist us not only with supplies and transport, but by sharing in the maintenance of our lines of communication.   Lord Roberts.

Throughout the nineties of the last century, especially from 1895 onwards, the frontier districts were abnormally disturbed. There were two main reasons for this: the forward policy pursued under Lord Lansdowne and Lord Elgin, and the intrigues of the Amir of Afghanistan. The opening years of the period under consideration witnessed punitive expeditions against the Shiranis inhabiting the slopes of the far-famed Takht-i-Sulaiman; the Orakzai clans in the neighbourhood of the Samana range; the Isazai tribes of the ill-omened Black Mountain; and the petty chiefs, or thums, of Hunza and Nagar.

To appreciate fully the Shirani situation, some knowledge of the Government of India's policy towards the tribes of the Gomal and Zhob valleys is necessary. We have already observed how the work of Sir Robert Sandeman in the Khan of Kalat's territories had resulted in the carving out of a new frontier district, the Baluchistan Agency. Between Baluchistan and the Panjab, that is, between the Bolan and Gomal

passes, stretched the Zhob and Bori valleys over which Sandeman desired to extend British control.[1] He pointed out that
for military, political, and commercial reasons the occupation
of Zhob was of paramount importance. It would shorten our
line of defence, and at the same time ensure the good behaviour
of the surrounding tribes, because it would secure the "back-
doors" or "bolt-holes" through which outlaws and raiding
parties escaped into Afghanistan. Situated on the southern
flank of the Gomal, it would serve as a protection for this
important trade route. In addition, the fact that no definite
information of this area had been acquired was a further
incentive for a more friendly understanding with the wild
banditti of these trans-frontier tracts.

In 1884, as the result of an expedition, the *maliks* of Zhob
and Bori professed their willingness to allow the location of
British troops in their respective valleys, whenever the British
should consider such a step desirable.[2] Three years later it
was necessary to locate troops at Loralai in the Bori valley,
for the purpose of protecting the frontier road connecting
Pishin with Dera Ghazi Khan. In the same year, Bori and
the adjoining territories of the Khetrans were brought under
the administration of the Baluchistan authorities. It was not,
however, until the year 1889, when it was decided to open and
attempt the pacification of the Gomal pass, that the Government of India sanctioned the occupation of Zhob. This task
was entrusted to Sandeman, who was ably assisted by Bruce,
the Deputy-Commissioner of Dera Ismail Khan. Sandeman
first proceeded to Appozai in Zhob, where an imposing
durbar was held, to which representatives of all the neighbouring tribes were invited. At this durbar he announced to
the assembled *maliks* and *jirgas* that in future Zhob was to be

[1] The Zhob river rises east of the Pishin valley, near Quetta, and flows
into the Gomal. Bori is now a sub-division of the Loralai district of
Baluchistan. It consists of a long valley forming the catchment area of
two branches of the Anambar river.

[2] Aitchison, xi, No. cxxvii.

looked upon as a British protectorate. From Appozai Sandeman proceeded along the Gomal to Tank, where another durbar was held. As a result of this three posts were established in the Gomal, and allowances, in return for the protection of the route, were granted to the Shiranis, Mahsuds, and Darwesh Khels.[1] Eventually, in the year 1890, the Gomal river, from Domandi to its junction with the Zhob stream, was declared the boundary between Baluchistan and the Panjab frontier.

It now looked as if the peace of this area were ensured, but there was still much to be done before the Gomal could be considered a royal high road. Some of the Darwesh Khels of Wana were dissatisfied with the allowances granted them at Appozai. Internal feuds amongst the Shiranis only served to complicate matters; and the Khiddarzai section of the Largha Shiranis, who had refused to attend the Appozai durbar, were still in open revolt. In addition, a notorious outlaw, one Dost Muhammad, was fomenting disturbances among the Kakar Pathans of Zhob. For this reason, towards the end of 1890, a punitive force under Major-General Sir George White overran the Khiddarzai country. This forced the Shiranis to come to terms. They agreed to guarantee the safety of caravans passing through the Zao, Khiddarzai, and Chuhar Khel passes; to furnish escorts for European officials entering their territories; to hand over hostages as a pledge of their good faith; and to surrender outlaws and fugitives from justice. They further agreed to the establishment of levy posts at certain points; and recognized that, if its orders were ignored, the Government of India would be at liberty to occupy the Shirani country.[2]

While these events were taking place on the borders of Baluchistan, the persistent misbehaviour of certain Orakzai clans across the Kohat frontier rendered the use of force

---

[1] *Moral and Material Progress of India*, 1889–90, p. 228.
[2] Aitchison, xi, No. xcii.

inevitable. The prevailing unrest was the result of two factors which have ever been instrumental in fomenting disturbances on the Indian borderland. First, considerable uncertainty existed as to the exact location of the boundary line between the settled districts and the independent hills. Secondly, negotiations with the tribesmen were carried on through the doubtful medium of a Pathan "middleman", the Khan of Hangu.

Roughly speaking the Samana range separated the independent Orakzais of the Khanki valley of Tirah from the Miranzai valley of the Kohat district, where dwelt the Bangash Pathans who were British subjects. The Orakzais, as we have observed, were divided into the Gar and Samil political factions. At this time, however, with the solitary exception of the Akhels, it was the five Samil clans who were disturbing the peace of the border. The anomalous position of the Malla Khels, who held lands both in the Miranzai valley and across the administrative border, where they were *hamsayas* of the Orakzais, proved a great obstacle to the good administration of the valley. Not only did they rob and plunder, but they also harboured outlaws and fugitives, and even acted as guides and spies for marauding bands from the independent hills. Unfortunately, there was a much more potent cause of unrest. It was a well-known fact that the Khan of Hangu intrigued with and stirred up discontent amongst the very tribes for whose peaceful conduct he was responsible. Indeed the Khan of Hangu was no ordinary person. His family was extremely influential, and, long before the British appeared upon the scene, had acquired a sort of hereditary right over the Bangash Pathans of the Miranzai valley. When the British occupied the district, it was found convenient to conduct relations with the inhabitants through this person, who became the Khan Tahsildar for the valley. The unrest prevalent on the Kohat borders at this time will go down to posterity as an example of the danger of raising a local and powerful khan to

the position of "middleman" or "go-between", for this
procedure inevitably results in his acquiring undue influence
and power. There can be no doubt that for years the Khan of
Hangu and his notoriously bad son, Baz Gul, had carried on
anti-British intrigues. Acting on his advice, the tribes had
refused to pay outstanding fines, and the Malla Khels in
particular had refused to be brought under British police
jurisdiction. In fact, the khan's disloyalty was at the root of
most of the disturbances in this area.

Sir James Lyall, the Lieutenant-Governor of the Panjab,
came to the conclusion that the British boundary, the red
line of the maps, should be advanced to the foot of the Samana
range, so as to include the Malla Khel villages. At the same
time the khan was warned that, if he did not collect outstanding fines, he would be deprived of his office and would
forfeit his allowances. As he seemed powerless to control his
son, it was proposed to remove Baz Gul from the district.
Lyall also recommended that a small body of militia should
be stationed at Hangu, and that the strength of the Border
Militia should be increased.[1] These recommendations, with
the exception of the last, received the sanction of the Government of India in July, 1889.[2]

Although the *tahsildar* and his son were removed from the
frontier, the tribes continued to misbehave and refused to
come to terms. On two occasions in the summer of 1890,
when it appeared as if matters could be arranged successfully
without resorting to armed intervention, the proposed expedition was cancelled, but, when all conciliatory methods
failed, and it became apparent that the clans mistook this
forbearance for weakness, it was resolved to coerce them by
punitive measures. Consequently, on 2 January, 1891, an
expedition was sanctioned. In January and February, troops
under Sir William Lockhart traversed the settlements of the

---

[1] *Parl. Papers*, 1891, LIX (C. 6526), 9–10.
[2] *Idem*, pp. 15–16.

offending clans, but, owing to the severity of the weather, encountered only slight opposition. The clans gave a very unwilling consent to the establishment of fortified posts on the Samana; and the withdrawal of British forces was the signal for a treacherous attack upon the troops protecting the working parties engaged in the construction of these forts. Thus the British temporarily lost possession of the crest. In the second Miranzai expedition of 1891, the British were faced not only by the Samil clans, but also by the Gar clans of the Akhel and Ali Khel, assisted by a detachment of Afridis. By 17 April, 1891, the crest was once more in British hands, and the enemy had been severely punished. It was now decided to hold the Samana range in force, for which purpose both military and militia posts were constructed. Fortunately for the peace of this part of the border the Orakzais gave no further trouble until the general frontier rising of 1897.

While we were consolidating our position on the Samana range, it became necessary to coerce the Black Mountain tribes of the Hazara border. The Black Mountain, so called because of its dark forests of Himalayan silver fir, stretches for a distance of about thirty miles between the Indus and Hazara, to the north of where the Indus becomes the western boundary of that district. Enclosed on the north and west by the Indus, bounded on the south by Tanawal and on the east by Agror, Pariari, Tikari, Nandihar, and Deshi, it rises to a height of about 8000 feet above sea-level. Its eastern face is the home of the Swati tribes of Deshi; its western slopes are inhabited by the cis-Indus Isazai clans of the Hassanzais, Akazais, and Mada Khels. Possessed of great natural beauty, it has assumed a somewhat melancholy importance in that it has been the haunt of fanatical bands, such as the Hindustani fanatics, who gave us so much trouble in the Ambela campaign of 1863. In 1888, twenty years of unprovoked outrages were punished by an expedition at the conclusion of which the Hassanzai and Akazai *jirgas* signed an agreement, whereby they recognized their responsibility for the conduct of Hashim Ali Khan of Seri, who was in open revolt against the British. They also agreed not to molest in any way or resist the march of British troops along the crest of the Black Mountain.[1]

This expedition served a useful purpose in proving to the recalcitrant tribesmen that a long series of outrages was inevitably followed by a day of reckoning; that they could not persist in their misconduct for ever; and that they could be coerced by troops operating even in the innermost recesses of their rugged and mountainous country. Although they had been severely punished and their *jirgas* had acquiesced in agreements which looked very well on paper, the authorities in India were not foolish enough to suppose that any lasting results would follow from a system of punitive expeditions devoid of any efforts to formulate a more conciliatory policy. Bearing this in mind they were desirous of evolving some arrangement by which a more effective control might be exercised over these tribes. There were several possible solutions. They could construct roads in order to facilitate the advance of troops into tribal territory; they could strengthen the frontier by holding selected points with posts garrisoned with levies or militia; and an attempt could be made to recruit a native militia from the disaffected elements across the border. In any case, it would be necessary to cultivate friendly relations with the trans-border headmen, but, in the case of the chief khan, Hashim Ali, the first overtures would have to come from him.

These Black Mountain tribes lived in a *cul de sac* which was of no importance either commercially or strategically. No great high roads gave access to Afghan territory; no important passes or trade routes connected their country with the bazaars of Central Asia. For these reasons, the Hazara

[1] Aitchison, xi, Nos viii and ix.

border, from Allai to Tanawal, differed in many respects from the Derajat and other parts of what was in those days the Panjab frontier. Even the outrages committed were different in origin and nature from those taking place near the entrances to the great passes of the south, where cattle lifting and camel stealing were everyday occurrences. The raids of the Black Mountain tribes were chiefly political in character, instigated by their leading men in pursuance of private feuds with persons residing in British territory. Mere plundering incursions were extremely rare, for the Black Mountain itself formed a barrier across which it was difficult to escape with cattle. These were the considerations which induced the local officials to advise the Panjab Government not to enlist the independent tribesmen in a border militia.[1] On 27 March, 1890, the Government of India sanctioned the construction of certain roads and border posts as the best means of controlling these clans.[2]

It will be remembered that the tribes, at the close of the 1888 expedition, had promised to permit the unmolested march of British troops along the crest of the Black Mountain. The Government of India now thought it advisable that this military demonstration should take place. It is to be regretted that the authorities ever made this decision, for, if they desired another expedition, this was one of the surest methods of creating fresh disturbances. It seems obvious that this trailing of our coat in the face of the enemy would be misconstrued by turbulent savages. To say the least the march was impolitic.

An attempt, in October, 1890, to march troops along the crest had to be abandoned, because of the hostile attitude of the tribes. Preparations were accordingly made for an expedition, but this time our *casus belli* was very weak. There were no kidnapped British subjects to release, no murderous

---

[1] *Parl. Papers*, 1891, LIX (C. 6526), pt ii, 50.
[2] *Idem*, pp. 61–2.

outrages remained unatoned. Neither was there any immediate urgency to settle the Black Mountain problem, for in importance it was vastly inferior to both the Gomal and the Khyber areas. But the fact remained that the clans had fired on British troops, and the authorities in India were of opinion that such an insult could be wiped out only by retaliation. The offending clans, the Hassanzais and Akazais, offered no opposition to a force which marched against them; and, on 29 May, 1891, agreed to the perpetual banishment of Hashim Ali Khan; to assist in protecting roads made within their borders; to allow the march of troops along the crest of the Black Mountain; to prohibit the settlement of Hindustani fanatics within their country; and to hold themselves responsible for the offences of their clansmen within British limits. Similar agreements were made with the Mada Khels and Chagarzais.[1] To protect the Hazara border the Government of India, contrary to the advice of its local officials, sanctioned the enlistment of the independent clans in the Border Police. The Swatis of Nandihar, Tikari, and Deshi joined in considerable numbers, but the service was unpopular with the Hassanzai and Akazai clans.[2] The return of Hashim Ali to Hassanzai territory led to another expedition in 1892, after which comparative peace reigned in the Isazai country.

Far more important than these petty wars was the peaceful acquisition of the Kurram valley, which was taken over in 1892, at the request of its Turi inhabitants. This was followed in 1893 by the delimitation of the Durand boundary, the effect of which will be discussed in the chapter dealing with Anglo-Afghan relations.

From what has been written it will be seen that, during the opening years of the 'nineties, there were marked signs of a more active policy along the entire length of the British border. We had advanced into Zhob; we controlled the Gomal; we

---

[1] Aitchison, xi, Nos. x, xi and xii.
[2] Mason, *Expedition Against Isazai Clans*, p. 2.

had taken over the Turi tribal area of Kurram; and we had occupied the crest of the Samana range. Our efforts at demarcating the Durand line only served to strengthen the suspicion, ever dormant in the minds of the tribesmen, that we had designs on their independence. It now remains to describe a further advance from the remote valleys of Chitral to the petty states of Hunza and Nagar lying under the shadow of the mighty, snow-capped Rakapushi.

British relations with Chitral arose as a result of our relations with Kashmir, which state recognized British suzerainty in the year 1846. For thirty years we hear little of Chitral, until, in the viceroyalty of Lord Lytton, it was deemed expedient, in view of Russian military activity in Central Asia, to obtain a more effective control over the passes of the Hindu Kush, from the eastern edge of Afghanistan to the northwestern confines of Kashmir. With this object in view the Maharaja of Kashmir was encouraged to extend his authority by means of peaceful penetration over Chitral, Mastuj, and Yasin.[1]

At this period in its history Chitral was governed by one Aman-ul-mulk, the Great Mehtar, the wisest ruler who has ever occupied that dangerous position and the first Mehtar to rule over both Upper and Lower Chitral. Recognizing that he was too weak and isolated to resist pressure from the hated Amir of Afghanistan, for there was no love lost between Pathans and Chitralis, he readily acquiesced in this offer of protection, and became the vassal of the Maharaja of Kashmir. By the engagement of 1878, Aman-ul-mulk was to receive a yearly *mawajib* (subsidy) of Rs. 12,000 from the ruler of Kashmir. As an acknowledgment of the Maharaja's paramount power the Mehtar was to present him annually with three horses, five hawks, and five *tezi* dogs (hounds).[2] At

[1] The fullest account of British relations with these states is to be found in F.O. 65, 1062.

[2] Aitchison, xi, No. xciv

the same time, the Amir of Afghanistan was warned that any interference on his part in the affairs of Bajaur, Swat, Dir, or Chitral would be regarded as an unfriendly act towards the Government of India. Towards the end of 1876 a British agent proceeded to Gilgit in order to ensure that this debatable area should be included within our sphere of influence, and to exclude all foreign interference. But the Amir of Kabul was constantly intriguing in Chitral, and even China exercised a vague suzerainty over Hunza and Nagar. In fact, all these petty chiefs were completely bewildered, and were "doubting to which quarter they should look for the safest barter of their allegiance in return for protection by some paramount power".[1] For five years, during which time he acquired much useful information concerning the ethnology and customs of the tribes of the Hindu Kush, Major Biddulph resided at Gilgit.[2] His work was productive of no other good results. Forced to deal with the tribes through local agents; hampered by the double dealing and jealous feuds of the petty chiefs; he had to report, not a desire for friendly relations, but a general feeling of disaffection. The British Agent was therefore recalled. Lord Lytton's dread of Russia had been the real reason underlying these tentative efforts at establishing British influence over the tribes in the neighbourhood of Gilgit; and it was this menace, real or fanciful, which prompted the Marquess of Lansdowne to re-establish the Gilgit Agency in 1889.

It was not long before trouble arose in the Hunza-Nagar quarter. These two states, divided only by the Hunza river, are situated in the angle formed by the junction of the mighty Mustagh and Hindu Kush ranges. Hemmed in practically on all sides by huge masses of mountains rising in parts to over 20,000 feet above sea-level, no part of the world is more rugged and inaccessible. Their only importance lies in the

[1] F.O. 65, 1062, No. 49 of 1879.
[2] See Biddulph, *Tribes of the Hindoo Koosh*.

fact that there is an extremely difficult caravan route leading to the Pamirs and the valley of the Yarkand river. For an accurate description of the physical difficulties presented by this region the reader's attention is invited to Sir Martin Conway's book, *Climbing and Exploration in the Karakorum Himalayas*.[1] The people of Hunza and Nagar were of the same stock and spoke the same language. Both professed to be Muhammadans, the inhabitants of Hunza being Maulais, those of Nagar, Shiahs. Quarrelsome and treacherous, often at enmity with one another, they had the common sense to unite in the presence of a common foe. Each state was ruled by its own chief or thum, but, of the two, the ruler of Hunza was the more important. Indeed, so important was this petty chief in his own estimation that he was reported to have exclaimed, "Mighty monarchs like myself and Alexander the Great, whose descendant I am, never leave their kingdoms". For centuries they had plundered the caravans journeying between Chinese Turkestan and India, and had profited from a lucrative slave trade. Nominally subordinate to Kashmir, their inaccessibility had been their salvation. It was in 1888 that these rulers drove the Kashmiri troops out of Chalt and Chaprot, two forts guarding the entrance to the Hunza-Nagar valley, but by the end of the same year the lost positions had been recovered.

It therefore came to pass that one of Colonel Algernon Durand's first tasks as agent at Gilgit was to pay a friendly visit to the rulers of these two states. On condition that they were granted annual subsidies in addition to the allowances they received from the Kashmir Durbar, both thums, in 1889, bound themselves to accept his control and to put an end to raiding on the Yarkand road. By the spring of 1891 it not only became obvious that they had no intention of abiding by their engagements, but it was also evident to

[1] See also *The Times*, 18 January, 1926; Visser, Ph. C., *Giants of the Karakorum*; F.O. 65, 1062, enclosures in No. 17, 11 June, 1877.

Durand that Thum Zafar Zahid Khan of Nagar, who was completely under the influence of his treacherous son, Uzr Khan, was preparing for war. As a precautionary measure Durand advanced to Chalt, where, in accordance with instructions received from the Government of India, he commenced to build a fort. At the same time it was decided to connect Gilgit and Chalt by means of a good military road. These proceedings met with the disapproval of the tribesmen, who, relying on the rugged nature of their valleys, determined to resist all attempts at opening up their country. After sharp fighting their power was completely broken and their country occupied.[1] British troops remained at Hunza until 1897, when they were replaced by the Hunza-Nagar levies.

No sooner had affairs been straightened out in this region than trouble began to brew in the Chitral valley. All went well as long as the Great Mehtar lived, but, in 1892, Aman-ul-mulk died, and for many years the valleys of Chitral resounded to the clash of fratricidal swords. He was succeeded by one of his sons, Afzal-ul-mulk, who immediately requested that a British agent should be sent to reside permanently in Chitral. Nizam-ul-mulk, the brother of Afzal, and an aspirant for the Mehtarship, knowing the fate of near relations and remembering the Persian proverb, that ten dervishes can sleep under one blanket, while two kings cannot be contained in one clime, fled for protection to the British Agent at Gilgit. Afzal reigned for two months and seven days. On the night of 6 November, 1892, his uncle, Sher Afzal, who for many years had been a political refugee in Badakhshan where he was in receipt of a large allowance from the Amir of Kabul, entered Chitral by the Dorah pass, surprised the fort, and slew his nephew. But his triumph was short-lived, for the advance of Nizam from Gilgit was followed by the flight of Sher Afzal to the Afghan commander-in-chief at Asmar. In

[1] For description of campaign see Durand, *The Making of a Frontier.*

answer to Nizam's request, a mission under Surgeon-Major Robertson was despatched to Chitral.[1]

With a view to establishing more firmly British authority in Chitral, Robertson laid certain proposals before the Government of India. He considered it a matter of great urgency that we should publicly declare that we considered Chitral and Yasin within our sphere of influence. He was also of opinion that it would be politic to recognize the *de facto* Mehtar. His other proposals were that British officers, protected by a sufficient escort, should be stationed in both districts; that the Gilgit garrison should be increased; that a local levy corps should be raised in Yasin; and that a road and telegraph line should be constructed in Chitral. All these suggestions were supported by Colonel Durand.[2] Towards the end of 1893, Lord Lansdowne, the Viceroy, issued instructions for the withdrawal of the Political Officer from Chitral, if no further complications occurred. Two factors were instrumental in reversing this decision. It was considered inexpedient to withdraw so long as the Pamir boundary dispute with Russia afforded an excuse for aggressive action from that direction. Further, it was feared that, owing to the hostile attitude of Umra Khan of Jandol on the southern borders of Chitral, our withdrawal would be followed by a period of anarchy.

In 1894, Nizam, forgetting that on the frontier a man's next-of-kin is generally his deadliest enemy, foolishly allowed his half-brother, Amir-ul-mulk, to return to Chitral, whence he had fled. Frontier history once more repeated itself, for, on 1 January, 1895, while out hawking, Nizam was murdered by one of his brother's followers. To make matters worse, Umra Khan of Jandol proclaimed a *jehad* throughout Dir, Swat, and Bajaur, and was joined by Sher Afzal.

---

[1] Other members were: Capt. F. E. Younghusband; Lieut. the Hon. C. G. Bruce; and Lieut. B. E. M. Gurdon.

[2] *Parl. Papers*, 1895, LXII (C. 7864), 29.

Because of the weakness of Amir-ul-mulk, who had entered into communication with Umra Khan, the British Agent recognized Shuja-ul-mulk as provisional Mehtar. Robertson now found himself besieged in Fort Chitral by a combined force of Chitralis and Pathans. This necessitated the immediate despatch of a relief column. It has not been thought necessary to lengthen the narrative with a description of the military operations that followed, for the simple reason that excellent accounts by eye-witnesses are already in existence.[1] The memorable siege from 4 March to 19 April, 1895; the heroic efforts of the defenders; Kelly's marvellous march of 350 miles in 35 days from Gilgit; and the advance of Sir Robert Low by way of the Malakand are well known to students of the frontier problem.

The siege raised, the hostile *lashkars* dispersed, it now remained for the Government of India, or rather the Home Government, to determine our future policy towards Chitral. The alternatives were: to maintain our position in Chitral, or to abandon all attempts at keeping an effective control over the external affairs of that state. Prior to Low's march over the Malakand, the only communication with Chitral was by way of Kashmir and the isolated position of Gilgit. Not only was this route circuitous and the roads bad, but Gilgit itself for many months in the year was also cut off by snow from both India and Chitral. The question of the retention of a garrison in Chitral, therefore, hinged on the proposal to construct a more direct road over the Malakand. This proposal dated back to 1889, but nothing more was heard of it until the famous proclamation of 14 March, 1895. As soon as it had been decided to move troops over the Malakand and Lowarai to Chitral, a proclamation had been issued to the people of Swat and Bajaur to the effect that, if they granted British forces an unmolested passage through their territories,

[1] (a) Younghusband, *The Relief of Chitral*; (b) Robertson, *Chitral*; (c) *Fortnightly Review*, July, 1895.

their country would not be occupied. On 8 May, 1895, the Government of India decided to retain a garrison in Chitral,[1] and, to ensure its safety, proposed the construction of a road from Peshawar through Swat. At the same time the Government of India pointed out that the annals of Chitral were nothing but anarchy, and that Afghan aggression had forced Aman-ul-mulk to seek the protection of Kashmir. Great stress was laid upon the fact that the history of Chitral for the previous twenty years had shown conclusively that it could not stand alone.

This decision did not meet with the approval of Lord Rosebery's cabinet and the Liberal government at home. Consequently, on 13 June, 1895, instructions were telegraphed to India to the effect that no military force or European agent was to be retained in Chitral; that Chitral was not to be fortified; and that the projected road was not to be constructed. Once more, however, was an important imperial problem to become the sport of English party politics, for this decision was reversed by Lord Salisbury's government in August of the same year.

It will be convenient at this stage to examine the arguments for and against the retention of Chitral. Had a Conservative government been in power in April, 1880, Kandahar would have been retained; had a Liberal government remained in power in 1895, we should have retired from Chitral. The Liberals considered the construction of the new road to be contrary to the spirit of the proclamation of March, 1895. It not only constituted a deliberate breach of faith with the tribes, but, in their opinion, it was also likely to lead to the annexation of tribal territory, the very thing we had pledged ourselves not to do. Sir Henry Fowler, speaking in the House of Commons, condemned it on military and financial grounds. Running for about 180 miles through hostile Pathan country over the Malakand (4000 feet) and the Lowarai (11,000 feet),

[1] *Parl. Papers*, 1895, LXXII (C. 7864), 46.

both its construction and protection would entail enormous expenditure, and involve grave military responsibilities.[1] But the breach of faith question was merely a party cry, for, with one exception, the tribes had paid no heed to the proclamation and had resisted the British advance. On 24 September, 1895, the Viceroy telegraphed to the Secretary of State as follows:

Occupation of Malakand is not regarded by tribes as infringement of the proclamation. On the contrary, petitions have been received from Ranizais, Swatis, and others, from Peshawar border to Panjkora river, asking for retention of troops to protect them, to help them in protecting road, and to maintain internal peace.[2]

The real problem was whether the fortification of Chitral was a strategic necessity for the protection of that part of the frontier. It was pointed out that the amir, by the Durand Agreement of 1893, had bound himself not to interfere in Swat, Bajaur, or Chitral: consequently all danger from Afghanistan had passed away. On the other hand, it should have been remembered that Afghan intrigues had played no small part in the recent struggles in Chitral. On 10 September, 1895, the Pamir boundary dispute came to an end, and the spheres of influence of England and Russia were definitely mapped out in that region. Some authorities were therefore of opinion that the danger of Russian aggression had passed away. The answer to this was that the Pamir agreement had brought to Russia a great extension of military and political prestige, because she had been allowed to advance her frontiers to the Hindu Kush. If, at the same time, we retired from Chitral, it would mean increased prestige for Russia and increased danger for the British. Military experts, as usual, were at loggerheads. Lord Roberts lent his support to the advocates of retention. Arrayed against him were formidable military authorities, such as Sir Donald Stewart, Sir Neville

[1] Debate on Chitral, House of Commons, 3 September, 1895.
[2] *Parl. Papers*, 1896, LX (C. 8037), 9–10.

Chamberlain, Sir John Adye, Sir Charles Gough, and Lord Chelmsford.[1] It is, however, difficult to see how any effective movement could be made by Russia from the direction of Chitral, unless she were in complete military occupation of Afghanistan, or in friendly alliance with the amir. In 1895 the danger of an attack upon India from the Chitral side was infinitesimal. Nevertheless, there was much truth in the contention that it was possible for a body of about 3000 Cossacks to cross the Kilik, Dorah, or Baroghil passes into Chitral. This would have constituted a serious menace, especially if our hands had been tied in other directions.

The retention of Chitral assured, the Government of India set to work to restore order out of chaos. Chitral was to be a part-sovereign state, for, while her internal affairs were left entirely in the hands of the Mehtar, Shuja-ul-mulk, and his advisers, the Government of India was to conduct and have control over all foreign relations. In addition to a permanent garrison in Chitral itself, both the Malakand and the crossing of the Swat river were to be temporarily guarded by British troops. In return for allowances, the Khan of Dir and the tribes between Swat and Peshawar engaged to carry the post, protect the telegraph line, repair the road, and grant unmolested passage to all reliefs.[2]

The closing years of the nineteenth century were fraught with great danger to the British Raj. To a large extent this was the outcome of the various advances which had taken place along the frontier, from the remote glens of Chitral to the stony nullahs of Waziristan. Before proceeding to discuss the causes leading up to the 1897–8 conflagration, it will be necessary to describe the course of events in Waziristan, especially around the Tochi, where the first outbreak occurred.

No more thorny problem than the settlement of tribal affairs in Waziristan has ever presented itself for solution on

---

[1] Series of articles in *Saturday Review*, 1895.
[2] *Parl. Papers*, 1896, LX (C. 8037), 24–8.

the frontier. There were really two problems awaiting solution. In the first place, it was necessary to demarcate that portion of the Durand boundary, which, in future, was to serve as the dividing line between Afghanistan and Waziristan. In the second place, a settlement of tribal affairs, such as the protection of trade routes and the prevention of raiding, was highly desirable.

The policy of Lord Elgin, the Viceroy, was to bring the tribes more under British control, but at the same time to repudiate all attempts at the annexation of tribal territory.[1] For several years the authorities had sought a solution in a system of tribal levies, but, owing to the absence of regular troops, this had proved a miserable failure, the number of raids increasing instead of diminishing. As far back as 1890, Mr R. I. Bruce, the Deputy-Commissioner of Dera Ismail Khan, had recommended the construction of a strong military post at Spin, in order to prevent the Mahsuds from raiding into Zhob. Once more, in 1894, Bruce advocated the establishment of a strong military station, this time at Wana, to the north-west of Spin. According to Bruce, Wana dominated not only the Mahsud country, but also the territories of the Suleman Khel, Dotannis, and Kharotis, all of whom were powerful tribes. In addition, its position on the lower slopes of the Marwatti mountain made it an admirable sanatorium. Bruce, a disciple of Sandeman and one of the Forward School, believed that the complete pacification of Waziristan was necessary; and, with this object in view, he advised the opening up of all trade routes and the construction of good lateral communications throughout the country from the Gomal to Kurram. Lord Elgin, however, advocated the construction of some well-situated and easily defensible post.

Certain members of the Viceroy's council objected to the new policy on the ground that it was a middle course between

[1] *Parl. Papers*, 1898, LXIII (C. 8713), 1, 3.

complete annexation and, what they termed, a policy of "dissuasive restraint".[1] The choice before Government was either to assume complete responsibility for the administration of Waziristan, or to influence Waziri affairs from the British side of the existing administrative boundary. The dissenting members recognized that the Durand Agreement had introduced a new factor into the already vexed cauldron of border politics, but held that in course of time it would tend to a peaceful solution of the frontier problem. In their dissenting minute of 6 July, 1894, they pointed out that a great danger would lie in the temptation to erect forts along the Afghan frontier. This, of course, would have been no solution to the problem, for, with our faces towards the unruly tribes of the Afghan border and with Waziristan behind us, we would have advanced only to find ourselves faced with a problem similar to that which we had left. They therefore were opposed to the establishment of any advanced military posts, and were convinced that the prevalence of a feeling of unrest in India, together with an urgent need for economy in all branches of administration, necessitated a policy of unaggressive watchfulness behind the existing frontiers. In forwarding their dissenting minute Lord Elgin pointed out that they were advocating a policy of inactivity tempered by punitive expeditions, which would inevitably bring about the annexation and administration of Waziri territory which they desired so much to avoid. On 24 August, 1894, Sir Henry Fowler, the Secretary of State for India, gave a rather reluctant consent to the proposals of the Government of India.[2]

On 3 November, 1894, the Mahsuds attacked the British Boundary Commission camp at Wana, for which they were punished by a force under Sir William Lockhart. This settled

[1] The dissenting members were: Sir Charles Pritchard; Mr J. Westland; and Sir Antony MacDonnell.

[2] *Parl. Papers*, 1898, LXIII (C. 8713), 30–1.

the Mahsud question for a few years. In return for allowances they guaranteed to keep open the Shahur Tangi route, and to prevent the commission of outrages and offences within British territory. They also agreed to surrender all offenders and permitted the construction of levy posts at Haidar Kach, and Sarwekai. No sooner had this temporary settlement been arranged than the Government of India proceeded to take over the administration of part of northern Waziristan.

We have already observed how the unwarlike Dawaris of the Tochi valley had been for generations at the mercy of their predatory Waziri neighbours. It was the desire for protection from their hereditary foes which prompted them, in the year 1895, to beseech the Government of India to take over and administer their fertile valley. It must not be imagined that the authorities in India were actuated solely by altruistic motives: there were other and far weightier reasons which brought about the advance into the Tochi. Wana was merely of local importance for guarding the Gomal, protecting Zhob, and coercing the Abdurrahman Khels, a truculent tribe of southern Waziristan. But it was also necessary to control northern Waziristan. In order to accomplish this and be in a position to coerce both the Darwesh Khels and the Mahsuds, the construction of a strongly fortified and easily accessible post in the Tochi was considered essential. With one post at Wana and another in the Tochi, it was thought, in those days, that the whole of Waziristan would be effectively dominated.

Within eighteen months practically all the tribes north of the Tochi had raised the standard of revolt, and the British were forced to cope with the most serious tribal disturbances in the blood-stained annals of the frontier. It is now proposed to analyse the causes underlying this general conflagration.

The first outbreak occurred in the newly acquired Tochi valley, where, on 10 June, 1897, the Political Officer and his escort were treacherously attacked in the village of Maizar.

Maizar is really a group of villages in the Upper Tochi above the junction of the Shawal Algad and the Tochi, about eleven miles from Datta Khel. It was occupied by certain sections of the Madda Khels who were under agreement to keep open the main road to Birmal and Ghazni which ran through this part of the Tochi. From Maizar the revolt spread to Swat, where the tribes rose under one Sadullah, known as the Mad Mullah, and attacked the Malakand and Chakdarra. Heavy fighting ensued before they were forced to retire. The next to rebel were the Mohmands, who, under Najm-ud-din, the Adda Mullah, attacked the village of Shankargarh and the neighbouring fort of Shabkadar in the Peshawar district. Finally, the Orakzais and Afridis, instigated by Mullah Sayyid Akbar, an Aka Khel Afridi, captured the Khyber forts, and laid siege to the Samana posts. The result was that troops had to be marched to Datta Khel in the Tochi, to Swat, Bajaur, Chamla, the Utman Khel country, and Buner. The Mohmands were punished by a force operating from Peshawar; and, lastly, a well-organized expeditionary force penetrated into the heart of Orakzai and Afridi Tirah.

In analysing the causes of these tribal insurrections, the following questions naturally arise. Did all these revolts result from a preconceived plan, that is, were they all connected? Was the treacherous outrage at Maizar intended as a signal for the risings which followed elsewhere, or was it the outcome of purely local grievances?

Our arrival in the Tochi had not been followed by an immediate cessation of outrages, for, since 1895, several persons had been the victims of murderous attacks. In 1896 a British subject had been murdered in the valley, and, in accordance with tribal custom, a fine, known as blood-money, had been levied on all concerned. But the Madda Khels of Maizar considered that they had been unfairly treated in this respect. Mr Gee, the Political Officer, was sent to Maizar, for the purpose of settling the payment of outstanding fines, and, at the same time, was instructed to select a site for a levy post somewhere between Sheranna and Maizar. The construction of this post, situated as it would have been at the Afghan entrance to the Tochi, and athwart the direct route to Birmal and Ghazni, was looked upon as an important link in the chain of frontier defence. What happened at Maizar has already been related. So treacherous was this attack, and so utterly at variance with the Pathan code of honour, that frontier officers found the greatest difficulty in ascertaining the exact cause. Bruce could not accept the view that it was a deliberate signal for the rest of the border to break out into open rebellion. He was convinced that each rising had its own particular local cause, and that in the beginning there was not the slightest connection between the Malakand, Afridi, and Maizar disturbances. That they occurred more or less simultaneously was, in his opinion, but an unfortunate coincidence. Sir Robert Warburton held similar views.

In support of the theory that the outrage was inspired by fanaticism, the coincidence of Gee's visit with the Muharram festival was cited. During this religious festival the Waziris kill sheep, congregate together, and consider the occasion to be an auspicious time for martyrdom. Fanatical outbursts were by no means uncommon amongst the Madda Khels, for on several occasions they had displayed strong fanatical tendencies. The mullahs therefore may have taken advantage of this to stir up the inhabitants to fresh acts of devilry. Gee, however, was convinced that there was no connection between Maizar and the Muharram.[1] At first, the Government of India was inclined to believe that the affair had been deliberately planned, but later it was compelled, owing to the lack of evidence, to reverse this decision. On the other hand, the presence at Shaktu of the Mullah Powindah, the head of the fanatical party in Waziristan, combined with the anti-British intrigues of the Afghan Sirdar, Gul Muhammad, should have thrown

[1] *Parl. Papers*, 1898, LXIII (C. 8713), 93–9.

some light on the situation. The relative importance of fanaticism, Afghan and other intrigues, and the feeling of unrest engendered by discontent at tribal allowances, as causes of the Maizar outrage, will perhaps never be definitely determined, but it seems certain that the exaggerated reports of this affair, disseminated by anti-British mullahs, did tend to affect the rest of the border—to some extent Maizar heralded the approaching storm.

The main factors underlying the 1897 risings were the active forward policy pursued in the 'nineties and the influence of fanaticism. There can be no doubt that this policy of intervention in tribal affairs had thoroughly alarmed and annoyed the Amir Abdurrahman Khan, whose complicity in the risings will be discussed in the chapter dealing with Anglo-Afghan relations. There were also certain minor causes of disturbance which now call for some comment.

In India the year 1897 had been one of plague, earthquake, famine, and flood. Contemporary writers had noticed a prevailing spirit of unrest from Bengal to the Panjab. So much so, that even Indian servants had adopted a more independent attitude towards their European masters. Mention has also been made of a curious innovation, the wearing of the Turkish fez by Muhammadans. The extent to which the prevailing discontent within India affected the frontier tribesmen cannot be gauged with any degree of certainty, but we have it on record that anti-British propaganda from the south did exercise some degree of influence: correspondence did take place between frontier mullahs and those of Delhi. The Afridis stated that their revolt was a protest against British encroachments, interference with tribal customs, and the enhancement of the salt tax. We certainly had interfered in that we had refused to hand over any of their women who had fled for protection into British territory. Although it was our policy to respect tribal rights and customs, it was not the policy of a Christian Government to surrender defenceless women to the bloody vengeance of their irate overlords.

Contemporary writers have dismissed the economic grievance in a few words. It is now proposed to enter into it more fully than has hitherto been attempted. Political considerations had necessitated the imposition of a light duty upon the salt produced at certain quarries in the Kohat district. Because of this low rate of duty, it was necessary to prevent the transit of Kohat salt from trans-Indus territory to the left bank of the Indus, where it would have a better market than the fully taxed salt of the cis-Indus districts. For this purpose a costly preventive line had to be maintained from Hazara to the junction of the Indus with the Sutlej. There were two reasons which prompted the local authorities to recommend the enhancement of the duty on Kohat salt to a rate approximating to that fixed for the cis-Indus salt. The maintenance of a costly preventive line was not a sound financial procedure, and, in addition, there was no longer any adequate reason for foregoing the revenue that might be raised by increasing the duty on trans-Indus salt. Since the year 1883, the duty on Kohat salt had been eight annas per Kohat maund, but in June, 1896, in order to abolish the Indus preventive line, it was decided to raise the duty from eight annas to two rupees per Kohat maund.[1] Now, if this increased duty can be regarded as one of the causes of discontent, why did not the Kohat pass Afridis, the carriers of salt, upon whom the duty fell heaviest, raise the standard of revolt? The answer is that in all probability their geographical position and their proximity to Kohat and Peshawar ensured their neutrality. The fact, however, remains that the Afridis and certain Orakzai clans did include this in their list of grievances. On the other hand, the Swat and Mohmand tribes, who were the first to rise and who were also affected by this increased duty,

[1] Sixteen annas are equal to one rupee: a Kohat maund is approximately 130 lb.

made no reference to it. The Government of India refused to
believe that the salt tax was anything more than a pretext. In
my opinion the essential point to remember is not that the
salt duty did or did not constitute a grievance, but that it was
cleverly utilized by the mullahs as an incentive.

In 1897 a spirit of fanaticism was in the air. Wholesale
massacres of Christians had taken place; the Turks had been
victorious over the infidel Greeks; the Arabs of the Sudan had
broken British squares; and behind it all was the sinister figure
of Sultan Abdul Hamid II. British prestige was very low
indeed until that crushing blow at Omdurman. It would be
difficult to state how far these happenings affected the Indian
frontier, but certain letters discovered in Mullah Sayyid
Akbar's house in the Waran valley of Tirah show clearly the
wild rumours that were prevalent. One quotation will suffice:

Aden, a seaport, which was in possession of the British, has been
taken from them by the Sultan. The Suez Canal, through which
the British forces could easily reach India in 20 days, has also been
taken possession of by the Sultan, and has now been granted on
lease to Russia. The British forces now require six months to reach
India. The friendly alliance between the British and the Germans
has also been disturbed on account of some disagreement about
trade...and fighting is going on in Egypt too against them.[1]

Wilder and more fantastic still were the rumours that
gained credence in Swat. Ignorant, bigoted, and priest-
ridden, the vast majority of the inhabitants believed that the
Mad Mullah had the heavenly hosts on his side, and that,
when the British advanced to the attack, the mouths of their
rifles and guns would be stopped. The fakir claimed that he
was endowed with miraculous powers. In his hands one
small pot of rice would be sufficient to feed multitudes; the
bullets of the enemy he would turn into water. In fact, he
had only to throw stones into the Swat river and each stone
would have the effect of a shot from a gun. He also claimed

[1] *Parl. Papers*, 1898 (C. 8714), Appendix, G, p. 39 c.

to be able to render himself invisible. More marvellous still, the tribesmen believed him. Even so notable a person as the Khan of Dir feared that he would be slain by an invisible foe. To satisfy the political aspirations of his Muhammadan followers, the Mullah had with him a young boy of about thirteen years of age whom he represented as the sole surviving heir to the throne of Delhi. Those who would consider these details as trivial know nothing of the border Pathan. Thousands of tribesmen whose ferocity was heightened by religious enthusiasm flocked to join him. Drunk with *bhang*, maddened by fanaticism, they fell upon our positions in the Malakand. Powerful too was the influence exerted by the mullahs on other parts of the frontier. Before entering Tirah, Sir William Lockhart had announced his intention of dictating terms from the heart of that country, and had pointed out that the length of operations would depend upon the opposition offered. The reply received from the Chamkannis shows how powerless they were to act for themselves:

Friendship and enmity are not in our choice; whatever orders we may receive from the Fakir Sahib of Swat, the Mulla Sahib of Hadda or the Aka Khel Mulla, and from all Islam, we cannot refuse to obey them; if we lose our lives, no matter.[1]

Contemporary opinion, especially that of officers and officials in the war zone, favoured fanaticism as the chief cause of the outbreak, but they have ever been ready to confuse fanaticism with the natural desire of the tribesmen for independence. How far then did the prevailing discontent have its origin in fanaticism, and to what extent did it result from the forward policy of Lords Lansdowne and Elgin?

From the distant north, where the snows of Rakapushi keep watch over Hunza and Nagar, to the confines of Baluchistan, we had extended our authority in many directions over the debatable area, known as independent territory. To the border Pathan there appeared the vision of a great mailed

[1] *Confidential, Frontier and Overseas,* II, 67.

fist, the fingers of which, in the 'nineties, seemed to be closing around him. Isolated forts garrisoned by British troops commanded the trade routes running through his territory, or frowned down upon his native hamlet or terraced fields. Dazzling white roads wound their way like serpents towards his fastnesses in the mountains. In the wake of demarcation commissions had sprung up long lines of white boundary pillars, enclosing his country and threatening that independence which was his proudest boast. It is therefore my considered opinion, after sifting all the available evidence, that the 1897 disturbances were mainly the result of the advances which had taken place in the 'nineties. Although many of these advances were justified from a military point of view, they nevertheless were looked upon as encroachments into tribal territory.

If then these risings were the result of a more forward policy, why did the movement not spread to Baluchistan and Kurram? A detailed answer to this question would rake up one of the greatest of frontier controversies, the respective merits and demerits of the Sandeman and Panjab systems. The answer lies in the difference between the Baluch and Pathan, in tribal constitution and in racial characteristics, and in the fact that Baluchistan had long enjoyed an ordered administration. Although minor disturbances did take place among the Sarawan Brahui chiefs and in Mekran, it would be difficult to connect them with the northern Pathan upheaval. As for the Turis of Kurram, they were Shiahs and at deadly enmity with their Sunni neighbours.

The chief part played by fanaticism was the way in which the frontier mullahs used it to stir up the latent passions of the turbulent tribesmen. Without the force of fanaticism and the sinister influence of Afghan intrigues, the risings would hardly have been so widespread, so united, or so simultaneous.

The results of the war and the work of reconstruction come within the province of the next chapter.

Chapter VI

LORD CURZON'S FRONTIER POLICY AND THE FORMATION OF THE NORTH-WEST FRONTIER PROVINCE, 1901

Her Majesty's Government are of opinion that the present arrangements are not satisfactory, and that it is desirable that the conduct of external relations with the tribes of the Punjab Frontier should be more directly than heretofore under the control and supervision of the Government of India.

Secretary of State for India to Government of India, 5 August, 1898.

If there is a field of policy in which rapidity of decision and swiftness of execution are essential, it is that of the Frontier.

Cd. 496 of 1901, p. 133.

On 6 January, 1899, Lord Curzon of Kedleston succeeded Lord Elgin as Viceroy of India. Many people thought that this appointment was going to be a complete triumph for the Forward School. They predicted that we should soon find ourselves fighting with Cossack hordes on the banks of the Oxus, and that the new Viceroy's policy would approximate to the worst features of that which had marred the administration of Lord Auckland. For many years Lord Curzon had made a close study of the geography of Asia, and its political and commercial problems. Unlike the majority of his predecessors, he had taken the keenest interest in Indian affairs and was by no means ignorant of the frontier and its turbulent inhabitants. To quote his own words: "I love India, its people, its history, its government, the absorbing mysteries of its civilization and its life".[1] To rule India had been his great ambition in life. What, then, had been his studies by way of preparation for his heavy responsibilities?

[1] Speech at dinner given by Old Etonians in London, 28 October, 1898.

Not only had he served as Under-Secretary for India in 1891–2, but he had also travelled extensively in the East. He had seen the principal cities of Japan and had visited Korea, China, Annam, Cochin-China and Cambodia. In 1888 he made his famous journey along the Transcaspian Railway to Bokhara the Noble and to Samarkand, the final resting-place of the mighty Timur. Thence he proceeded in a tarantass to the city of Tashkent. The following year found him in Persia. In 1894 he discovered the source of the Oxus to be a huge glacier at the eastern end of the Wakhan Pamir. From the Pamirs he proceeded to Chitral, making the acquaintance of the thums of Hunza and Nagar on the way. After leaving Chitral he visited Kabul as a guest of Abdurrahman Khan, and, at one time, was reported as having been murdered. From Kabul he rode along the historic road to Kandahar and eventually reached the British outposts in Baluchistan. The new Viceroy had, therefore, completed a tour of the north-western frontiers of India which few have been privileged to undertake.

When Lord Curzon arrived in India, the Government of India had successfully brought to a conclusion a series of punitive expeditions against widespread and violent tribal risings, which had taken place at a most critical juncture, when India was suffering from the effects of widely diffused famine and plague. The frontier seemed calm, but the conflagration of 1897 had left bitter memories in its wake, and the echoes of the Tirah expedition had scarcely died away. The Afridis of the Khyber were clamouring for allowances which they had forfeited by their own acts; and British forces were locked up in lonely outposts and isolated forts in tribal territory. The new Viceroy found more than 10,000 British troops cantoned across the administrative border, in the Khyber, on the Samana range, in Waziristan, and in the Malakand area. Not only were these advanced positions many miles from a base, but they were also entirely unconnected by lateral communications, and were consequently in constant danger of being overpowered before supports could be rushed to their assistance. This state of affairs was extremely dangerous, in that the presence of troops, cooped up in miserable caricatures of forts from which, in many cases, they were too weak to sally forth, constituted a source of irritation to the tribesmen and an invitation to strike one more blow in defence of their independence. The lesson of 1897–8 seemed to have had no effect upon the authorities in India, for, not only were they still persisting in a policy of dispersion instead of concentration of forces, but proposals were also being brought forward for the construction of fresh and costly fortifications in tribal territory.[1] Fortunately, wiser counsels prevailed under Lord Curzon, whose policy can best be described as one of withdrawal and concentration.

Towards the end of Lord Elgin's viceroyalty, Lord George Hamilton, the Secretary of State for India, had, in his despatch, 28 January, 1898, sent a timely note of warning to the Government of India. Recognizing that the events of the 'nineties had considerably increased our responsibilities and the chances of collision with the tribes, he recommended certain measures which would be of essential importance in any reconstruction of our frontier policy. The most important of these were the avoidance of interference in the tribal zone; the best possible concentration of military forces; and the maintenance of the Khyber pass as a safe artery of communication and trade. Even before the termination of hostilities, he had telegraphed to the Viceroy that "no new responsibilities should be taken unless absolutely required by actual strategical necessities and the protection of British Indian border".[2] In other words the forward policy of the 'nineties was to be replaced by one of non-interference resembling in many respects the old "close-border" system.

[1] *Parl. Papers*, 1901 (Cd. 496), p. 116.
[2] *Idem*, 1898 (Cd. 8714), p. 26.

Lord Curzon belonged to no particular school of frontier policy, and it soon became apparent that, with the exception of Chitral, the retention of which he favoured on imperial grounds, he objected to any advance beyond the existing administrative boundary. At the same time, he was of opinion that the policy of *quieta non movere* associated with the name of Lawrence had become obsolete, owing to the lapse of time and the change of circumstances, such as improved communications. It was no longer possible for us to remain inactive behind a sort of Chinese Wall, when the Durand Agreement of 1893 had extended our sphere of influence over the so-called independent tracts. He had definite views on frontier policy before he reached the shores of India. In a speech delivered to Old Etonians before leaving England he maintained that it was the duty of a Viceroy "to preserve intact and secure, either from internal convulsion, or external inroad, the boundaries of that great and Imperial Dominion". In his second Budget speech, 27 March, 1901, he gave a list of twelve reforms, which it had been his intention to carry out ever since he had arrived in India. First in importance he placed the creation and pursuit of a sound frontier policy. What he accomplished can be best summed up in his own words:

Withdrawal of British forces from advanced positions, employment of tribal forces in defence of tribal country, concentration of British forces in British territory behind them as a safeguard and a support, improvement of communications in the rear.[1]

The system of tribal militia and local levies was necessary for the protection of the tribal country, but it was also hoped that it would, by offering increased facilities for military employment, solve, to a certain extent, the poverty and unemployment question, one of the abiding problems of the unadministered hills. This system naturally differed on various parts of the frontier, from the crude and rudimentary native levies, who were employed in Chitral, to the Khyber Rifles,

[1] Budget speech, 30 March, 1904.

who were well-equipped and trained by British officers. The important point to remember about his militia scheme is that he recognized that a tribal militia would inevitably break down, if called upon to perform the duties of regulars, as had been the case in the Khyber in 1897. Consequently he arranged for their protection and support by movable columns and light railways. In addition, he paid a personal visit to the frontier, where, at an imposing durbar held at Peshawar and attended by the local khans and sirdars, he assured them that we had no intention of interfering with their religion or their independence, and that we were prepared to pay them allowances, if the roads and passes were kept open and offenders handed over to justice.

By 1904 the new system was in operation along the whole frontier from Chitral to Baluchistan. All regular troops had been withdrawn from Gilgit, and the protection of that isolated position had been left in the hands of the Kashmir Imperial Service troops. In Chitral alone, for reasons already given, were regular forces to be found. These were concentrated at Kila Drosh in the extreme south, at a discreet distance from the Mehtar's capital. Mastuj was the headquarters of the Chitrali irregulars. In 1902, the Khar Movable Column was withdrawn and regulars stationed at Chakdarra, Malakand and Dargai. Chakdarra was of great importance owing to the fact that the Swat river had been bridged at that spot, and because it was the starting-point of the famous road to Chitral. All the outlying posts were held by the Dir and Swat levies, who were responsible for the safety of the road. To support the Malakand garrisons, a light railway was constructed from Nowsherra to Dargai. Similarly, regular troops were withdrawn from the Khyber, which was guarded by the reorganized Khyber Rifles, consisting of two battalions under British officers. For their support a flying column was kept in constant readiness at Peshawar, which was connected with Jamrud by an extension of the broad gauge railway, with Landi Kotal by a road running through the Mullagori country, and with Kohat by a cart road running through the Kohat pass. The Mullagori road was an alternative route to the Khyber and its construction had been previously advocated by Sir Robert Warburton. The bridge over the Indus at Kushalgarh and the extension of the railway from Kohat to Thal were not completed during Lord Curzon's term of office. In the Orakzai country the Samana Rifles were raised, and were supported by British troops at Kohat. British garrisons were withdrawn from Kurram and were replaced by two battalions of the Kurram Militia, equipped and officered on the same lines as the Khyber Rifles. In the Waziri country, the Northern and Southern Waziristan Militia were raised for the protection of the Tochi and Gomal passes respectively, and were supported by movable columns stationed at Bannu and Dera Ismail Khan. In Baluchistan the Quetta-Nushki railway was commenced, but it was not completed until 1905. This line played an important part in the later development of the Nushki-Seistan caravan route.

The creation of the North-West Frontier Province was the consummation of all his frontier policy: to quote his own words, it was "The Keystone of the Frontier Arch". It must not be imagined, however, that the idea of forming a new province across the Indus emanated from the fertile brain of Lord Curzon. For at least a quarter of a century, viceroys, administrators and generals had, tentatively or otherwise, put forward proposals for the creation of a new administrative unit, which they hoped would usher in an era of peace on the blood-stained border and prove a panacea for most of the evils to which it was subject.[1] In 1843, six years before the

---

[1] The following had, at different times, been in favour of the creation of a separate frontier administration: Sir Bartle Frere, Sir Henry Durand, Lord Roberts, Sir James Browne, Sir Robert Warburton, Sir Robert Sandeman, Sir William Lockhart, Lord Lytton, Sir Charles Aitchison, Sir George Chesney, and Lord Lansdowne.

Panjab was wrested from its Sikh owners, Sind had been placed under the Government of Bombay. Had the Panjab been annexed first, in all probability Sind would have been incorporated with it, for these two areas were connected by the strongest of all natural links, a large river. During the governor-generalship of Lord Dalhousie a proposal had been made to join the two, but, for financial reasons, it was not sanctioned by the Court of Directors.[1] After the Mutiny the question was reconsidered, but, owing to the backward state of communications along the Indus, Lord Canning refused to give his consent. Moreover, Sind was prospering under the excellent administration of Sir Bartle Frere. The *status quo* was, therefore, maintained, and even to-day, in spite of distance, Sind remains under the Government of Bombay. Frere, however, was always in favour of the proposal, in order that there might be one Government from the seaboard to Kashmir, but, at the same time, he objected to any scheme under which the distinctive features of the Sind system would be abandoned. In 1876 Lord Northbrook was of opinion that Sind should be joined to the Panjab, but, in the following year, Lord Lytton, who succeeded him as Viceroy, sought to solve the problem by the creation of an enormous trans-Indus province, consisting of the six frontier districts of the Panjab and of the trans-Indus districts of Sind.[2] At the head was to be a chief commissioner and agent to the Governor-General. Under him were to be two separate commissioners for the Pathan and Baluch tribes respectively. Lytton argued that:

The Viceroy would, by means of this arrangement, command the services of his own specially selected agent, in whose hands the threads of all our border politics and tribal relations would be

[1] *Parl. Papers*, 1878, LVIII (Cd. 1898), 5.
[2] Six frontier districts of the Panjab, viz. Hazara, Peshawar, Kohat, Bannu (except the cis-Indus tracts), Dera Ismail Khan (with the same exception), Dera Ghazi Khan, and trans-Indus Sind (with the exception of Karachi).

concentrated. The time of such an agent could be devoted almost entirely to purely frontier duties; and he would be better able than any Lieutenant-Governor of the Punjab can possibly be to visit...all parts of the frontier.[1]

There were three objections raised to this scheme: that certain of these districts were integral parts of the Panjab; that their internal administration would suffer by separation; and that frontier affairs could be best supervised and administered by the Panjab Government. Lytton replied that these districts were separated from the Panjab geographically, historically and racially. He also pointed out that "all unnecessary links in an administrative chain admittedly weaken the strength of it". In his covering despatch, 17 May, 1877, he proposed that Bombay should receive the whole or part of the Central Provinces, in order to compensate it for the loss of trans-Indus Sind. It was this proposal which raised a storm of indignation and contributed largely to the non-acceptance of his scheme. The Secretary of State was unable to accept the scheme as proposed by Lytton, and suggested a compromise in the form of a separate commissioner for both the Pathan and Baluch tribes, but there was to be no chief commissioner. Both Sir Charles Aitchison, the Foreign Secretary, and Sir Robert Egerton, the Lieutenant-Governor of the Panjab, vigorously protested against a compromise so full of "the seeds of future misunderstanding, confusion and divided responsibility". Lytton, however, accepted the proposal of the Secretary of State and had appointed Sir Frederick (afterwards Lord) Roberts as the first northern commissioner when the Second Afghan War, 1878–80, broke out, whereupon his plans automatically fell to the ground. With the end of the first phase of the war, 1879, he once more endeavoured to put this proposal into practice, but his plans were once more upset by the murder of Cavagnari. When the war came to an end, in 1880, Lord Lytton had been succeeded

[1] *Parl. Papers*, 1878 (Cd. 1898), p. 134.

by Lord Ripon, who objected both to the separation of the trans-Indus districts from the Panjab and to the transfer of Sind. During the viceroyalty of Lord Lansdowne, 1888–94, the proposal was revived in its original form, namely, the transfer of Sind to the Panjab; but, owing to the formation of the Baluchistan Agency, Sind had ceased to be a frontier district. Nevertheless Lansdowne was of opinion that the Durand Agreement, which had increased our responsibilities north of the Gomal, necessitated the creation of a separate frontier charge in direct communication with the Government of India. Lord Elgin, who succeeded Lord Lansdowne, found his time fully occupied in suppressing the 1897 risings. When the wave of fanaticism had rolled away and the preaching of the Mad Mullah was heard no more, the Secretary of State in his despatch, 5 August, 1898, pointed out the desirability of placing tribal policy more directly under the control and supervision of the Government of India.[1] Lord Elgin, on receipt of this despatch, consulted the officials of the Panjab Government, but found that the majority of them objected to any dismemberment of the Panjab. At the same time, many of them confessed that an entirely new province was the only alternative to the existing system.

This was the state of affairs when Lord Curzon became Viceroy. Since the days of Dalhousie some change had been thought desirable, while, from 1877 onwards, the idea of forming a separate frontier province had steadily gained ground. After carefully considering all previous proposals, Lord Curzon determined to carve out a new frontier province across the Indus. The reasons which led him to take this step are clearly laid down in his minute, 27 August, 1900. The most important reason for the change was that between the frontier system and the authority of the Viceroy there was placed a subordinate government through whose hands all frontier questions had to pass before they

[1] *Parl. Papers*, 1901 (Cd. 496), p. 71.

reached the Government of India. As Lord Salisbury had pointed out in 1877, the Panjab Government was placed in charge of the frontier at a time when communications were tedious, when Russia was a great but distant power, and when the Government of Lahore was not overburdened with internal affairs.[1] But since that date the Russian menace had steadily increased, vast tracts of tribal territory had been absorbed, and the extension of railways and the introduction of the telegraph had brought Calcutta into close touch with the remotest parts of the Indian Empire. Lord Curzon pointed out that under the existing system, with its long official chain of reference, rapidity of action and swiftness of decision, both of which were essential on an exposed frontier, were well-nigh impossible. Weeks, even months, passed before the Viceroy's decision arrived. Some system which would accelerate the receipt of reports and the transmission of orders was absolutely essential. Not only was delay inevitable, but the very fact that the Government of Lahore neither originated, nor was responsible for, India's foreign policy, produced inefficiency.

I venture to affirm that there is not another country or Government in the world which adopts a system so irrational in theory, so bizarre in practice, as to interpose between its Foreign Minister and his most important sphere of activity, the barrier, not of a subordinate official, but of a subordinate Government, on the mere geographical plea that the latter resides in closer proximity to the scene of action—a plea which itself breaks down when it is remembered that for five months in the year the Supreme and the Local Governments are both located at the same spot, Simla.[2]

In refutation of the argument that the Panjab officers, who had spent long periods on the frontier, knew more about border politics than a Viceroy whose knowledge was only acquired during his term of office, Lord Curzon gave detailed

[1] *Parl. Papers*, 1878, LVIII (Cd. 1898), 153.
[2] *Idem*, 1901 (Cd. 496), p. 131.

facts to show that in reality Panjab officials had not spent very long periods on the frontier itself. At the same time he was careful to point out that the best administrators were those who had spent most of their lives in the settlement of tribal affairs, and instanced Lord Lawrence, Jacob, Nicholson, Edwardes, Mackeson, Warburton and Sandeman. It was obvious that the results of inexperience were "departmental irresolution, dissipation instead of concentration of responsibility, and long and injurious delays". There can be no doubt that the Panjab officials were offended, both by the pointedness of Lord Curzon's remarks and by a certain brusqueness with which he carried his decision into effect. Sir Lepel Griffin's reply to Curzon's statement, that none of the chief secretaries of the Panjab had previously served on the frontier, deserves to be recorded:

He asserts that I never served on the Frontier before I was appointed Chief Secretary. The truth is that I was in camp at Dera Ghazi Khan on the border when I was first appointed to officiate as Chief Secretary, and that for several previous years, under three different Lieutenant-Governors, I had received a singularly exhaustive frontier political training. There was no frontier district which I did not know; no outpost or pass from Hazara to Sind which I had not visited, nor was there a single chief, Baluch or Afghan, with whom I was not personally acquainted.[1]

Mr Herbert Fanshawe, who had been Chief Secretary of the Panjab Government, resigned the service because he considered that a grave public indignity had been thrust upon the administration of the Panjab.[2] There were many who sympathized with Fanshawe for sacrificing a high career to voice a serious grievance. Nevertheless, Fanshawe was obviously in the wrong, for officials in his position were not colleagues of the Viceroy but executive agents, permitted to advise, even with great freedom, but bound, when a decision

---

[1] *Empire Review*, April, 1901. The final sentence must be taken *cum grano salis*.

[2] *Spectator*, 15 June, 1901; 22 June, 1901.

had been arrived at, to carry it out loyally to the best of their ability.

Having decided to create a new province, Lord Curzon had to consider several possible forms of new administration. The grandiose scheme of Lord Lytton was rejected on the grounds that it was too cumbersome and too immense a burden for any single man to shoulder. In addition, owing to the fact that Sind was no longer a frontier district and Baluchistan was being successfully administered under the Sandeman system, he considered that no alteration of the existing administrative organization of the southern border-lands was needed. What he proposed to rearrange was the form of administration to the north of the Gomal where dwelt the most fanatical and turbulent of the border tribes. Another suggested form of administration had been to create a frontier province stretching from Chitral to Dera Ghazi Khan, including within its limits the districts of Rawalpindi and Jhelum. This he rejected because it meant a needless dismemberment of the Panjab. It had also been proposed to retain the existing system, that is, to keep the management of frontier affairs in the hands of the Panjab Government, but to appoint a lieutenant-governor well versed in tribal politics and customs. This, however, would have been very unfair to the settled districts, the interests of which would have been sacrificed to those of the border tracts. Perhaps the greatest objection to this was that it would be contrary to the instructions contained in the Secretary of State's despatch, 5 August, 1898, and would not tend to place the conduct of external affairs more directly under the control of the Government of India.

Numerous compromises, which could not possibly have survived the test of time, were also put forward as solutions. The most important of these was to make the commissioner of Peshawar directly responsible to the Government of India as far as his external policy was concerned, while for internal affairs he was still to remain answerable to the Panjab authorities. Fortunately, Lord Curzon, a student of the frontier problem, was well aware that, for at least a quarter of a century, this suggestion had been reprobated by all the greatest frontier authorities. Neither did he fail to realize that the administrative boundary was an arbitrary line drawn through the limits of a more or less homogeneous population, and that the people on either side were closely connected socially, ethnically, and commercially.

Thousands of our subjects are constantly visiting independent territory, many thousands of the hillmen regularly migrate to our districts, whole clans live for half the year on this and for the other half of the year on that side of the border; where the residents within and without the frontier are not men of the same clan or of the same tribe, they are connected by the intimate ties of common race, of marriage, neighbourhood and of an association, territorial and social, which has endured for many generations.[1]

Lord Curzon came to the conclusion that none of these schemes was suitable. Some were too ambitious; some had become obsolete owing to changed circumstances; while many of them were based upon a false assumption, that the politics of the hills could be separated from those of the plains.[2] After a careful consideration of all previous proposals he put forward his scheme, which he believed to be the only workable remedy at that time. The frontier districts were to be separated from the Panjab by the creation of an entirely new administrative unit, the North-West Frontier Province.

Politically, the new province was divided into two parts: the settled districts of Hazara, Peshawar, Kohat, Bannu, and Dera Ismail Khan; and the trans-border tracts which lay between the administrative and Durand boundaries. It should be remembered that the trans-border area, in addition to the five political agencies of the Malakand, Khyber,

---

[1] *Parl. Papers*, 1901 (Cd. 496), p. 75.
[2] See also *Bray Report*, p. 4.

Kurram, Tochi, and Wana, also contained tribal tracts under the political control of the deputy-commissioners of the adjoining settled districts. The cis-Indus tract of Hazara was not included in the scheme as originally drafted by Lord Curzon. It is interesting to note that between Dera Ismail Khan and Hazara there was only one trans-Indus tract which was not taken away from the Panjab: the transriverain *tahsil* of Isa Khel, the inhabitants of which were non-Pashtu-speaking Pathans, remained within the limits of the Panjab. The head of the new unit was to be a chief commissioner and agent to the Governor-General, to be appointed by and responsible to the Government of India. In addition, there was to be both a revenue and a judicial commissioner.

The first chief commissioner was Lieutenant-Colonel H. A. Deane, whose staff consisted of officers of the Political Department of the Government of India, members of the provincial and subordinate civil services, police officers, and officers specially recruited for the Militia, Engineering, Education, Medicine, and Forestry Departments.[1] The civil and judicial administration of the settled districts approximated to that obtaining elsewhere in British India. Each of the five districts was placed under a deputy-commissioner who was assisted by the usual *tahsildars, naib-tahsildars, kanungos,* and *patwaris.* The judicial commissioner, Mr C. E. Bunbury, was the controlling authority in the judicial branch of the administration, his court being the highest criminal and appellate tribunal in the province. Subordinate to him were the two divisional and sessions judges of Peshawar and the Derajat. The revenue administration of the whole settled area was likewise under the control of the revenue commissioner, Mr (afterwards Sir) Michael O'Dwyer.

---

[1] A good account of the early administrative system will be found in O'Dwyer, *India As I Knew It,* ch. VII. For later changes in the staff of the chief commissioner see *N.W.F.P. Administration Report,* 1921–2, p. 17.

Four objections were raised to the creation of this new province: the existing revenue system would be disturbed; it would entail a succession of territorial rectifications and compensations; it would deprive the Panjab Government of the opportunity of training officers in frontier affairs; and it would lead to a more forward policy. Lord Curzon replied that it was not proposed to revolutionize the revenue system. Secondly, only the Panjab was to be dismembered. He pointed out that under his scheme, which did not at first include Hazara, he took away from the Panjab only about one-fourteenth of its area, one-fifteenth of its total revenue, and about one-eighteenth of its population. As far back as 1864 Sir Henry Maine had written:

> The association with the Punjab of districts so essentially different from it in character and conditions as those which lie beyond the Indus, is quite as likely to delay the progress of the Punjab as to hasten that of their less civilized populations.[1]

As has already been shown, the trans-Indus tracts, especially the hilly country, were distinct from the Panjab, both historically and geographically; and the Pathan tribes, speaking a different language and living under different social conditions, were ethnically unlike their cis-Indus neighbours. In Lord Curzon's opinion there was no need to compensate the Panjab for the loss of its frontier districts; this proposal had been instrumental in shipwrecking Lord Lytton's scheme. Even in the 'seventies the Panjab had been a rapidly expanding province with an overworked executive. This was still more true of the beginning of the twentieth century when its population, revenue and trade had increased by leaps and bounds. In fact, the canalization and irrigation schemes of the Chenab river, Lower Bari-Doab and Sind-Sagar would serve as ample compensation. The following opinion of a contemporary Panjab official will make this point clearer:

[1] *Parl. Papers*, 1878, LVIII (Cd. 1898), 134.

D F   8

Towns have grown, Municipalities have been created under new and complex laws, the whole machinery of Local Self-Government has been started, hundreds of miles of railway and canals have been opened, the cultivated and, what is more important, the irrigated area has been enlarged by scores of thousands of acres,—in a word development in all directions has been so great that it is questionable whether there is not enough cis-Indus to occupy the full energies of a great administration.[1]

The third objection, that it would deprive the Panjab Government of the opportunity of training officers for frontier service, was answered by placing the officers employed upon the list of the political department of the Government of India. Under this arrangement the cream of the Indian civil service would be available, and any officers showing special aptitude for dealing with frontier tribes could be permanently posted, if this were thought desirable. Therefore, in his opinion, the opportunity of training officers would be enhanced rather than diminished.

That the new system would be "a measure of defence and security" was his reply to the fourth objection, his opinion being it would not lead to a more aggressive frontier policy. He pointed out that it could not be said the Panjab had served as a barrier against aggression, for, during the fifty years of Panjab control, at least forty expeditions had been needed against the tribes. Arguing in the same strain as that adopted by Lord Curzon, it cannot be said that the creation of the North-West Frontier Province prevented the two expeditions of 1908, or settled the Waziristan problem. Referring to the case of British Baluchistan, he was able to state that its creation had not been followed by any marked martial activity. This, however, was a particularly weak argument, for it does not follow that a system of administration, which was successful in that area, would have a corresponding effect in the northern Pathan country.

[1] *Parl. Papers*, 1901 (Cd. 496), p. 101.

The greatness of Lord Curzon's frontier policy does not lie in the fact that he originated the idea of a new frontier province—to hold that opinion, as has been shown in this chapter, would be utterly false. It lies rather in the fact that he carried out a reform which had been discussed and generally approved for nearly twenty-five years. He knew full well that finality can never be reached on the Indian frontier; and did not claim that his solution of the problem would last for ever.

Were his expectations fulfilled? He gave India a longer period of rest from border warfare than she had experienced for many weary years; and he was truthfully able to refer thus to the creation of the new province:

> You will all remember the outcries of the prophets of evil. It was going to inflict an irreparable wound upon the prestige of the Punjab Government. It was to overwhelm the Foreign Department with tiresome work. It was to encourage ambitious officers to gasconade upon the frontier. It was the symbol of a forward and Jingo policy, and would speedily plunge us in another Tirah campaign....I am content with the simple facts that for seven years we have not had a single frontier expedition, the only seven years of which this can be said since the frontier passed into British hands; and that, whereas in the five years 1894–9 the Indian taxpayer had to find 4½ million pounds sterling for frontier warfare, the total cost of military operations on the entire North-West Frontier, in the last seven years has only been £248,000, and that was for the semi-pacific operation of the Mahsud blockade.[1]

[1] Speech at the United Service Club, Simla, 30 September, 1905.

Chapter VII

THE MAHSUD BLOCKADE, 1900–2

As a punitive measure, the effects of the blockade have been severe; the Mahsuds have paid a fine of one lakh (the largest fine ever paid by a frontier tribe); they have lost their allowances for 15 months; also profits of trade and wages of labour and the pay of 250 Mahsuds in the Militia, or, at the rate under these heads of Rs. 10,000 per mensem, a sum of Rs. 1,50,000; they have surrendered 65 rifles taken during the blockade, worth at least Rs. 24,000; they are restoring animals taken during the blockade, worth Rs. 15,000; the property and live-stock lost by them during the active operations were worth about 2½ lakhs; their total pecuniary losses have been about Rs. 5,39,000. Besides, they have lost about 130 Mahsuds killed and some 250 wounded.

Parl. Papers, 1902 (Cd. 1177), p. 286.

The method claims three main advantages over that of punitive expeditions, the first, that of enforcing joint responsibility (among the members of the tribe). The second is the enormous saving of money, the cost in this instance working out at about Rs. 1500 as against Rs. 100,000 per day. At this rate a blockade can be kept up for three years for about the same expenditure as would be necessary for an expedition lasting sixteen days. The third advantage of a blockade is that it enlists instead of alienates the sympathy of the surrounding tribes.   *The Times*, 17 August, 1901.

It can be safely affirmed that the problem presented by the Mahsuds inhabiting the heart of Waziristan has been the one abiding difficulty on the Indian frontier. Practically every conciliatory method and every form of coercion have been attempted, but, after the lapse of more than three-quarters of a century, no real solution has been discovered. There still remains, as a last resort, the complete occupation and administration of Waziristan.

To explain the state of affairs along the borders of Waziristan in the opening years of the twentieth century, a short historical retrospect is essential. We have it on record that, during the days of Sikh rule, the Mahsuds were the scourge of the Bannu and Derajat borders.[1] The annexation of the Panjab, in 1849, made little difference, for they still continued to plunder and to devastate the country in the vicinity of Tank. The history of British relations with this tribe has been one of constant friction, of raids and counter-raids, of fanatical murders, bloodshed and rapine. At times the list of outrages has been so long, the insolence of the Mahsud so great, that nothing less than a punitive expedition has been able to restore that prestige, the loss of which is attended by such disastrous results, where civilization and barbarism come into contact. These expeditions have been followed, in some cases, by brief periods of peace during which the Mahsuds awaited an opportunity for fresh acts of devilry. Secure in their almost inaccessible mountain retreats, able to operate along interior lines of communication, a tremendous advantage, they boasted that they had paid tribute to no ruler of Hindustan, that their *pardah* had never been lifted, and that they had never been conquered. Unfortunately for them, their rocky fastnesses commanded the Gomal and Tochi, two of the five main passes connecting India with Afghanistan.

As far back as 1855, Sir John Lawrence had urged the Government of India to move against them; but in those early days it was a far cry to the Panjab and still farther to the extreme outposts of Empire. The result was that the dwellers on the plains were left unavenged. However, on three occasions, in 1860, 1881, and 1894, the Mahsuds became so troublesome and so utterly reckless was their behaviour that the British were forced to undertake punitive expeditions against them. In 1860, a long series of raids and robberies culminated in an unsuccessful attempt by about 3000 Mahsuds to burn the frontier town of Tank. The Government of India now determined to exact reparation for past offences, with the result that a force under

[1] Davies, *Report*, August, 1864.

Brigadier-General N. B. Chamberlain, after encountering a pertinacious opposition both at Palosina, near Jandola, and in the ill-omened Barari Tangi, a narrow cleft in the mountains cut by the Tank Zam, succeeded in occupying Kaniguram and razing Makin to the ground.[1] On the conclusion of this expedition a temporary peace was patched up, by which each of the three main sections, the Bahlolzai, Alizai, and Shaman Khel, agreed to hold themselves responsible for outrages committed by their respective clansmen.[2] But the promises of the Mahsuds were written in water, for, in less than two months, they were once more on the war-path.

From 1862 to 1874 various sections of the tribe were at one time or another placed under a blockade, until, in 1873 and 1874 respectively, the Shaman Khels and Bahlolzais, finding their continued exclusion from British territory irksome, made full submission.[3] On New Year's Day, 1879, a band of Mahsuds, whose leaders were acting under instructions from Kabul, burned Tank to the ground. This and other outrages eventually led to the expedition of 1881, when a British force once more penetrated Waziristan as far as Kaniguram and Makin. For the next ten years the cultivators of the Derajat and the banias of Tank and other frontier hamlets were left practically unmolested, and the whole of the Waziri border enjoyed a period of comparative peace. So peacefully disposed were the Mahsuds that, in 1883, they even rendered assistance in the survey of the country around Khajuri Kach, and, in 1890, were granted allowances for the watch and ward of the Gomal. The history of Waziristan in the 'nineties has been dealt with elsewhere.[4] Although the Mahsuds took no part in the 1897 risings, it would be wrong to suppose that peace reigned on the borders of Waziristan. It would be more correct to state that affairs were normal, which meant that raids

---

[1] *Confidential, Frontier and Overseas Expeditions*, II, ch. VIII.
[2] Aitchison, XI, 152–4.
[3] *Idem*, XI, 154–9.   [4] *Vide* ch. v.

and depredations were carried on with almost unabated fury.

From 1897 to the commencement of the Mahsud blockade on 1 December, 1900, the sufferings of British subjects in the settled districts can be best compared with those of the French settlers on the outskirts of Montreal and along the banks of the St Lawrence, who always moved about in constant dread of the Iroquois tomahawk. But the inhabitants of the Derajat and Bannu were much worse off than either of these, for the Government of India, in order to prevent counter-raids by border villagers, had disarmed them, thereby depriving them of the means of defending their own homes. The Mahsud was everywhere in evidence, his track being marked by looted *serais*, plundered villages and mutilated corpses. British subjects were utterly panic stricken, while the arch fiend swaggered about in broad daylight and broke with impunity all the laws that had been framed for the protection of human society. This terrorism engendered by raids and outrages extended to respectable *zamindars*, to the Border Military Police, to the ordinary police, and even to higher government officials.

It would, of course, be an exaggeration to say that the Mahsuds ever attempted directly to intimidate British officers: they were far too clever for this. But they actually did intimidate superior native officials.[1]

Mr Pipon, who was assistant commissioner at Tank during the years 1899 and 1900, cites several instances of Mahsud insolence and intimidation, which throw considerable light upon the state of the border during those troubled years. On one occasion during the hearing of a case in a *tahsildar's* court some Mahsuds, who were present to make a petition on behalf of one of their tribesmen, when they saw that the case was going against them, began to threaten the *tahsildar* in order to force him to give a decision in their favour. Anyone who had

---

[1] *Parl. Papers*, 1902, LXXI (Cd. 1177), 273.

crossed the path of a Mahsud, even in the discharge of Government duties, ever afterwards went about in continual dread, not knowing the moment when swift retribution was sure to follow.

During these two years, so far as I know, not one Mahsud was ever killed or even wounded by the Border Military Police, and this in spite of the Zam massacre, the shooting of four Border Military Police sepoys at Wana, and the many rifle thefts. It was well known that no Border Military Police sepoy would shoot a Mahsud. He would fire, but be careful to miss.[1]

It is obvious that the police were useless from fear; rare were the occasions on which even notorious raiders were arrested, and it was a well-known fact that, when the police had mustered up enough courage to do so, they were afraid to handcuff Mahsuds. Innumerable petty robberies were committed, *serais* were broken into, flocks and herds were carried off, shops in the Tank bazaar were pilfered, and men stabbed within twenty yards of Pipon's bungalow. Bands of Mahsuds used frequently to loot the crops of the Mianis whose lands lay near the Gomal, but no Miani ever dared complain. Villagers had been known to go to prison rather than disclose the names of offenders; and, what was worse, had been forced to assist the Mahsud in his depredations. Pipon attributed all this to the grant of large allowances which enabled the Mahsud to purchase more and better rifles; to the fact that border villagers had been disarmed; to the "invariable consideration shown to Mahsuds of all classes in British territory"; and to the Mahsud colony.

The last-named scheme gave every Mahsud *badmash* an explanation for his presence; it afforded a perfect rendezvous for raiding gangs, and a handy repository for arms and stolen property....It was as a Gundapur Khan dryly described it, a "school of *badmashi* opened by Government for the instruction of our young men".[2]

---

[1] *Parl. Papers*, 1902, LXXI (Cd. 1177), 274.　　　　[2] *Ibid.*

A Mahsud could carry arms openly on the highway; a British subject would be tried under the Arms Act for carrying even a dagger. All Mahsuds were exempt from *begar* (*corvée*); no Mahsud colonist was expected to perform irrigation labour, his share was done for him by British subjects. It is not, in these circumstances, to be wondered at that there was a widespread belief that the Mahsud was a privileged person whom even the British wished to propitiate rather than offend.

Most of the offences leading up to the blockade were cases of petty theft, robbery, house-breaking or lurking trespass, too numerous, and, in many cases, too insignificant to warrant separate description, but a brief account of some of the more important outrages will not be amiss at this stage in the narrative.

On 14 April, 1898, a Hindu marriage procession was proceeding along the road from Kulachi to Draband, when it was attacked by a gang of Mahsuds and robbed of a large number of valuable jewels. Not content with this, on the way back to their own territory, they committed another outrage by firing on a party of Zarkannis who were peacefully watering their fields. On 3 September of the same year, a band of Guri Khel Mahsuds raided the Jani Khel flocks grazing in British territory, kidnapped the shepherds and children in charge, killed several British subjects, and returned to their homes with large numbers of cattle, sheep and goats. This outrage was committed and the raiders had retreated across the border long before the garrison of the adjacent Jani Khel post had started off in pursuit. This post, manned by infantry and situated ten miles from the actual border, should have been garrisoned by cavalry, whose mobility would have rendered pursuit far easier. Merk, the Commissioner of the Derajat, held that a raid of this nature was much more damaging to British prestige than depredations taking place in the grazing lands adjacent to the border. The fact that it had taken place in British territory and that British subjects had been murdered rendered immediate reprisals imperative. The plundering propensities of the Mahsuds and their hereditary feuds with the Jani Khels, who were Darwesh Khel Waziris, were assigned as the probable causes of this outrage. There can be no doubt that the inefficiency of the border police, the fact that the border villagers were disarmed, and that British troops were in possession of arms decidedly inferior to the breech-loading rifles used by the Mahsuds, facilitated the task of the raiders and rendered the work of pursuit parties more difficult.

In the following year Mahsud outrages took the form of acts of open hostility to the British Raj. In May, 1899, they fired upon a party of Zhob Levy Corps sepoys who were proceeding along the bed of a nullah between Girdao and Mir Ali Khel; in June, they cut the telegraph line on the Khajuri Kach road, and fired upon a party of sepoys sent out to repair the damage; in July, they attacked a ration convoy in the now well-known Shahur Tangi, one of the narrowest of frontier defiles; and, on the twentieth of the same month, fired upon Mr Watson, the Political Officer for Wana, killing his *chaprassi*. In the opening months of 1900 they became more reckless than ever, and even commenced attacking fortified posts. In January, they suddenly fell upon the Zam post, murdered the garrison, and carried off all available arms and ammunition. Four more serious outrages need recording.

Some Miani Powindahs were travelling up the Gomal on the way to their summer quarters in Khurasan. On the night of 23 April, 1900, when their camels were grazing, they were attacked by a gang of about eighty Mahsuds and Zalli Khel Waziris, who, having killed one Powindah, made off with 170 camels as booty. The mails were robbed in the Tiarza nullah on 21 May of the same year, and, four days later, fifteen raiders attacked the water picket at Khajuri Kach.

Lastly, on 23 October, the Border Military Police post at Kot Nasran was attacked and looted. Lieutenant Hennessey of the 45th Sikhs, who went in pursuit, was killed by a wounded raider.

From this it will readily be seen that the state of affairs on the eve of the blockade rendered immediate reprisals essential. The causes of unrest were partly economic, partly political. The failure of the rains and the consequent lack of food and fodder across the border had resulted in innumerable petty raids and robberies. But the later attacks directed against British troops and Government officials were political in origin, and were believed to have been instigated by the Mullah Powindah, the evil genius of Waziristan. For years the Mahsud had preyed upon his less warlike neighbours. All attempts at conciliation had failed; large fines remained outstanding; and people were beginning to blame the Government for the almost unchecked licence of the Mahsud. But the hour was at hand when they were to be shown that forbearance could not last for ever; that they could not with impunity spread havoc and desolation through the border districts. It was essential to strike and to strike hard, the only form of chastisement ever understood by refractory savages.

It is now necessary to give some account of the system which regulated our relations with the Mahsuds; and to explain how far it was responsible for the difficulties experienced in preserving the peace of the border.

Until 1861 there was no systematic basis of political relations with the Mahsud tribe, but in that year the three main sections of the tribe accepted responsibility for the misdeeds of their respective members.[1] Although this arrangement was a step in the right direction it cannot be said that it ushered in a reign of peace on the Derajat borders. From 1875 to the outbreak of the Second Afghan War in 1878, and from the expedition of 1881 to the

[1] Aitchison, xi, 152–4.

year 1889, the most peaceful years in the history of Anglo-Mahsud relations, full tribal responsibility was enforced, that is, the complete tribal *jirga* was held responsible for any outrages committed by a Mahsud or body of Mahsuds. In other words, the coercion of recalcitrant members became a tribal, not a sectional, duty. In the 'nineties, however, a new scheme, already referred to as the Bruce or *maliki* system, was introduced by Mr R. I. Bruce, the Commissioner of the Derajat.[1] Bruce, who had previously served under Sandeman in Baluchistan, attempted to introduce into Waziristan, amongst the intensely democratic Mahsuds, the system which had proved so successful in dealing with the Baluch tribes of the southern frontier. It seems to me that Bruce made three mistakes. In the first place, he made a fatal mistake when he attempted to introduce his system into Waziristan without first occupying some commanding central position with troops. Secondly, he entered upon his new duties with preconceived ideas that the Mahsud republic, a republic bordering on anarchy, could be controlled in the same way as the Baluch and Brahui tribesmen, who, to say the least, were far from democratic. Lastly, he completely underestimated the turbulence of the Mahsuds. After his retirement, he wrote a defence of this system, from which the following quotation has been taken:

I do not believe there is a single tribe with whom we have had intimate dealings up to the present, including the great Waziri tribe, so difficult to manipulate as were the Marris and Bugtis when we went at them in 1866.[2]

That Bruce failed to realize the difficulty of controlling the inhabitants of Waziristan, becomes apparent when it is remembered that the most pressing problem on the whole frontier, since 1919, has been the settlement of Waziri affairs.

[1] *Vide* ch. II, p. 34.
[2] Bruce, *Forward Policy and its Results*, p. 18.

Bruce based his system upon three principles.[1] First, certain *maliks* were selected by him, not by the tribe, and were graded according to their supposed power and influence. Secondly, these *maliks* had to produce a certain number of Mahsuds for service as levies. Lastly, in return for allowances, the *maliks*, supported by the levies, were expected to surrender offenders to justice and to control the *ulus*, the name given to the body of the Mahsud tribe. It was an attempt to bring home offences to the guilty, to procure the surrender of the actual culprits, and not to make the whole tribe suffer for the sins of its unruly members. In fact, its exponents defended it on the ground that it was ethically superior to the enforcement of tribal responsibility, under which the innocent were forced to share punishment with the guilty.

Coercive pressures are the essential basis of this system, and they are not conducive to the cultivating of really friendly and sympathetic relations. Punitive expeditions mark our attempts in the past to manage the Mahsud tribe, dealing with it as a whole.[2]

The argument that tribal responsibility had been productive of punitive expeditions falls to the ground, when it is remembered that the years, during which this system was enforced, were some of the most peaceful in the stormy history of Waziristan. The greatest argument against the *maliki* system was the unanswerable contention that it had failed. From the most democratic of Pathan tribes, possessing at that time a fighting strength of something like 10,000 men, Bruce had selected and subsidized about 270 *maliks*. Merk, the commissioner on special duty during the blockade, pointed out that the very fact that the headmen were chosen by Bruce, and not by the tribe, meant that they did not fully represent the *ulus*. If the Mahsuds were allowed, or compelled to select their own representatives, the most powerful men would naturally come to the front. Watson, the Political Officer for

[1] *Parl. Papers*, 1902 (Cd. 1177), pp. 125–6.
[2] *Idem*, p. 63.

Wana, cited instances where influential men had been passed over by the local British authorities; and he recorded his opinion that some of the worst characters were also the most influential.

The result of all this was that internal government had collapsed in the Mahsud hills. The *maliki* system had been tested; it had failed ignominiously. The *maliks*, who had accepted allowances in return for which they were expected to control the tribe, had become absolutely powerless. In 1893, the headmen, who had been instrumental in handing over to justice the murderers of Mr Kelly, a British official, had themselves been murdered by their own tribesmen.[1] Again, in 1894, the attack on the British boundary demarcation camp at Wana had been instigated by the Mullah Powindah in defiance of the subsidized *maliks*. Indeed, so powerless had these *maliks* become that on several occasions they had begged the local officials to persuade the Government of India to annex their country. According to Merk, in the old days the coercion of recalcitrant tribesmen had been performed by the *chalweshtis* or tribal police, in accordance with instructions received from the tribal *jirga*. He, therefore, advocated the bolstering up of the internal government of the Mahsud country by reverting to full tribal responsibility, which had been tried, and tried successfully, in the past. If this policy were not adopted, anarchy would reign supreme in Waziristan, and the British would eventually be faced with the occupation and administration of that country. To cut a long story short, the Panjab authorities came to the conclusion that the procedure in force in the Derajat for the settlement of tribal cases was too cumbersome.

The process of ascertaining and, if possible, of effecting the surrender and punishment of individual offenders, and, failing this, of dealing first with small sub-sections, then with sections,

[1] On 30 June, 1893, Mr Kelly, a subordinate officer in the Public Works Department, was shot by raiders near Mughal Kot.

and so on till the whole clan or tribe is reached, seems to be productive of delay and complications.[1]

Having come to the conclusion that the Mahsuds were deserving of punishment, the Government of India had to decide whether it would be better to coerce them by means of a blockade or by a punitive expedition. A strict blockade has for its object the exclusion of all members of a certain tribe from British territory; it aims at preventing any trade or intercourse with the outside world; and, if successful, should starve the recalcitrant tribe or section into complete submission.

The blockading method was no new departure on the frontier. It had been employed with good effect in the past, either against particular clans or against the tribe as a whole. Many Afridi clans, especially those of the Kohat pass, had been blockaded on several occasions. While the fate of the Mahsuds hung in the balance, the Aka Khels, who, during the winter months, inhabit the hills between the Kohat pass and the Bara river, were suffering from this particular form of punishment. The Gaduns of the Hazara border had been blockaded on three separate occasions. It had also been applied with varying degrees of success to certain of the Yusafzai and Orakzai clans. Except for brief periods of peace, the history of British contact with the Mahsuds had been one of blockades enlivened by occasional expeditions.[2]

At the time under consideration the condition of affairs in Waziristan was admirably suited to a stringent Mahsud blockade. Our troops in the Tochi and at Wana commanded their northern and southern borders respectively; access to Bannu and the Derajat was rendered more difficult by the

[1] *Parl. Papers*, 1902 (Cd. 1177), p. 58.

[2] In 1878, after a blockade, the whole Mahsud tribe came to terms. "This blockade demonstrated what a powerful engine of coercion such a measure was against the Mahsuds for the redress of all ordinary border crime"—Paget and Mason, *Record of Expeditions*, p. 527.

friendly co-operation of the Bhittannis, armed for this purpose by the Government of India; and, so long as the Badar
land dispute with the Darwesh Khels remained unsettled, the
Mahsud retreat into Afghanistan was blocked by their
deadliest enemies. In addition there was supposed to be a
great scarcity of food and fodder in their country. It was
therefore predicted that all these factors would combine in
bringing the blockade to a successful and speedy termination.
At the same time, it was considered essential that the blockade
should be one of the whole tribe and not merely of the
offending sections, for, under a sectional blockade, there was
always the danger of members of the blockaded sections
trading with British territory under the guise of friendlies.
There was, however, a far more important reason for resorting to this particular form of coercion.

   To punish the Mahsuds was not the sole aim of the Government of India: it was also necessary to reform the internal
administration of the tribe, that is, to replace the *maliks* by a
fully representative tribal *jirga*. As Merk pointed out, to produce a political reformation of this nature a somewhat
lengthy blockade would be required. It must be remembered, however, that all these arguments refer to a particular
case, the Mahsud tribe as it existed in the closing years of the
nineteenth century. Where it is desired signally to punish a
recalcitrant tribe, the punitive expedition still holds the field.
Even in this particular case, as will become apparent, a mere
passive blockade without military operations of any kind failed
to bring the tribe to terms. Indeed, a blockade is often a mere
euphemism for an expedition.

   A fine of one lakh of rupees for past offences was imposed
upon the Mahsud tribe. Having failed to pay half of this fine
within fifteen days, they were blockaded from 1 December,
1900. The blockade can be divided into two stages, the passive
and the active. During the latter it was varied by a series of
sudden punitive sallies into their mountain retreats.

To ensure the success of the blockade, a cordon of posts was established between Bannu and Dera Ismail Khan, while small movable columns were stationed in readiness at Jani Khel and Zam. The Gomal line of defence was strengthened by regular garrisons at Murtaza and Manjhi and by a cordon of posts on the Zhob border. In addition to the existing posts at Jandola, Haidari Kach, Sarwekai, and Khajuri Kach, new posts were established at Tormandu, Khwuzma Narai, and on the Spin plain. These troops received instructions to prevent the export of grain from British India into Waziristan and to prevent any Mahsud from crossing the administrative border. A reward of twenty rupees was paid for every Mahsud discovered trading or working in British territory. To increase the economic distress in Waziristan these Mahsuds were not imprisoned but sent back to their own country.

Surrounded by an almost impenetrable ring-fence of about 300 miles in length, deprived of all the luxuries and of many of the necessaries of life, the Mahsuds at first began to pay the fine in real earnest. The severity of the blockade may be inferred from the fortnightly reports of Merk. As time went on, prices rose to famine rates; salt, tobacco, cloth and *gur* were practically unobtainable; and when the *jirgas* came in, every man appeared to be suffering from dyspepsia. Within seventeen days of the imposition of the blockade, Merk was able to telegraph the following report:

Complete cessation of raids, robberies and thefts along borders of Tochi, Bannu, Dera Ismail Khan and Wana...proves, firstly, that the Mahsuds alone were the disturbers of the peace; and, secondly, that the tribe is perfectly capable of combining for a common purpose and of controlling its bad characters if it chooses.[1]

The second part of this report was far too optimistic, for, about the middle of January, 1901, all payments towards the fine ceased and there was a general recrudescence of raiding

[1] *Parl. Papers*, 1902 (Cd. 1177), pp. 184–5.

along the British borders. To explain the deadlock, a short description of events in Waziristan is necessary.

There were two political factions in the Mahsud country, the one headed by the *maliks*, the other by their enemy, the Mullah Powindah.[1] It seems that, when the mullah used his influence to pay off the fine, the *maliks*, fearing that it would restore him to the Government's favour, deliberately encouraged the tribesmen to commit fresh depredations. They hoped in this way to force the Government of India to undertake punitive operations which the mullah, as religious leader, would have to resist. The *maliks* hoped that the termination of hostilities would find the mullah discredited in the eyes of the British authorities, while they would still be in receipt of their usual allowances.

The result was that the year 1901 witnessed a series of raids, some of an extremely daring nature. For the first six months the Mahsuds confined their attention to mail-runners, small escorts, sepoys on picket duty and lonely outposts; but August found them attacking police and militia posts in broad daylight. The most daring raid of all took place on 23 September, 1901, when a band of Mahsuds attacked a village twenty-five miles within the Bannu district. The raiders were headed by one Nabi Bakhsh, a desperate outlaw, who had been previously wounded by a wealthy money-lender, Attar Shah Singh. Nabi Bakhsh, after the manner of his race, had sworn eternal enmity, and the chief motive for his attack was to settle his account with the money-lender. Attar Shah Singh, his children and three other persons were killed, and the surrounding houses and shops looted. Thus did a desperate ruffian, in the heart of a British district, wreak vengeance on a respectable British citizen.

A raid of this magnitude is unknown within the memory of the present generation, and it is no exaggeration to say the whole

[1] A priest of the Shabi Khel, Alizai, section of the Mahsuds. He was nicknamed the "Pestilential Priest" by Lord Kitchener.

countryside is terrified and appalled at the knowledge that it is possible....At present a feeling of insecurity prevails throughout the *ilaka*,[1] and a growing belief that Government is unable to protect its subjects.[2]

This was followed, on 3 November, by a well-prepared ambush, in which the escort detailed for the survey party at work on the Murtaza-Sarwekai road sustained heavy casualties.

At last, the Government of India realized that a merely passive blockade would not bring about the desired result; that only about three-fourths of the fine had been collected, while the account for fresh outrages, committed since the commencement of the blockade, was steadily increasing. Worse than this, it was apparent that the attitude of the tribe had changed to one of open hostility. Later events proved that the blockade had not been so effective as had been expected. Indeed, Merk's fortnightly reports on the state of affairs inside Waziristan had been somewhat too optimistic, for, when British columns penetrated the Mahsud country, they discovered large stores of grain and food, and found that the Mahsuds were comfortably settled in some of the lower valleys. The Khaisara was found to be a valley of extreme fertility containing a considerable area of arable land, well irrigated by canals.[3] Two courses were therefore open to the Government of India: either to continue the blockade throughout the winter months and settle affairs by means of an expedition in the spring; or to dispense with an expedition, but to vary the blockade by sudden punitive sallies into the Mahsud hills.

It was eventually decided to carry out the second of these proposals. At the same time, it was pointed out that the success of the second stage of the blockade, that is, the active stage, could only be ensured by surprise attacks; and that the

[1] District.   [2] *Parl. Papers*, 1902 (Cd. 1177), p. 243.
[3] *Idem*, p. 266.

Mahsuds would have to be kept in a continual state of anxiety and uncertainty. This could only be accomplished by making it impossible for them to discover from which corner of the cordon of blockading troops these harassing counter-attacks were to be expected. Climate, one of the chief factors in the physiographic environment, plays a very important part in determining the nature of punitive operations in the frontier hills. The intense cold which sets in after the middle of November forces the Mahsuds to migrate from the upper ranges to the warmer valleys. If operations were undertaken in the cold weather it would be extremely difficult for the tribes-men to escape with their flocks and herds across Shawal into Afghan territory. The military officers in charge of these operations had also to remember that the Mahsuds possessed the tremendous advantage of being able to operate on interior lines and could therefore collect quickly. Active operations commenced on 23 November, 1901, and took the form of four series of raids, at intervals of about a fortnight, each series lasting from four to five days. They were directed against the Mahsuds inhabiting the Khaisara, Shahur, Dwe Shinkai, Guri Khel, Shaktu, and other parts of Waziristan, and were completely successful.[1]

At last the Mahsuds were forced to comply with Govern-ment terms,[2] with the result that, on 10 March, 1902, the blockade was raised. They were forced to pay a fine of a lakh of rupees; they accepted full tribal responsibility, and agreed to hand over all outlaws and fugitives from justice; and, as Merk pointed out, they came to realize that their country could be penetrated from north, east, and south, "without the hope of successful resistance on their part". It must, however, not be forgotten that a mere blockade, unvaried by punitive sallies, had proved a failure.

---

[1] For detailed description of operations see: (*a*) *Parl. Papers*, 1902 (Cd. 1177), pp. 254–69; (*b*) *Confidential, Frontier and Overseas*, II, 440–5.
[2] For the text of the Agreement, see Aitchison, XI, 160–1.

Merk's account ends on a note of hope for the future, but later events, combined with the pernicious effects of the arms traffic, show the futility of prophesying about the frontier. Government officials were inclined to be too optimistic: the more accurate opinion of the inhabitants of the border was far from being so:

The native opinion on the border is definitely that the Mahsuds will submit and will later again break out; that the tribe cannot be reformed and induced to relinquish their old ingrained habits of murdering, raiding and thieving by anything short of permanent occupation of their country.[1]

It should have been realized that, with an expanding, virile and unruly tribe like the Mahsuds, it was impossible to predict the continuance of peaceful conditions for any length of time. For a few years, indeed, there seemed to be a genuine desire on the part of influential *maliks* for keeping the peace, with the result that the conduct of the tribe was excellent; but, unfortunately, the Mullah Powindah, owing to the lack of real co-operation amongst the *maliks*, became paramount in the Mahsud council chamber, and several dastardly assassinations were traced to his direct instigation.[2] To this ambitious follower of the Prophet may be traced the murders of Captain Bowring in September, 1904; of Colonel Harman in February, 1905; and of Captain Donaldson in November of the same year. These murders led to the disbandment of 400 Mahsud Militia sepoys, and the imposition of a fine of Rs. 25,000. In 1908, the Mahsud question became more acute, and once more a series of raids into British territory under two notorious outlaws, Mianji and Surab, was found to have originated in the machinations of the Mullah Powindah. Although the Government of India issued a warning to the whole Mahsud tribe, several attempts were made to murder the British Political Agent. The state of affairs on the

[1] *Parl. Papers*, 1902 (Cd. 1177), p. 257.
[2] *Secret Border Report*, 1907–8, pp. 7–8.

borders of Waziristan can be gauged from the following report:

...the gang met the Political Agent's bearer and the Political Tahsildar's Munshi and killed them both, mutilating the former's body and leaving most of the property as an indication of the real animus of their act. On receipt of the report of this offence the Political Agent effected a general reprisal on Mahsuds and their property in the protected area of the Agency and on the Dera Ismail Khan border, capturing 379 Mahsuds and 1884 head of cattle. The Chief Commissioner then summoned the Mahsud Jirga to Tank with the exception of the Mulla Powindah, who under the orders of the Government of India was expressly ignored. In retaliation the Mulla did his utmost to prevent Mahsuds from attending the jirga, and eventually only the Maliks and their immediate adherents attended at Tank at the close of the year.[1]

The death of the mullah did not solve the Mahsud problem, for he nominated his second surviving son, Fazal Din, as his successor. His real successor, however, was Mullah Abdul Hakim, who "left no stone unturned to preserve the continuity of his late master's policy, namely the fostering of a united Mahsud country hostile to the British Government".[2]

[1] *Secret Border Report*, 1907–8, p. 8.   [2] *Idem*, 1913–14, pp. 19–20.

Chapter VIII

RELATIONS WITH THE AFRIDIS AND MOHMANDS, 1898–1908

The Zakka Khel, who were the most powerful clan, who blackmailed the rest by right of occupation of lands stretching from the farther mountains to the frontier of India; who lent no soldiers to the ranks of the British Army and had no pensions to lose—the traffickers in salt and (it is said) in slaves with Afghanistan, the wolves of the community, were all for war.   Holdich, *The Indian Borderland*, p. 347.

Waziristan and the Khyber have been the two main zones of disturbance on the Pathan frontier. In fact, they present a striking and interesting parallel. Both are inhabited by war-like and predatory tribes, proud of their independence; both command important routes between India and Afghanistan, the Gomal of the south and the Khyber of the north; and the fact that neither of them is capable of providing the necessaries of life for its turbulent inhabitants forces the tribesmen to raid and lay waste the open plains contiguous to their mountain retreats. If the Mahsud has been the curse of the Derajat, it is equally true that the Zakka Khel Afridi has been the scourge of the Peshawar border.

The Khyber, as its name implies, runs through the Khyber hills from the Shadi Bagiar opening, about three miles beyond the fort of Jamrud, for about thirty-three miles in a north-westerly direction, until it finally debouches, just beyond the old Afghan fort of Haft Chah, on to the barren plain of Loi Dakka, which stretches to the banks of the Kabul river opposite the Mohmand village of Lalpura. There is a very steep ascent at the mouth of the pass, but afterwards it rises gradually to Fort Ali Masjid (3174 feet), where the Khyber stream is first encountered, and where it also leaves the pass to flow through the Kuki Khel country. From Ali Masjid the pass winds through the village of Sultan Khel to Landi Kotal (3518 feet), where its highest point is reached, and whence a route leads into the Shilmani country. The main pass, however, descends from Landi Kotal through Shinwari territory to Landi Khana, where British control ends and the limits of Afghanistan are reached. In and around the Khyber dwell the Khyber Afridis.[1]

Our first skirmish with the Afridis dates back to the invasion of Afghanistan during the war of 1839–42. From 1849 to 1898 no less than eight expeditions, during which the British sustained casualties amounting to 1287, were required to coerce them. Three of these were directed against the Zakka Khels: it now remains to record the events leading up to a fourth, that of 1908.

At the time under consideration the Zakka Khels of the Khyber and the adjacent Bazar valley of Tirah were the most important and powerful of all the Afridi clans. Inhabiting lands stretching from the slopes of the Safed Koh to the borders of Peshawar, they were able to force their neighbours to pay exorbitant tolls for the privilege of passing through their territories. Even amongst robbers distinctions are possible, for, though every Zakka is a born thief, Warburton has described one of their sections as "that most thieving community the Zya-ud-din Zakka Khels".[2]

The first agreement with the Zakka Khels dates back to the days of the Mutiny, when their two factions under Bostan Khan and Aladad Khan respectively, on condition that they

---

[1] From Jamrud to Ali Masjid the Khyber winds through the territories of the Kuki Khel, Sipah, Kamrai, and Kambar Khel; from Ali Masjid to the Kandar ravine, near Garhi Lala Beg, it passes through the habitat of the Malikdin Khel and Zakka Khel.

It should be remembered that the opening of a railway through the pass on 2 November, 1925, has completely revolutionized the problem presented by the Khyber.

[2] Warburton, *Eighteen Years in the Khyber*, p. 303.

would be allowed free access to British territory, promised that they would neither harbour outlaws nor associate with the enemies of the Sarkar.[1] The peace of the Khyber was not abnormally disturbed until the Second Afghan War, 1878–80, when the harassing attacks of the Afridis upon the Khyber line of communications forced the British to undertake retributive measures, with the result that, both in 1878 and in the following year, our troops marched through the Zakka Khel country, destroyed their crops and razed their forts and villages to the ground. That part of the treaty of Gandamak, 1879, which related to the Khyber, read as follows:

> The British Government will retain in its own hands the control of the Khyber and Michni Passes, which lie between the Peshawar and Jalalabad Districts, and of all relations with the independent tribes of the territory directly connected with these Passes.[2]

Within four months Sir Louis Cavagnari was treacherously murdered at Kabul and the treaty of Gandamak became mere waste paper. At Zimma, on 31 July, 1880, although no formal treaty was drawn up, Abdurrahman Khan, the new amir, pledged himself to recognize a state of affairs similar to that contemplated in the above article. It now remained for the British to make arrangements with the Khyber Afridis. On 17 February, 1881, the Afridi clans,[3] together with the Loargi Shinwaris of Landi Kotal, accepted responsibility for the safety of the Khyber, and, on condition that their independence was recognized, agreed to have no dealings with any other foreign power. This agreement is of supreme importance, in that it regulated our relations with the Afridi tribe for the next sixteen years. It also arranged for the protection of the Khyber by the creation of a force of *Jezailchis*, or tribal levies, to be paid by the Government of India;[4] the

---

[1] Aitchison, XI, 92–6.   [2] *Idem*, p. 346.
[3] Kuki Khel, Kambar Khel, Malikdin Khel, Zakka Khel, Sipah, and Kamrai.
[4] The yearly cost of the *Jezailchis* was Rs. 87,392.

granting of annual allowances of Rs. 87,540; and, what is very important, bound the Afridis not to commit dacoity, highway robbery, or murder in British territory, under penalty of forfeiture of these allowances.[1] The Afridis, who were the last to join in the tribal risings of 1897-8, were coerced by the Tirah Expeditionary Force under Sir William Lockhart. Early in 1898, Lord George Hamilton, the Secretary of State for India, informed the Government of India that the safety of the Khyber was of essential importance in any fresh agreement with the Afridi tribe.[2] Thereupon the Government of India set to work to examine various proposals for the future management of the pass.

There were four possible solutions: the pass could be held and garrisoned by regular troops; by a force partly regular, partly irregular; by irregular troops alone; and, lastly, it could be placed entirely under tribal management. There were many reasons against employing regular troops: their presence would serve as a source of irritation to the tribesmen; the Government of India had been warned not to accept fresh responsibilities by locking up regular forces in isolated posts across the administrative border; and, as Merk pointed out, there was always the danger of the presence of troops in the Khyber paving the way for the annexation of the surrounding tribal territory.[3] The other extreme, that of tribal responsibility alone, would, it was argued, prove still more dangerous, for it postulated a power of cohesion and combination which did not exist among the Afridis, whose never-ending bloodfeuds and intensely democratic nature rendered tribal cohesion and united action well-nigh impossible. Eventually, it was decided to revert to the system which had proved so successful for seventeen years, 1881-97; but, at the same time, the Khyber Rifles were to be reorganized under British

[1] Aitchison, XI, 97-9.
[2] Parl. Papers, 1901, XLIX (Cd. 496), 15.
[3] Idem, pp. 41-2.

officers and supported by a movable column at Peshawar. The employment of British officers was a distinct step forward, for, under the 1881 Agreement, the Afridis themselves were responsible for the force of *Jezailchis*, whereas, under the new system, the British accepted full responsibility for the Khyber Rifles and the safety of the pass.

In October, 1898, a new Agreement, which regulated our relations with the Afridis until the year 1908, was drawn up between the Government of India and a representative *jirga*.[1] Amongst other things they agreed to have no dealings with any other foreign power, and signified their willingness to co-operate with the British in keeping the Khyber open as a caravan route. On condition that they would commit no offences in the pass and comply with all the terms of the agreement, their former allowances were restored and an *inam*, or award, of three months' allowances was granted to the *jirga*.

The peaceful construction of the Mullagori road and of a telegraph line through the Khyber during the opening years of the twentieth century proved that the Afridis were making determined efforts to remain loyal to their engagements. But subtle and sinister forces were working beneath the surface. The mullahs were constantly exhorting the tribesmen to rise against the hated *Feringhi* Government, and the activities of the anti-British party at Kabul had for their object the fomenting of disturbances along the whole frontier. Although the attempt of Khawas Khan, a proscribed *malik*, to raise an Afridi bodyguard for the amir was doomed to failure, and although, towards the end of 1902, the death of the Adda Mullah put an end to his nefarious influence over the tribesmen, the Zakka Khels were soon to commence a series of raids and depredations, which caused widespread ruin along the Kohat and Peshawar borders.

It would be as absurd to hope for the complete cessation of

[1] *Parl. Papers*, 1908 (Cd. 4201), pp. 14–15.

outrages on an exposed frontier inhabited by savage tribes, as it would be to expect that burglary would ever become extinct in any of the large cities of Europe. But, when waves of fanaticism and anti-British propaganda disturb the face of the waters, the inevitable result is an increased spirit of lawlessness. Towards the end of the year 1904, large numbers of Afridis visited Kabul, where they were favourably received by Habibullah, the amir, and his brother, Nasrullah. This visit was followed by several marauding incursions into British territory, in which the Zakka Khels, assisted by other Afridi clans, by Orakzais, and even by bands of Afghan outlaws, such as the Hazarnao gang, were the chief offenders. Amongst the Zakkas the most uncompromising in their hostile attitude towards the British were the members of the Zia-ud-din sub-section.

On 3 September, 1904, a gang of raiders hid themselves on the outskirts of Darshi Khel, a village in the Teri *tahsil* of the Kohat district. Under cover of darkness they entered the village, looted the shop of a Hindu *bania* whom they murdered, and forced the women of the adjoining houses to hand over the jewellery they were wearing. A party, who went in pursuit of the raiders, lost five killed and six wounded. The failure of the pursuit party can be explained by the fact that the raiders were in possession of Martini-Henry rifles and were, therefore, easily able to keep at a distance the villagers who were armed only with Snider and Enfield rifles. When it is remembered that the night was dark; that the raiders retreated by sections in an orderly fashion over difficult ground; and that, when day broke, their tracks had been obliterated by heavy rainfall, the failure of the pursuit party is more easily appreciated. Major Roos-Keppel, the Political Officer for the Khyber area, was convinced that the Darshi Khel outrage was no ordinary raid, but a deliberate act of defiance against the British. The object of the anti-British party, or, as they would term themselves, the patriotic party, was to induce all Afridi clans to commit themselves beyond all hope of pardon, so that the Government of India would be compelled to undertake a punitive expedition, not against the Zakkas alone, but against the whole Afridi tribe.

It was openly hatched in Tirah and committed, in defiance both of the Zakka Khel maliks and of Government, by the party who were benefiting by the intrigues of Khawas Khan at Kabul, at a time when the Afridi clans generally were breaking their agreements with Government by visiting Kabul.[1]

The first three months of 1905 witnessed no less than ten dacoities culminating in an attack on the police post of Matanni near Peshawar, all of which were carried out by a gang of Afghan outlaws from Hazarnao. It was always possible to mete out temporary punishment, if financial considerations permitted, to tribes living on the British side of the Durand boundary: it was an entirely different matter when the marauders were Afghan subjects outside our sphere of influence. From 1905 onwards large gangs, composed of Afghan subjects, outlaws from British territory, and unruly tribesmen expelled from tribal limits, continued to ravage the frontier districts, kidnap wealthy Hindu *banias* and hold them to ransom. The situation assumed a very critical aspect when it was discovered that the Afghan Government, though professing complete ignorance of the presence of these gangs, was secretly encouraging them to raid British India. To quote the words of a contemporary report:

The outlaws provide the local knowledge, the exiled tribesmen the arms, and the Afghans a secure retreat and base, where, under the patronage of the local Afghan Governor, who shares their profits, they can hold British subjects to ransom for many months, can dispose of their loot and settle their plans for their next adventure.[2]

Everything humanly possible for the protection of our subjects was done by the local authorities; and, to cope with

[1] *Parl. Papers*, 1908 (Cd. 4201), p. 24.
[2] *Secret Border Report*, 1908–9, p. 3.

the situation, a special system of patrolling was introduced. There were, however, several factors militating against success. The physical features of the Peshawar and Kohat borders, where cultivation extended almost to the mouths of the very passes through which the raiders entered the plains, constituted an invitation to the lawless to lay waste the settled districts; and an intricate maze of nullahs and defiles afforded them a speedy and safe line of retreat to their mountain fastnesses. Possessing an unrivalled knowledge of the ground and an elaborate system of espionage, they were able to avoid fortified posts, permanent pickets, villages and other places, where serious opposition might be expected. When it is remembered that the raiders were well aware of the defenceless state of the border villagers, who, against the almost unanimous opinion of the greatest frontier authorities, had been disarmed in 1900, it becomes obvious that the position of our subjects resembled that of sheep exposed to ravening wolves; so much so, that the Chief Commissioner of the Frontier Province was of opinion that it would be impossible to cope with these raiding gangs unless the border villagers were rearmed.

Rifles and pistols are now denied to them except under licence, so that villages which formerly could and did hold their own, can now turn out armed only with *jezails*, swords, and sticks to combat a gang armed with weapons of precision and reckless of life.[1]

Far worse than this, the tribesmen were better armed than either the Border Military Police or the Militia, the very forces maintained for the purpose of reprisals. We have it on record that, by 1909, the state of the Border Military Police had become so disgraceful, that twenty-five out of every hundred sepoys were either unfit or too old for frontier service, which, to say the least, is very exacting. Both native officers and the non-commissioned ranks were selected, not for their military efficiency, but for political reasons, because

[1] *Parl. Papers,* 1908 (Cd. 4201), p. 32.

they happened to be the sons or relatives of influential border landowners. In addition, the rank and file were so badly paid for their extremely strenuous duties, that it was practically impossible for them to make both ends meet, unless they were stationed in close proximity to their native villages.[1] Not only were the border villagers disarmed, the tribesmen well armed, and the Military Police inefficient and undisciplined, but the morale of the Militia was being rapidly undermined by the knowledge that their obsolete weapons could be easily outranged by those of their foes across the border. Before 1914 these abuses had been remedied as far as possible by the arming of the border villagers and by the creation of a more efficient and better armed Frontier Constabulary to take the place of the Border Military Police.

To revert to the Zakka Khels, it must not be imagined that Afridi *maliks* and *jirgas* made no attempts to prevent this intractable clan from ravaging the British borders. On the contrary, *lashkars* were raised and forcibly billeted on the recalcitrant Zakkas, until the culprits in the Darshi Khel raid were either surrendered or banished from the country. When this failed, the fortified towers and haunts of these desperadoes were attacked and levelled to the ground. In many cases well-known outlaws were slain. But Tirah, like Waziristan, had its evil genius, and the efforts of loyal *maliks* were frustrated by a quondam *malik*, Khawas Khan, who was constantly coquetting with Afghan officials. It will be remembered that the Waziri *maliks*, who were instrumental in arresting the murderers of Mr Kelly, were themselves murdered by Mahsud tribesmen. An almost parallel case occurred in the Afridi country, where a headman, who attempted to prevent the passage of raiders through his lands, was attacked by the whole clan. Not content with killing him, they destroyed his native village and turned his relatives adrift.

[1] *Secret Border Report*, 1908–9, p. 17.

In the spring of 1905, the Zakkas promised not to allow certain outlaws to return to the Bazar valley, but their promises on this and many other occasions were flagrantly broken. In fact, those Zakkas who remained loyal and attempted to carry out their engagements with the British were looked upon as traitors to their country. Notwithstanding all conciliatory efforts on our part, the anti-British section of the population increased in numbers, raiding broke out afresh, and the breach between the Zakkas and the British authorities widened from day to day. From 1905 to 1908, affairs grew from bad to worse, and bands of well-armed Afridis ravaged the British borders.[1] To give but one example: on 15 December, 1906, a gang of raiders attacked the police post at Pabbi, twenty-five miles on the British side of the administrative boundary, and, had it not been for the presence of a detachment of the 53rd Sikhs, would also have sacked a flourishing bazaar in the immediate neighbourhood. It was in the year 1907 that the insolence of the Zakkas reached its height, for, when the friendly Afridi clans came in to receive their allowances, the Zakka Khels, seeing that the Government of India had no intention of summoning them as well, sent an uninvited *jirga* to Landi Kotal, in the Khyber, where they insolently announced that the system of deducting fines from allowances must cease; that they refused to accept responsibility for raiders passing through their limits; that they would not surrender offenders for punishment; and that all restrictions on members of the tribe going to Kabul must be removed.[2]

During July and August of the same year, large numbers of Zakkas visited Kabul, where the anti-British party, headed by Nasrullah, the brother of Amir Habibullah, not only increased their allowances, but also afforded them facilities for

---

[1] Towards the end of 1907 there were five separate raiding gangs under the following notorious outlaws: Dadai, Multan, Gul Baz, Muhammad Afzal, and Usman.

[2] *Parl. Papers*, 1908 (Cd. 4201), p. 72.

purchasing large numbers of rifles which had become available from the Persian Gulf source of supply.[1] Their return was the signal for a general recrudescence of raiding along the British borders, the outrages increasing both in numbers and in boldness. Large raiding gangs under notorious raiders made well-organized attacks upon villages within the British administrative border; ambushed parties of Military Police; fired upon detachments of regular troops; and, on one occasion, even attempted to abduct the extra assistant commissioner of Peshawar. Zakka Khel misconduct culminated in an attack upon Peshawar city by a gang of about eighty men, on the night of 28 January, 1908, when the value of loot taken from the house of a Hindu banker, Chela Ram, was estimated at a lakh of rupees. It was therefore only natural that the local authorities should be approached by a deputation of Hindu merchants and shopkeepers complaining of the great state of insecurity prevailing even in the heart of a British cantonment, which was strongly fortified and garrisoned by British troops.

At last the patience of the Government of India was exhausted. For at least nine months efforts were made to persuade the Home Government to sanction a punitive expedition. It was pointed out that no system of fines would solve the problem, for the Zakkas owed in compensation for their past misdeeds an amount which would not be covered even by the stoppage of all allowances for the next three years. Immediate reprisals were essential, for, as the Indian authorities pointed out, if the Zakkas were not speedily punished the British might find themselves faced by a tribal rising approaching that of 1897–8. As it was, the persistent misbehaviour of the Zakkas, combined with their continual immunity from punishment, were already beginning to affect the surrounding tribes, especially the Mohmands and Orakzais.[2] Sir Harold Deane, the Chief Commissioner of the

[1] *Confidential, Frontier and Overseas*, ii, Supplement A, p. 3.
[2] *Parl. Papers*, 1908 (Cd. 4201), pp. 39–41.

Frontier Province, was convinced that retributive measures were the only means of forcing them to see the error of their ways.

The steady misconduct of this troublesome section is illustrated by the fact that during the last seven years no less than 32 British subjects have been murdered, 29 wounded, 37 kidnapped and held up to ransom by members of this tribe.[1]

Major Roos-Keppel, who possessed an unrivalled knowledge of Afridi politics and characteristics, was even more convinced of the necessity for drastic and immediate action. That the Zakkas were bitterly hostile to the British becomes apparent from the following report:

> Every man, woman and child in the clan looks upon those who commit raids, murders and robberies in Peshawar or Kohat as heroes and champions. They are the crusaders of the nation; they depart with the good wishes and prayers of all, and are received on their return after a successful raid with universal rejoicings and congratulations.... Year after year the evil has grown, and each year the necessity for punishing the Zakka Khel has become more pressing. Circumstances, larger questions of policy, and the natural dislike of Government to strong measures, have saved the clan from the punishment which it so richly deserves.[2]

But the local frontier officials and the Government of India recommended much more than a mere invasion of the Bazar valley, for both Deane and Roos-Keppel strongly advocated permanent occupation.

The Bazar valley of northern Tirah is shut off from the Khyber by the Alachi mountains and from the Bara valley and the rest of Tirah by the Sur Ghar range. Its eastern extremity is a narrow defile debouching on to the Peshawar plain; its western and south-western outlets are connected with Tirah and Afghanistan by the Mangal Bagh, Bukar, Thabai, and Tsatsobi passes. Hence, the key to the problem of Zakka control is to command these "back-doors" through

---

[1] *Parl. Papers*, 1908 (Cd. 4201), p. 56.   [2] *Idem*, p. 44.

which the tribesmen are wont, on the approach of a punitive column, to escape into Afghanistan. The local officials were convinced that no permanent effects would result from a mere punitive expedition into the Bazar valley. To enter the valley for such a purpose was tantamount to punishing the law-abiding portion of the population who would, in all probability, remain behind when the malcontents and culprits, whom we desired to coerce, had fled to the friendly asylum afforded by the ruler of Afghanistan. If, on the other hand, Bazar were occupied, a useful purpose would be served both from a military and a political point of view. They therefore recommended the conquest of the country and the subjugation of the inhabitants by troops. This accomplished, the next step, in their opinion, was to dominate the valley by permanent posts, manned by the Khyber Rifles, at China, Mangal Bagh, and Sassobi. Major Roos-Keppel emphatically declared that this was the only satisfactory solution to the problem.

Lord Minto, the Viceroy, was in favour of the occupation but not of the administration of tribal territory. In a private letter to Mr Morley, the Secretary of State for India, he wrote:

There need be no necessity for taking the country in the sense of forcing upon it British administration, collection of revenues, etc. We could simply hold it by the creation of one or two roads, or rather by the improvement of the existing roads by means of tribal labour...and the establishment of a few advanced posts, leaving the tribes as heretofore to carry on their own tribal administration.[1]

As soon as the Secretary of State for India became aware of the intentions of Lord Minto and his advisers, he telegraphed instructions to the effect that permanent occupation of tribal territory was contrary to the policy laid down in Lord George Hamilton's despatch of 28 January, 1898;[2] and

---

[1] Quoted Buchan, *Lord Minto*, p. 268.   [2] *Vide* ch. VI, p. 101.

that, if possible, operations should be restricted to a blockade carried out on the same lines as the Mahsud blockade of 1900–2. The Viceroy replied that geographical conditions did not favour a blockade and that disaster would result from the employment of small bodies of troops in the Bazar valley. An effective blockade of the Zakka Khel country, in addition to the securing of the distant passes leading into Afghanistan, would also involve the temporary occupation by troops of the territory of other Afridi clans. It was feared that such action would lead to friction and possibly to a general Afridi rising. In fact, Lord Kitchener strongly deprecated any action which might produce a general tribal revolt, because the tribal areas by this time had been flooded with arms of precision. It was finally decided to attempt the coercion of the Zakkas by means of an ordinary expedition, but the Home Government took the necessary steps to ensure that operations should be limited to the punishment of the offending clan. For political reasons the following *kharita* was despatched to the amir at Kabul before British troops entered the Bazar valley.

I write to inform you that the Zakka Khel section of the Afridis have faithlessly broken their engagements with the Government of India and, notwithstanding the very kind and too compassionate treatment that I have meted out to them, have misunderstood my leniency and, by constant raids and murderous attacks on my law-abiding people, have filled up the cup of their iniquities. I can no longer shut my eyes to these nefarious proceedings, and I therefore write to inform you that I intend to punish these people, who deserve severe treatment, and I hope that, through the friendship that exists between us, Your Majesty will issue stringent orders to prevent any of these people from entering your territories or receiving assistance from the tribes on your side of the frontier.[1]

The result of this expedition was that the Zakkas were speedily coerced by troops under the command of Major-General Sir James Willcocks.[2] The exemplary conduct of the

[1] *Confidential, Frontier and Overseas*, II, Supplement A, p. 8.
[2] For operations see *London Gazette*, 22 May, 1908.

Khyber Rifles and the other Afridi clans; the invaluable assistance rendered by Roos-Keppel, the Political Agent; and the rapidity of the advance, were the chief factors contributing to this success. No frontier tribe had ever been punished so effectively or so rapidly before, and their casualties were so heavy that they exceeded those sustained by the whole Afridi tribe during the Tirah campaign of 1897–8. On 28 February, 1908, a *jirga* of *maliks* and elders of the Afridi tribe accepted responsibility for the future good behaviour of the Zakka Khels. The following day witnessed the complete evacuation of the Bazar valley, but, unfortunately for the peace of the frontier, trouble was brewing in the Mohmand hills to the north of the Khyber.

The Bar (Hill) Mohmands can be divided into three main groups, the Tarakzai, Khwaezai, and Baezai.[1] To a large extent the Khyber area is at the mercy of these tribes. During the First Afghan War, 1839–42, one of their chiefs, Saadat Khan of Lalpura, had been deprived of his position by the British. Therefore, when Dost Muhammad, the amir, thought it necessary to harass the British borders in the years following the annexation of the Panjab, he found a willing ally in the person of this discontented chief. In the years that followed, these fanatical and priest-ridden tribes were a constant source of irritation and annoyance to the British in India. There were many reasons for this. The barren nature of their almost waterless hills compelled them to obtain the necessaries of life by raiding the rich plains around Peshawar. Their commanding position on the northern flank of the Khyber constituted a standing invitation to plunder the caravans passing between India and Afghanistan. In receipt of allowances from the amir, who exercised some sort of vague suzerainty over them, and easily swayed by the fanatical utterances of their mullahs, they were not inclined to be amicably disposed towards the unbelievers who had, in 1849,

[1] *Vide* ch. IV, p. 61.

pushed their outposts across the Indus. Add to this a naturally turbulent disposition, and it is not to be wondered at that seven expeditions had been required against them before 1908.[1] But this much can be said in their favour, that from 1880 to the general uprising of 1897 Mohmand raids were more economic than political in origin.

The Durand Agreement of 1893 placed certain clans within the British sphere of influence, but it was not until the year 1896 that the Halimzai, Kamali, Dawezai, Utmanzai, and Tarakzai, hereafter known as the eastern or "assured" clans, accepted the political control of the Government of India.[2] On condition that they remained faithful to the British they were granted allowances in lieu of those which they stated had been paid them in the past by the Amir of Afghanistan. The very year after this agreement was made the whole tribe, incited by the utterances of that fanatical agitator, the Adda Mullah, joined in the general tribal rising, and attacked the village of Shankargarh and the neighbouring fort of Shabkadr. The punishment meted out to them, both in the Bedmanai pass and in the Jarobi glen, kept them quiet until the year 1902, when some of the Baezais, influenced by anti-British propaganda, refused to come to Peshawar for their allowances. Their example was followed by several other "assured" clans; in fact the Tarakzais and Halimzais alone remained loyal to their engagements.[3] In 1903, Muhammad Husain Khan, the Sartip of Dakka, insolently despatched Afghan *khassadars* to punish the villagers of Smatzai and Shinpokh for their friendly intercourse with the British. There was another cause of friction. At the time under consideration there was considerable uncertainty as to the exact location of the Indo-Afghan boundary at this par-

[1] 1851–2, 1852, 1854, 1864, 1879, 1880, 1897.

[2] Called "assured" to distinguish them from clans not under British political control. The following allowances were granted: Halimzai (Rs. 8480); Kamali (2800); Dawezai (1200); Utmanzai (720); Tarakzai (3600). *Vide Parl. Papers,* 1908 (Cd. 4201), p. 125.

[3] *Confidential, Frontier and Overseas,* I, Supplement A, p. 5.

ticular spot. For this reason the Viceroy requested the amir to arrange for an exact demarcation in conjunction with Major Roos-Keppel. Nothing was done by Habibullah, whereupon the proposal fell to the ground. In 1905, the Sartip of Dakka once more attempted to punish the inhabitants of these two villages, with the result that the Viceroy suggested to the amir that his troublesome official should be replaced.

The amir emphatically declined to call the Sarhang to account, and even forwarded and endorsed a decidedly impertinent letter from Muhammad Husain Khan laying claim to Smatzai as Afghan territory.[1]

The whole affair was evidently caused by the Durand Agreement and its defects. In his heart of hearts Habibullah, like his father Abdurrahman before him, was not favourably disposed to this partition of tribal territory. Neither did the tribesmen themselves understand an arrangement, whereby their lands had been parcelled out, without their consent, amongst foreign powers. For our present purpose it is enough to remember that these causes of friction led to a great recrudescence of raiding along the British borders.

Towards the end of the Zakka Khel expedition of 1908, mixed Afghan and Mohmand *lashkars* hovered around ready to join in the fray, but fortunately they arrived at a time when the Zakkas had been severely chastized, and were clamouring for peace.[2] In April, 1908, news arrived that the Sufi Sahib of Kot, together with other notorious mullahs, had raised large *lashkars* for the purpose of invading British territory.[3] To cope with the situation, British troops were hurried to the frontier. By 23 April, it was reported that these *lashkars* were being reinforced by tribesmen from far and near;

---

[1] *Confidential, Frontier and Overseas*, I, Supplement A, p. 5.

[2] *Parl. Papers*, 1908 (Cd. 4201), p. 109.

[3] The total fighting strength of the Mohmands was estimated in 1907 at 21,500 men with about 1850 breech-loading rifles. Of the above about 11,000 men and 750 rifles belonged to the Afghan clans. Later, because of the arms traffic, the number of rifles increased. *Confidential, Frontier and Overseas*, I, Supplement A, p. 1.

that they were being supplied with grain, ammunition, and cash from Afghan territory; and that their attitude was becoming more aggressive every day. Although brushes with the enemy took place all along the line, the movements of British troops were strictly confined to defensive operations. For this purpose, namely the dispersion of hostile gatherings, the eighteen-pounder quick-firing gun was used for the first time.[1]

Extreme caution was the keynote of Mr Morley's policy, and it was not until the enemy had actually attacked the fort of Michni Kandao in the Khyber, that the Secretary of State for India consented to an expedition. General Willcocks received the following instructions:

> The policy of Government is the same as that announced in the case of the expedition against the Zakka. Punishment and the reduction of the Mohmands to submission as soon as possible are the objects of the expedition. The absence of all desire or intention on the part of the Government to annex Mohmand territory or to interfere with the status quo in respect of the general relations between Government and the Mohmands should be made widely known by you.... Complications with tribes or sections who may be settled on Afghan side of the Durand line must be avoided.[2]

Throughout the expedition, despite the efforts of the Sufi Sahib, the Afridis made no attempts to join in the struggle. Had they done so, the British, in all probability, would have been faced with a general revolt from Swat to Waziristan, for the frontier tribesmen are only too ready to follow where the Afridis lead.[3] Operations were short and successful. In less than a month the recalcitrant sections had been forced to comply with British terms, and British troops had recrossed the administrative border. Thus ended the last frontier expedition that comes within the scope of this history.

---

[1] Nevill, *Campaigns on the N.W. Frontier*, p. 337.

[2] *Parl. Papers*, 1908 (Cd. 4201), p. 145.

[3] For attitude of Russian press see *British Documents on the Origins of the War* (ed. Gooch and Temperley), v, 242.

Chapter IX

THE AFGHAN PROBLEM, 1890–1908

Modern Afghanistan is indeed a purely accidental geographical unit, which has been carved out of the heart of Central Asia by the sword of conquerors or the genius of individual statesmen.   Lord Curzon.

Afghanistan may be termed the Achilles' heel of India, for, before the advent of the European nations by sea, India had been peculiarly susceptible to invasion through the gates of the North-West. As the rich and fertile soil of Italy tempted the inhabitants of the more barren uplands to descend and lay waste, so did the Panjab plains prove an irresistible attraction to the virile highlanders of the north. Both Italy and India were the prey of marauding bands, until the Romans and English respectively, by marshalling the forces of the south, were able to raise up bulwarks of defence. To continue the parallel: Switzerland, like Afghanistan, has become the home of many languages, the meeting-place of numerous races.

It can be safely affirmed that modern Afghanistan owes its independence to its peculiar geographical position, which makes it the glacis of the fortress of Hindustan. Had it not been for the fact that the British in India recognized the importance of a friendly and semi-independent buffer state between them and the Russians in Central Asia, in all probability Russia would have advanced beyond the Oxus, and the British would have adopted the Kabul, Ghazni, Kandahar line as their frontier of resistance. Although other factors, such as the intrigues of the amirs with the frontier tribesmen, have, in recent years, played their part in determining Anglo-Afghan relations, by far the most important has been Russia's steady march across the steppes of Central Asia. To a large extent our Afghan policy has been regulated by the pressure of the political barometer in Europe, for friction between England and Russia in Europe has nearly always been followed by complications in Central Asia. If Napoleon and the Czars of Russia had not entertained ideas of an invasion of India; if they had not intrigued to our detriment both in Persia and Afghanistan; if the Black Eagle had never winged its flight across the Caucasus, in all probability, our relations with Central Asian states would have been purely commercial in character. It was French intrigues in Persia and the success of General Gardane's mission to Teheran, in 1807, that alarmed Lord Minto, whose counterstroke was to despatch Malcolm to the court of the shah and Elphinstone to the camp of Shah Shuja at Peshawar. The task of our envoys was considerably facilitated by Napoleon's sacrifice of Persian interests at Tilsit, 1807, with the result that on 12 September, 1809, Sir Harford Jones was able to report to Canning: "I now consider myself able to announce the complete abolition of the French influence in Persia". The great controversy, both at this period and later, was whether Persia could be better coerced by means of a naval demonstration in the Gulf, or by an army operating in the neighbourhood of Teheran. Fortunately those in authority favoured the former proposal.[1]

Nearly thirty years separated the missions of Elphinstone and Burnes. Those years had witnessed a dynastic revolution in Afghanistan, where the Sadozais had been replaced by the Barakzais. For this reason Shah Shuja found himself a refugee in Ludhiana in British territory.

In England, in the year 1835, Melbourne came into power with Palmerston as Foreign Secretary; and, in the same year, Lord Auckland proceeded to India as Governor-General. In

[1] For French intrigues in Persia and the question of a naval demonstration see F.O. 248, 9; 249, 14, 91; 251, 35.

those days the Russian menace was at its height. At Teheran, Simonich, the Russian envoy, had persuaded the shah to lay siege to Herat; while, at Kabul, Burnes, whose hands were tied by his instructions from India, had been outmanœuvred by the Russian agent, Vickovitch. The impression gained from a perusal of the correspondence of Burnes, as presented to Parliament in 1839, is that the amir, Dost Muhammad, was entirely hostile to the British.[1] Unfortunately these despatches were printed in a mutilated form, and it was not until 1859, when the ungarbled correspondence was placed before Parliament, that it became evident how a little patience on the part of Lord Auckland might have prevented the First Afghan War, 1839–42.[2] Lord Auckland, influenced by his private secretaries, decided to champion the cause of the Ludhiana refugee, but the responsibility for this attempted resuscitation of the Sadozai dynasty must also be shared by the Home Government.[3] Although no one would attempt to justify this practically unprovoked war, yet the Auckland policy, in so far as it attempted to interpose a strong and friendly power between India and Russia, was entirely commendable. At the same time, it should be remembered that, in the days of Auckland, both Sind and the Panjab were independent states. The result of this war was to leave the Barakzais the paramount power in Afghanistan.

Thirteen years passed before the reopening of diplomatic negotiations led to the Anglo-Afghan treaty of 1855. Some historians have erred in attributing this treaty to the efforts of Sir John Lawrence, when, in reality, it was the work of Sir Herbert Edwardes acting in accordance with the instructions of Lord Dalhousie.[4] But Dalhousie, in order to ensure that

---

[1] *Parl. Papers*, 1839, XL, 131 (II and IV).

[2] *Idem*, 1859, XXV, 7; and F.O. 257, 45.

[3] F.O. 248, 91. Secret Despatch to Lord Auckland, 24 October, 1838.

[4] (a) For latest writer to fall into this error see: Repington, *Policy and Arms*, p. 228. (b) For correspondence between Dalhousie and Edwardes see: *Life and Memorials of Sir H. Edwardes*, I, 236–45.

the first overtures came from the Afghan side, was forced to curb the ardour of Edwardes.[1]

Caution was the keynote of the Afghan policy of the Government of India until the days of Lord Lytton's viceroyalty. In 1874, Gladstone fell from power and was succeeded by Disraeli. At the same time Lord Salisbury became Secretary of State for India. In the 'seventies Russophobia became even stronger than it had been in the 'thirties, for Russia was no longer the distant power she had been in the time of Lord Auckland. Our pro-Turkish policy, Disraeli's action in bringing Indian troops to Malta, and the passage of the Dardanelles by British warships, brought the two countries to the verge of war. Russia's reply was the Stolietoff mission to Kabul. The refusal of Sher Ali, the amir, to allow Sir Neville Chamberlain's mission to cross the frontier furnished Lord Lytton with his famous *casus belli* for the Second Afghan War, 1878–80. Thus on two occasions, in 1839 and 1878, Russian intrigue had led to the invasion of Afghan soil. The proper solution to the problem would have been to bring pressure to bear upon Russia in Europe, for estrangement between the amir and the Government of India was obviously to the advantage of Russia. Lord Lytton must share with the Home Government the responsibility for this war, for, although he had been warned that the tension between England and Russia was at an end, he still persisted in his idea of forcing a mission upon Sher Ali.[2]

We now come to the accession of Abdurrahman Khan, perhaps the most important event in the history of Afghanistan. In July, 1880, Abdurrahman Khan, the most powerful candidate in the field, was informed that the British were prepared to recognize him as Amir of Kabul provided that he acknowledged their right to control his foreign affairs. At the same time he received the following communication:

[1] Lee-Warner, *Life of Dalhousie*, II, 83–4.
[2] Buckle, *Life of Disraeli*, VI, 383–7.

If any Foreign Power should attempt to interfere in Afghanistan, and if such interference should lead to unprovoked aggression on the dominions of your Highness, in that event the British Government would be prepared to aid you to such extent and in such manner as may appear to the British Government necessary in repelling it.[1]

These terms were accepted by Abdurrahman Khan at the conference of Zimma, 31 July–1 August, 1880. Three years later this promise was renewed by the Marquis of Ripon, who also bestowed upon the amir an annual subsidy of twelve lakhs of rupees, to be devoted to the payment of troops and to other measures essential for the protection of his north-western frontier.[2]

History proves that an ill-defined boundary is a potential cause of war. The above agreement pledged the British to protect a country of unknown limits. Bearing this in mind, it will be recognized that the most important event in the reign of Abdurrahman Khan was the delimitation and demarcation of the boundaries of Afghanistan. The Russian occupation of Merv, in 1884, gave the necessary impetus to negotiations which ended in the appointment of an Anglo-Afghan Boundary Commission. By the year 1886, although the Panjdeh incident of the previous year had almost wrecked hopes of a peaceful settlement, the northern frontier of Afghanistan had been demarcated from Zulfikar to the meridian of Dukchi, within forty miles of the Oxus. After a dispute as to the exact point at which the boundary line should meet the Oxus, the process of demarcation was completed in 1888. The last frontier dispute in which Russia was concerned was settled by the Pamir Agreement of 1895, by which the Afghan boundary between Lake Victoria and the

---

[1] F.O. 65, 1104. (Papers, printed for the use of the Cabinet, relative to the recognition of Sirdar Abdul Rahman Khan as Amir of Kabul.)

[2] *Parl. Papers*, 1884, LXXXVII (c. 3830), 85. For negotiations see F.O. 65, 1173, No. 115 of 1883, and enclosures.

Tagdumbash was mapped out by a joint commission.[1] The report of this commission proved the absolute impracticability of any Russian invasion of India from the direction of the Pamirs. Thus, in the closing years of the nineteenth century, the recognition of a definite frontier between Russia and Afghanistan led to a decided improvement in the Central Asian question.

The next task that faced British statesmen was the delimitation and, where possible, the demarcation of the southern and eastern boundaries of the amir's dominions. Considerable uncertainty existed as to the respective spheres of influence of the amir and the Government of India over the tribes of the Indo-Afghan border. When it is realized that the frontier tribesmen are, in many cases, of the same racial stock as the inhabitants of south-eastern Afghanistan, and are, with rare exceptions, orthodox Muhammadans of the Sunni sect, it becomes apparent that the amir is able, when Anglo-Afghan relations are strained, to exploit their marauding proclivities. In war, there is always the danger of large bodies of tribesmen joining his forces as soon as he proclaims a *jehad*; in peace, the amir, if so inclined, can persuade them to harass the British borders. For this reason it was fortunate for the British during the Mutiny that diplomatic negotiations had resulted in the Anglo-Afghan treaty of 1855. The outbreak of war with Afghanistan in 1878 was the signal for increased disturbances throughout the tribal zone. The Hazara border was in a perpetual ferment; the Khyber was constantly raided by Zakka Khels and Mohmands; Zaimushts harassed the Kohat line of communications; and Mahsuds from the heart of Waziristan raided and laid waste the country in the vicinity of Tank.

[1] (a) For Ridgeway Commission see *Parl. Papers*, 1887, LXIII (c. 5114); c. 5235): 1888, LXXVII (c. 5254); (c. 5518). (b) For Panjdeh incident see *Parl. Papers*, 1884–5, LXXVII (c. 4387); (c. 4418). (c) For Pamir Commission see *Parl. Papers*, 1895, CIX (c. 7643); and *Report on the Proceedings of the Pamir Boundary Commission*, Calcutta, 1897.

On the other hand, the Turis of Kurram, who, because of their Shiah beliefs, had for many years been subjected to oppression by Afghan officials, hailed with delight the arrival of British troops in their valley. By the treaty of Gandamak, 1879, Kurram was declared an assigned district, to be administered by the Government of India. In the following year, Abdurrahman was informed that whereas the Jagi *ilaka* of Hariab was to be considered Afghan territory, Kurram proper, the dwelling-place of the Turi and Bangash tribes, was to be independent of his control.[1] As a result of complaints on the part of the amir regarding Turi feuds with the neighbouring tribes of Afghanistan, a British delegate was sent to the valley to confer with the amir's representative. This resulted for the time being in an amicable settlement of outstanding disputes. Fresh disputes, however, led to the appointment of an Anglo-Afghan Commission in 1888, the efforts of which were entirely unsuccessful. Although the British escort was withdrawn from the valley, yet the amir was informed that the Government of India would brook no interference with the independence of the Turis. At length, in the year 1892, by the request of the Turis themselves, the British occupied their country.[2]

Between 1890 and 1898, Anglo-Afghan relations were so strained that on several occasions war seemed imminent. For some time before the Durand Mission set out for Kabul, rumours reached the ears of the amir that the British were desirous of an exact demarcation of the Indo-Afghan frontier. This may have been the reason why Abdurrahman increased his intrigues amongst the various border tribes with the object of securing some of their territory before it was too late. In 1892, a detachment of Afghan troops arrived at Gustoi in the Zhob district; and, at the same time, Afghan intrigues com-

---

[1] Aitchison, xi, 133–4. See also F.O. 65, 1062. Proclamation to *maliks* of Kurram, 26 December, 1878.

[2] *Panjab Administration Report*, 1883–4, pp. 3, 12; 1892–3, p. 2.

menced in Waziristan. The advance into Zhob constituted a distinct threat, for that district had only recently been annexed by the British. The tribes of Waziristan became divided into two opposing camps, the Kabul and Loyal factions. When representatives of the former were received with great honour by the amir at Kabul, the Government of India became alarmed, and a strong remonstrance on its part led to the recall of the Afghan agents responsible for these intrigues. Throughout the years 1892 and 1893, a state of unrest and disquietude continued to exist along the whole frontier from the snow-capped peaks of Chitral to the barren deserts of Baluchistan. To quote a contemporary government report:

A general uncertainty prevailed as to the limits of the two Governments, and the tribesmen constantly took advantage of this uncertainty, playing off the one against the other. In Chitral apprehension of aggression under cover of Afghan protection stood in the way of any settled Government. The people of Bajaur and Swat were in uncertainty whether they might not any day be exposed to an Afghan invasion. There was anarchy in Kurram, where the Turis were kept in fear by local disturbances fomented by Afghan officials, and by raids carried on by Afghan subjects. And, south of Kurram, the whole Waziri tribe was in a state of ferment, and intrigues were frequent in the Zhob and Gomal Valleys.[1]

Before the Durand Mission reached Kabul, the amir despatched a letter to Lord Lansdowne in which he stated his opinion as to the best method of dealing with the tribes, and warned the Viceroy of the results of a more forward policy.

"If you should cut them out of my dominions", he wrote, "they will neither be of any use to you nor to me. You will always be engaged in fighting or other trouble with them, and they will always go on plundering. As long as your Government is strong and in peace, you will be able to keep them quiet by a strong hand, but if at any time a foreign enemy appear on the borders of India, these frontier tribes will be your worst enemies.... In your cutting

[1] *Moral and Material Progress of India*, 1892–3, p. 156.

away from me these frontier tribes, who are people of my nationality and my religion, you will injure my prestige in the eyes of my subjects, and will make me weak and my weakness is injurious to your Government."[1]

Nevertheless, Lord Lansdowne was desirous that something should be done to settle the frontier problem; and, with this object in view, the amir was invited to visit India. Abdurrahman replied that the disturbed condition of Afghanistan prevented him from accepting this invitation. The Viceroy's next step was to inform the amir that Lord Roberts would visit him at Jalalabad. This suggestion, that the hero of the Second Afghan War and the champion of the forward policy should once more enter Afghanistan, proved still less acceptable to the amir; and, eventually, it was decided to despatch an unescorted civilian mission to Kabul. That part of the Durand Agreement of 1893 which affected the Indo-Afghan frontier resulted in the delimitation of a line, afterwards known as the Durand line, across which neither the amir nor the Government of India was to interfere in any way.

The importance of this agreement has been somewhat overrated. It is true that by putting an end to the existing uncertainty the demarcation of this boundary should have considerably facilitated frontier administration, but a knowledge of frontier history, since 1893, shows that this agreement has not only increased the responsibilities of the Government of India, but has also increased the chances of collision with the tribes and of war with the amir. The new boundary line was not based upon sound topographical data, for, during the process of demarcation, it was discovered that certain places, marked on the Durand map, did not exist on the actual ground. Many ethnic absurdities were perpetrated, such as the handing over to the amir of the Birmal tract of Waziristan, which was peopled by Darwesh Khel Waziris, large numbers of whom were included within the British

[1] Abdurrahman, *Autobiography*, II, 158.

sphere of influence. The worst blunder of all was the arrangement by which the boundary cut the Mohmand tribal area
into two separate parts. It seems that this could not have
been a tripartite agreement, for there is no evidence that the
tribesmen were consulted before 1893. In fact, it was not
until the year 1896 that the Halimzai, Kamali, Dawezai,
Utmanzai, and Tarakzai Mohmands, afterwards known as
the eastern or "assured" clans, accepted the political control
of the Government of India. In all probability political considerations produced this sacrifice of ethnological requirements. If the amir had not been promised the Birmal tract
it is quite likely that he would have refused his consent to the
inclusion of Wana within the British sphere of influence. In
the light of subsequent events it is difficult to understand the
reasons which prompted the amir to sign this agreement.
Perhaps his consent was purchased by the increase of his subsidy to eighteen lakhs of rupees, and by the recognition of his
right to import munitions of war.

The demarcation of the new boundary took place during
the years 1894 and 1896. By the year 1895, that part of the
frontier lying between Nawa Kotal on the outskirts of the
Mohmand country and the Bashgal valley on the borders of
Kafiristan had been demarcated, and an agreement concluded on 9 April, 1895, between Mr Udny and Ghulam
Haidar Khan, the amir's representative. A similar agreement,
as far as the Kurram frontier was concerned, had been completed on 21 November, 1894, the agents being Mr J. Donald
and Sardar Sherindil Khan. The Afghan-Baluch boundary
from Domandi to the Persian frontier was not finally demarcated until 1896. A small portion of the line in the Khyber
area remained undemarcated until the conclusion of the
Third Afghan War of 1919.

Before proceeding to discuss Afghan intrigues since 1893,
some reference to the amir's policy in Kafiristan is necessary.
Kafiristan, the land of the unbelievers, is bounded on the

north by the Hindu Kush; on the south by the Kunar valley; on the east by the eastern watershed of the Bashgal river; and on the west by the ranges above the Nijrao and Panjshir valleys. The origin of the Kafirs is lost in the mists of obscurity, but what directly concerns the point at issue is that they were non-Muhammadan tribes, who, throughout the ages, had successfully resisted all attempts at conversion, until in 1893, for political reasons, they were sacrificed to the tender mercies of the amir and militant Islam. It was from this secluded spot in the Hindu Kush that Afghan nobles obtained their household slaves, and Abdurrahman his concubines. When the news of the amir's forcible conversion of these so-called infidels reached England, the Secretary of State for India received numerous petitions from the Anti-Slavery Society and the Aborigines' Protection Society, beseeching the Government of India to use its influence to protect the defenceless Kafirs of the Hindu Kush. It was obvious that the poor Kafir stood no chance with his rude weapons against Afghan regular troops armed with Martini-Henry rifles. Although the Government of India stated in reply that the amir's action was not a direct result of the Durand Agreement, yet many authorities, whose opinions carried great weight, held that British policy was in no small measure responsible for the sacrifice of these rude savages to the amir.

Quickly following in the wake of the process of demarcation came a period of dynastic struggles in Chitral. The Mehtar (ruler) of Chitral had scattered his Maker's image throughout the land with the result that his death was the signal for fratricidal conflicts between his numerous offspring. A detailed account of our relations with this state has already been given.[1] It is, however, necessary to point out that Afghan intrigues and interference in this quarter were largely responsible for the expedition of 1895; so much

[1] *Vide* ch. v.

so, that Sir Thomas Holdich contends, in his *Indian Border-land*, that Afghan troops were present at the siege of Chitral.

The echoes of the Chitral expedition had no sooner died away than the frontier was abnormally disturbed by the con-flagration of 1897.[1] The charges brought against Abdurrah-man were that he had received deputations from the British tribal zone; that he had failed to prevent his regular troops and subjects from joining tribal *lashkars*; and that he had granted an asylum to the enemies of the Government of India. It is a well-known fact that he addressed an assembly of mullahs from all parts of Afghanistan and the frontier, and impressed upon them that it was the duty of all true believers to wipe out the infidel. It is significant too that at the same time he assumed the title of *Zia-ul-Millat wa ud-Din*, the "Light of the Nation and Religion". The publication of the amir's book, entitled *Taqwim-ud-Din* (Catechism or Almanac of Religion), which dealt with the question of a *jehad*, was, to say the least, inopportune. A correct interpretation of this book may have been perfectly harmless; the construction placed upon it by frontier mullahs and its distribution within the British frontier zone were not calculated to promote peaceful relations. During the struggle the anti-British intrigues of local Afghan officials, combined with the actual support afforded to the insurgents, called forth a sharp remonstrance from the Viceroy. The following statement, which I have been allowed to quote from one of the Government of India's confidential publications, throws considerable light on the question of Afghan complicity.

Yet another factor, and one of whose importance we have the most ample proof, was the universal feeling amongst the tribesmen that they could rely not only upon the approval and moral sup-port, but also upon the active intervention in their favour, of the Amir of Afghanistan.[2]

[1] *Vide* ch. v.
[2] *Confidential, Frontier and Overseas*, II, 65.

Abdurrahman persistently refused to admit the least degree of Afghan complicity in the risings, but qualified his remarks as follows:

No tribesmen from my territories can do such an act in an open manner. Some of them, however, have great faith in Mulla Hadda, and it is possible that they may have joined him during the night, travelling like thieves by unfrequented roads. How is it possible to keep watch on thieves during nights along such an extensive frontier? My kind friend, such an arrangement could only be possible by posting about ten thousand soldiers on all the mountain tops and at all the fords in that district.[1]

It had long been prophesied that the death of Abdurrahman Khan, which took place on 3 October, 1901, would be followed by the usual internecine and fratricidal conflicts within Afghanistan; and that it would be the signal for bloody struggles in Central Asia. Nevertheless, Habibullah Khan, his son, was the first amir who had not waded to his throne through streams of blood. It cannot be said that Anglo-Afghan relations ran smoothly throughout Abdurrahman's reign. He had viewed with no friendly eye the forward policy of Lords Lansdowne and Roberts. Regarding the extension of the Quetta railway to New Chaman as a "knife in his vitals", he had prohibited his subjects from using it; and, when the Viceroy had placed an embargo upon the importation of arms and ammunition into Afghanistan, he had shown his displeasure by refusing to draw his subsidy and by writing a direct letter of complaint to Lord Salisbury. He informs us in his *Autobiography* that he had taken great exception to the dictatorial style of Lord Lansdowne's letters.[2] His failure to obtain diplomatic representation at the Court of St James, which was the real object of Nasrullah's visit to England in 1895, only served to increase his displeasure. The amir's annoyance was reflected in the disquieting reports

[1] *Parl. Papers*, 1898, LXIII (c. 8714), 122–3.
[2] II, 135.

received from the Indian borderland. Although it can be safely asserted that he viewed with suspicion any attempts by the Government of India to extend its control over the frontier tribes, yet, on the larger issues, such as the Russian question, Abdurrahman undoubtedly was favourably inclined to the British alliance.

The accession of the new amir, Habibullah Khan, was followed by a wave of unrest which swept along the frontier from Buner to the confines of Baluchistan. This can be accounted for in many ways. Fanatical preaching was very prevalent, owing to the fact that there was a widespread belief in the ultra-religious attitude of the new amir who was, to a large extent, under the influence of his fanatical brother, Nasrullah Khan. In addition, a new province had been carved out of the frontier districts towards the end of 1901; and the construction of the Thal-Kohat railway had been misunderstood.

The early conduct of Habibullah was the reverse of friendly, for, in order to win the support of the fanatical party in Afghanistan, he not only received tribal deputations from British territory, but also commenced intriguing with certain frontier fanatics and freebooters. Shortly after his accession he attended the Id service at Kabul, when, for the first time in history, the amir himself performed the duties of *Imam*. Because the agreement between the Government of India and the late amir had been of a personal nature, it was hoped that Habibullah would visit the Viceroy at Calcutta. The new amir, however, declined this invitation on the plea that he considered the agreements contracted with his father to be still in force. In November, 1901, a Muhammadan deputation left India for the purpose of congratulating Habibullah upon his accession, and in order to try and persuade him to accept the Viceroy's invitation. He assured the members of the deputation that, in all his relations with the Government of India, he would follow in the footsteps of his father, and would adhere to Abdurrahman's policy, in so far as it was hostile to the introduction of railways and the telegraph, and to the appointment of European agents in Afghanistan. He made a similar declaration to a gathering of the leading men of Afghanistan, who had journeyed to Kabul for the *Fateha* ceremonies. In addition, he promised to protect the country from foreign aggression; and, in order to conciliate the religious party, he announced his intention of excluding missionaries.[1]

The reverses sustained by Russian troops in the war with Japan were not calculated to make an Oriental potentate, like Habibullah, a willing tool in the hands of the Government of India. Perhaps it would not be far wrong to suggest that the total defeat of an Occidental power by an Oriental nation was looked upon as a symptom of general Occidental decadence. At length, the unrest prevailing in the British tribal zone; the fact that the new amir did not seem so favourably disposed towards us as his father had been; and his persistent refusal to come to Calcutta, convinced the authorities in India that the time was ripe for a fresh treaty with Afghanistan. For this purpose the Dane Mission set out for Kabul in November, 1904. Owing to the haughty attitude adopted by Habibullah, and the anti-British counsels proffered by his brother, Nasrullah, negotiations were carried out in an extremely laborious manner. The reception afforded to Mr (afterwards Sir) Louis Dane and the other British delegates was far from cordial, but a treaty was eventually concluded on 21 March, 1905.[2] In some quarters the treaty was regarded as of little political importance, except in so far as it constituted a renewal of the Agreement of 1893. It has also been asserted that the reception afforded the mission at Kabul temporarily

---

[1] For the substance of this paragraph I am indebted to *Nairang-i-Afghan*, Syed Muhammad Husain Aghlab, ch. VII, pp. 230–46; and to the pages of the *Indian Pioneer Mail*, January–March, 1902.

[2] *Parl. Papers*, 1905, LVII (c. 2534), 9.

lowered British prestige in the eyes of the inhabitants of India and Afghanistan.[1] The mission, however, was soon to bear important fruits, for, in the year 1907, Habibullah announced that he was desirous of visiting India. The first Barakzai amir, Dost Muhammad, had entered British territory as a prisoner, in the year 1840; Sher Ali had crossed the Indus as an honoured guest of Lord Mayo, in 1869; and the Earl of Dufferin accorded a similar reception to Abdurrahman at Rawalpindi, in 1885. Habibullah's visit to Lord Minto turned out to be a complete success, for, in his farewell speech, the amir gave a promise which he loyally kept even through the critical period of the Great War, 1914–18.

At no time will Afghanistan pass from the friendship of India. So long as the Indian Empire desires to keep her friendship, so long will Afghanistan and Britain remain friends.[2]

The period covered by this volume ends, so far as imperial strategy is concerned, with the Anglo-Russian Convention of 1907. It is now necessary to deal briefly with the reasons which forced England and Russia to compose their differences in Central Asia.

Russia had repeatedly declared Afghanistan to be outside her sphere of influence. As far back as 1869, Prince Gortchakoff had instructed Baron Brunnow to assure the Earl of Clarendon that the Czar regarded Afghanistan as entirely beyond Russia's sphere of action. This assurance, repeated on several occasions between 1869 and 1885,[3] was as formal as anything could be which was not the subject of a treaty or convention. But in the past Russian assurances concerning their policy in Central Asia had been one thing, the actions of their generals another.

By the close of the nineteenth century the scene of Anglo-Russian rivalry had been transferred to the Far East. It

[1] For adverse criticism see *Fortnightly Review*, Hamilton, A., LXXVIII, 1905, 75 *et seq.*

[2] Quoted in *Lord Minto*, Buchan, J., pp. 250–1.

[3] 1874, 1876, 1877, 1878, 1882, 1883, 1884 and 1885.

seems probable that this friction, coinciding as it did with British reverses in South Africa, prompted Russia to interfere once more in Afghan affairs. In a memorandum communicated by the Russian Embassy on 6 February, 1900, a proposal was made for the establishment of direct relations between Russia and Afghanistan with regard to frontier matters. At the same time an assurance was given that these communications would have no political character; that Russia would maintain her former engagements and regard Afghanistan as outside her sphere of influence.[1] On 22 February of the same year, M. Ignatieff, the Russian Political Agent at Bokhara, forwarded a letter to the Amir of Afghanistan by one of the amir's trading agents. This communication, which concluded with the hope that it would prove the first step towards the establishment of direct friendly relations between Russia and Afghanistan, combined with the concentration of Russian troops on the Afghan frontier, was contrary to the friendly tone of the original Russian memorandum. In reply to this request on the part of Russia, the British Government pointed out that the proposed change could not be taken into consideration unless the Russian Government were prepared to give more definite information with regard to the methods to be adopted for the exchange of such communications; the limitations to be placed on them; and the means of ensuring that such limitations would be observed.[2]

But Russian interference did not cease, for, at a durbar held at Kabul, on 5 September, 1902, Habibullah read out the following Russian communication:

In the opinion of the Russian Government the time has now come for closer commercial relationship between Afghanistan and Russia. The Afghans have nothing to fear from Russian aggression, since the friendliness existing between England and Russia

---

[1] *British Documents on the Origins of the War*, ed. Gooch and Temperley, I, 306–7; IV, 512.

[2] *Idem*, IV, 514; *Parl. Debates*, Commons, No. 113, 1902, p. 208.

would be endangered if further annexations were made by the Government of the Czar.... The Russian Government, therefore, invites the Amir to throw open to Russian caravans the trade routes between Khushk and Herat and Khushk and Kabul.[1]

In return for this concession the Russian Government was prepared to allow Afghans to trade without restriction in Russian territory. At the same time it was pointed out that the British Government had already been approached on this subject, and that a favourable reply from the amir would considerably facilitate negotiations. Habibullah announced in durbar that his policy was the same as that which his father, Abdurrahman, had laid down in his pamphlet, the *Nasaih Namchah-i-Afghani* (Advice to the Afghan People concerning their Present Policy). The policy advocated by the late amir in this pamphlet was decidedly anti-Russian.[2] Habibullah, perhaps remembering the disastrous results of the Sher Ali–Kaufmann correspondence, sent a reply requesting that all future communications should be addressed through the Government of India.

Viewed from the Russian standpoint, it was only natural that she should desire the right to communicate directly with a contiguous state on purely local and commercial matters. But the British, remembering that on two occasions Russian attempts at direct negotiations with the ruler of Kabul had resulted in Anglo-Afghan conflicts, regarded with distrust all steps in this direction. Nevertheless, Russian officers continued to correspond with Afghan officials, and some of these communications were undoubtedly of a political character. Indeed the whole affair hinged on the construction to be placed upon the term "non-political". Experience proved that the Russian Government regarded the reparation of boundary pillars as a purely local question and a matter for direct understanding between Russian and Afghan authori-

[1] Quoted in *Fortnightly Review*, Hamilton, A., LXXX, 1906, 993.
[2] *Indian Pioneer Mail*, 24 October, 1902.

ties. To this the British could not agree; and there was much truth in the British contention that questions relating to the maintenance of a frontier demarcated by British and Russian officers could scarcely be included in a non-political category. The Russian reply to this protest contributed to the Anglo-Russian crisis of 1903.[1]

The defeat of Russia by Japan, however, proved that the feet of the Colossus were but of clay. The Anglo-Japanese Pact of 1902 had provided that England and Japan should come to each other's assistance in case of attack by any two states. The Agreement of 1905 substituted one Power and unprovoked aggression for two Powers; provided for joint military and naval action in such a case; and extended the sphere of action to include the north-west frontier of India.[2] The obligation on the part of Japan was proposed in the first instance by Baron Komura[3] at the suggestion of "some eminent Japanese soldiers" and was taken up by Lord Lansdowne.[4] It was apparently disapproved of by the British General Staff, but was ultimately accepted by the British Government. This stipulation was widely quoted at the time as a proof of the decadence of the British Empire in arranging for the defence of its own frontiers by the troops of another Asiatic power. Many people were convinced that the best guarantee of our Indian possessions lay in a Russian and not in the Japanese alliance; that English and Russian interests were not so widely divergent in Central Asia as to render it impossible for them both to live in amity. Sir Edward Grey held that it was essential to come to some understanding with Russia.

[1] *British Documents etc.* ed. Gooch and Temperley, IV, 621.

[2] *Parl. Papers*, CXXXVI (Cd. 2690). In all probability the sphere of action was extended because the inequality of advantage under the Pact of 1902 made Japan look as if she were in the position of a protected state.

[3] *British Documents etc.* ed. Gooch and Temperley, IV, 121.

[4] *Idem*, p. 124.

Our interests were so important and in such intimate contact
in Asia that, without an understanding, there was bound to be
friction increasing to the point of danger.[1]

He further pointed out that, since both England and Russia
were friendly with France, we could not at one and the same
time pursue a friendly policy towards France and the reverse
towards Russia. In his opinion, "an agreement with Russia
was the natural complement of the agreement with France".
The real cause; however, of the Anglo-Russian entente was
the growing German menace in Asia and elsewhere.

Those articles of the convention, signed with Russia in
1907, relating to Afghanistan were five in number.[2] We
declared that we had no intention of altering the political
status of Afghanistan, while Russia, on her part, renewed her
assurances that she considered the territories of the amir to
be outside her sphere of influence. A stipulation that the
British would not encourage the amir to take any measures
threatening Russia resulted from what Sir Edward Grey considered a real apprehension on the part of Russia that we
might adopt, in conjunction with Afghanistan, an aggressive
policy in Central Asia.[3] It should, however, have been
obvious to Russian statesmen that it was as much against
British as against Russian interests to convert Afghanistan
into a powerful state. All that was needed for the defence of
our Indian Empire was to build up an Afghan state with
powers of intermediate resistance sufficient for the protection of India while regular troops were being moved to the
amir's assistance. Nevertheless, Russia did not want Afghanistan transformed from a buffer state into an *avant-garde* of the
Indian Empire. At the same time, it must be confessed that
the British, in pledging themselves not to alter the political
status of Afghanistan, weakened their control over the amir,

[1] Grey of Fallodon, *Twenty-Five Years*, I, 159.
[2] For text see *Parl. Papers*, 1908, cxxv (Cd. 3750).
[3] *British Documents etc.* ed. Gooch and Temperley, IV, 532.

for one of the amir's chief incentives to observe his treaty obligations towards the Government of India was his dread that the British might at any time annex Afghan territory.

By this convention Russian and Afghan frontier officials were empowered to settle local questions of a non-political character. Finally, it was agreed that both countries should enjoy equal commercial opportunity in Afghanistan. This stipulation that Russia was to enjoy equality of commercial opportunity, while Indian traders were almost excluded from Russian territory, was violently attacked in several of the leading English journals.[1]

To my mind, the strength of the agreement, so far as Afghanistan was concerned, lay in the fact that Russia for the first time recognized by treaty that Afghanistan lay entirely outside her sphere of action. At last, the period of vague diplomatic assurances was at an end, and Russia had pledged herself openly by an international agreement not to encroach upon Afghan territory; to conduct all her political relations with Afghanistan through the intermediary of His Majesty's Government; and to abstain from sending agents into Afghanistan, thereby removing the danger of any further Russian advances in the direction of the Indian frontier. On the other hand, the refusal of the Home Government to consult the amir[2] only served to add more fuel to the smouldering fires of Habibullah's resentment. His displeasure was reflected, to a certain extent, in the wave of fanatical unrest which swept over the Afridi and Mohmand valleys in the year 1908.

---

[1] (a) *Asiatic Quarterly Review*, 1908, xxv, 1 *et seq.* (b) *United Services Magazine*, 1907–8, p. 257 *et seq.*

[2] *British Documents etc.* ed. Gooch and Temperley, IV, 577.

Chapter X

SUMMARY OF POLICY AND CONCLUDING REMARKS

No man who has read a page of Indian history will ever prophesy about the frontier.

Lord Curzon. Freedom of City of London Speech, 20 July, 1904.

The more one studies the problem presented by the North-West Frontier the more one becomes convinced of the truth of Lord Curzon's remark. For this reason it has been considered advisable to avoid prophecy and to devote this concluding chapter to a general survey of our frontier policy, the lessons to be learned, and the dangers to be avoided. The pages of Indian history are strewn with false prophecies. Time after time our local officials have entirely failed to appreciate the situations in which they have been placed. "All quiet from Dan to Beersheba" was the last message of the ill-fated Macnaghten. The same is true of our envoy in the Second Afghan War, for Cavagnari's private letters and official diaries can be searched in vain for any evidence that he expressed at any time the slightest apprehension for his personal safety or for that of the members of his mission and escort. On the contrary all his reports referred to the increasing freedom with which both he and his staff were able to move about the city of Kabul and its environs.[1] The last words penned by the over-sanguine Cavagnari were:

> The religious element at Kabul is wonderfully quiet. At none of the mosques has a single word disapproving of the English alliance been uttered. I cannot hear that there is any really anti-English party.... [2]

[1] F.O. 65, 1069. No. 202 of 1879 Government of India to Secretary of State for India, dated 15 September, 1879.

[2] F.O. 65, 1098. Report on the circumstances of the attack on the British Embassy at Kabul in September, 1879.

To give but one more example. On 17 August, 1897, the commissioner of Peshawar telegraphed to the Government of India that everything was quiet, and that reports from a reliable source showed that the Afridis were unaffected. That very evening an Afridi *lashkar* of about 10,000 men was reported as marching to attack the Khyber forts. So on the Indian borderland everything may appear peaceful and quiet, even to experienced observers, when all the while sinister forces are working beneath the surface, groups of hungry tribesmen are listening to the utterances of fanatical mullahs, and discontented *maliks* are planning fresh raids in the *hujra* of some isolated village. Uncertainty and the lack of finality are the factors underlying every problem connected with the Indian frontier. The sun may rise upon silent valleys and deserted nullahs which, before the day is spent, may be the scene of some treacherous ambush or dastardly assassination; and the smallest border fray may set the whole frontier ablaze from the waterless Mohmand hills to the confines of Baluchistan.

Certain years stand out like great landmarks in frontier history. The conquest of Sind, in 1843, and the annexation of the Panjab, in 1849, advanced the British administrative boundary across the Indus making it coterminous with the territories of the independent Baluch and Pathan tribes. The year 1863 saw the authorities in India faced by the most formidable rising since their troops had come into contact with those wild caterans of the independent hills. The Durand Agreement of 1893 extended our sphere of influence and increased our responsibilities, while the creation of the North-West Frontier Province, in 1901, marked a new departure in frontier administration. The year 1890, at which date our detailed consideration of the frontier problem begins, marks an epoch in the history of frontier expeditions, for, with the exception of the Ambela campaign of 1863, no very serious tribal risings had taken place before. Since 1890, gun-running in the Persian Gulf and other causes, such as the generosity of the Amir of Kabul and thieving in British cantonments, have flooded the tribal areas with arms and ammunition, so that in the later expeditions the combatants have been more equally matched. The possession of arms of precision has also produced a change in Pathan tactics, for, with the exception of certain *ghazi* rushes, there has been a tendency for the recklessness which characterized the earlier struggles to disappear. Indeed, there have been but few instances of that absolute disregard of life which was a marked feature of the fighting of the Hindustani fanatics and of the attacks upon Crag Picket, in 1863. Besides this change in the character and conduct of frontier warfare, the 'nineties witnessed the commencement of a more forward policy, to the discussion of which an entire chapter has been devoted. In view of the fact that the influx of rifles and ammunition into tribal territory has completely changed the nature of border warfare, some account of the arms traffic is essential.

The Pathan has always recognized the importance of obtaining possession of arms and ammunition. For years his only hope of doing so was by means of robbery under cover of darkness, at which dangerous trade he soon became an adept. In spite of the fact that the loss of a rifle meant a court martial for the unfortunate sepoy, many rifles found their way across the border in this manner. So cunning a thief did the Pathan become that even to-day, when near the frontier, Indian sepoys sleep with their rifles chained to their bodies. Many devices and stratagems have been adopted to run rifles and ammunition into tribal territory. Instances have occurred where rifles have been strapped underneath goods waggons destined for Peshawar, at which place the wily Pathan would devise some means of conveying them into the independent hills, where a ready market would be found. Again, large quantities of ammunition cleverly concealed in bales of merchandise have been carried through the Khyber. When these methods failed, there still remained the Kohat rifle factory, owned by Pathans, and situated in the strip of independent territory which separates Peshawar from Kohat. Although certain writers have magnified out of all proportion the importance of this factory, nevertheless its existence still remains an example of the absurdity of carrying the policy of non-intervention to extremes.

There would, however, have been small cause for apprehension, had it not been for the enormous growth of the arms traffic in the Persian Gulf, which, both at Bushire and Muscat, was at first in the hands of British traders. The evil effects of this traffic, which flooded the tribal areas with arms of precision, first became apparent during the Tirah campaign of 1897–8, but ten years were to pass before adequate attempts were made to suppress it. From 1906 onwards there was an alarming increase in the number of rifles imported into Afghanistan, the number increasing from 15,000 in 1907 to 40,000 in 1909.[1] During the Tirah expedition only one Afridi in every ten was in possession of a Martini-Henry rifle, while the remainder were armed with Sniders, muzzle-loading Enfields, and *jezails*. It has also been stated on the highest authority that during this campaign the total number of Lee-Metford rifles possessed by the Afridi tribe amounted only to seven. But, in 1908, a Martini was the rule, not the exception. Some idea of the volume of trade may be gained from the fact that whereas, in 1906, the price of a Martini rifle in Tirah was approximately Rs. 500, in 1908 it had dropped to Rs. 130. Although the Chagai caravan route was effectively blocked in 1908 by the strengthening of the British detachment at Robat in Baluchistan, the real result of this precautionary measure was to deflect the traffic to more westerly routes through Persian territory. The necessity for immediate

[1] *Secret Border Report*, 1908–9, p. 5.

repressive measures becomes apparent from the following report:

It is estimated that over 16,500 rifles, 352 revolvers and pistols and 1,079,100 rounds as well as 137 boxes of ammunition were landed between the 31st March 1909 and 1st April 1910.[1]

It was not until 1910, when the British established a rigorous blockade of the Gulf, that this pernicious traffic was in any way checked. Unfortunately these repressive measures came too late. In Baluchistan this illicit traffic produced a weakening of the system of tribal responsibility under which tribesmen within our sphere of influence were held responsible for raids committed by trans-frontier desperadoes, so much so that it became exceedingly difficult to enforce tribal responsibility for trans-border raids with any show of justice.[2] Reference has already been made to the change produced in the tactics and in the powers of resistance of the Pathan tribes. It can therefore be safely affirmed that this arming of the border tribes with modern weapons in place of the old-fashioned *jezails* has not only greatly aggravated the difficulty of dealing with the frontier problem, but has also radically altered the whole situation. A knowledge of the later struggles, since 1919, only serves to confirm this opinion.

But the arms traffic is only one of the many causes of unrest. Certain factors, such as the geographical and economic, have been operative from the dawn of history: others, such as Bolshevik propaganda, are of more recent origin. To appreciate some of the causes which have outlawed these wild tribesmen it is essential to have an intimate knowledge of frontier topography. "O God, when Thou hadst created Sibi and Dadhar, what object was there in conceiving hell?"—so runs a local proverb. There is also much truth in another proverb that, when God created the world He dumped the rubbish on the frontier. Life in the independent hills is as much a struggle

[1] *Baluchistan Agency Report*, 1909–10, p. 2.
[2] *Idem*, 1911–12, p. 4.

between man and nature as between man and man. We can never hope to solve the frontier problem until the tribesmen are able to gain a livelihood without being forced to raid the settled districts. So long as hungry tribesmen inhabit barren and almost waterless hills, which command open and fertile plains, so long will they resort to plundering incursions in order to obtain the necessaries of life. Indeed, the plundering of caravans, as they wind their way through the Khyber, has been forced upon the Afridi by his environment. The same generalization also applies to the Mahsuds and Darwesh Khels, for the greater part of Waziristan is a region of stony nullahs and barren plains, with only occasional stretches of cultivated land in the warmer valleys. In close proximity lie the fertile plains of the Derajat, while to the south runs the famous Powindah caravan route to Central Asia. The very fact that from 1849 onwards the British have sought to coerce the inhabitants of Waziristan by means of blockades proves that the country is not self-supporting, and that the tribesmen are soon faced by the grim spectre of starvation. When writers describe the Pathan as having the lawlessness of centuries in his blood, when they state that the plundering of caravans and the raiding of the *daman* have been his occupation from time immemorial, what they really mean is that he has been forced by his environment to play this rôle in the drama of life. Environment has definitely shaped the national character of the frontier tribesmen. It has produced a race of men who are the most expert guerilla fighters in the world; it has made them hardy mountaineers, possessed of great powers of endurance; it has developed in them a freedom born of their wind-swept mountain sides, a hatred of control, and a patriotic spirit approximating to a religion. In the same way the dwellers on the plains have waxed fat and indolent, with the result that they have been at the mercy of their more warlike neighbours. In the cold weather, from November to April, the tribesmen enter British India to engage in agricultural pursuits and for the purpose of trade. In April they receive their allowances, after which they return to their hills. For this reason, "the political barometer of the North-West Frontier is always more nearly at 'fair' in April than at any other season of the year".[1] Therefore, the hot season, when no hostages remain in British territory, is the Pathan's opportunity.

Although it is often stated that the economic factor is at the root of almost every frontier disturbance, it is my considered opinion that political propaganda, especially from 1890 onwards, has been the most potent cause of unrest. It has been Afghan intrigues, either instigated directly from Kabul with the full cognizance of the amir, or carried on by his local officials, which have from time to time incited the tribes to rebel against the British Raj. Deserters from British forces, dastardly assassins, murderers and kidnappers of women, raiders and outlaws have been welcomed with open arms in Afghanistan. Anti-British mullahs and discontented *maliks* have been granted rewards and pensions; and *jirgas* from the British side of the Durand line have been entertained at Kabul, where they have been presented with or given special facilities for the purchase of arms to be used against us. The important point to remember is that, had it not been for these intrigues, a certain measure of success would have been our reward in taming these wild tribes and in inducing them to make some sort of effort in the direction of law and order.[2] In the colony of Hindustani fanatics, who for years disturbed the peace of the Hazara border, and who were reinforced by a steady stream of recruits from Bengal and other parts of India, we have a notorious example of anti-British intrigues originating in British territory. As Hunter pointed out, instead of attempting to fight these fanatical outlaws in their mountain fastnesses, we should have crushed the organization by which they were fed.[3]

---

[1] *Secret Border Report*, 1917–18, p. 1.   [2] *Idem*, 1908–9, p. 4.
[3] Hunter, *The Indian Musalmans*, ch. II.

Considerable unrest also resulted from our practice of dealing with the tribes through *arbabs* or Pathan middlemen. This system, the adoption of which was to a certain extent inevitable in the early days of British rule, when our frontier officers were ignorant of the language and customs of the tribes, was one of the evils inherited from our Sikh predecessors. In the year 1877, a raid committed by Bunerwals on the Yusafzai border was traced to the direct instigation of Ajab Khan, a middleman and leading khan of the Peshawar district.[1] In the same year Lord Lytton pointed out the evils of employing these "go-betweens" and recommended as a remedy the personal intercourse of British officers.[2] Twenty years later we find Sir Robert Warburton and Lord Curzon advocating the abolition of this system. Referring to the practice of deliberately fomenting disturbances, Warburton wrote: "My experience of the Asiatic is that he is certain to do so if he can better himself or injure an enemy or rival by so doing".[3] Those whose experience is confined to the West will find it difficult to reconcile this sweeping generalization with the fact that Warburton himself was of Asiatic extraction.

From this brief survey of the chief causes of unrest the extremely complicated character of the frontier problem becomes apparent. Repeated references have been made to the fact that the British have never had and never could have had a uniform policy for the whole frontier zone. To hope for any scheme of this nature is absurd. But, the chief charge which can be laid at the door of British frontier administration is that they have never had, what could be called, a settled policy. In February, 1921, it was pointed out in the Indian Legislative Assembly that the policy of the Government of India had always been one of non-interference in the internal affairs of the tribes, so long as their behaviour did not injure the welfare

---

[1] *Panjab Administration Report*, 1882–3.
[2] *Parl. Papers*, 1878, LVIII (c. 1898), 141.
[3] Warburton, *Eighteen Years in the Khyber*, ch. XIX.

of British subjects in the settled districts.[1] This statement of policy cannot, however, be accepted, for there are many examples of the sacrifice for strategical reasons of the rights and even of the independence of the inhabitants of certain districts. On several occasions the British have annexed tribal territory at the request of the inhabitants. It should, however, be remembered that no plebiscite was ever taken. In every independent tribe, however, there are certain *maliks* who hope to profit by making such an offer. Again, it must not be forgotten that there are two distinct problems calling for solution, that of tribal control and that of imperial strategy. By far the more important is that of adequately protecting India's only vulnerable land frontier. With this object in view roads have been made, railways constructed, and tribal territory annexed. The Government of India may make a declaration to the effect that its past policy has been one of non-intervention: a knowledge of the events of the 'nineties leads one to a very different conclusion.

The truth is that the baneful effect of party politics in this country has prevented the adoption of any consistent and settled frontier policy. With shame be it confessed India has been the sport of English political factions. In a country where, more than anywhere else, continuity and firmness are essential, on an Asiatic frontier where vacillation spells loss of prestige, our administration has been marked by sudden advances and ill-timed retreats. Not only have violent changes in frontier policy been caused by general elections in this country, but the feeling has always existed that a change of Government in England would in all probability lead, if not to a complete reversal, at least to a considerable modification of the policy in vogue. Both the First and Second Afghan Wars became party questions, for which reason the student of Anglo-Afghan relations rarely, if ever, comes across an impartial account. To further party interests innumerable

[1] *Indian Pioneer Mail*, 25 February, 1921.

extremely biased pamphlets were written on the Afghan problem; for this purpose the correspondence of Burnes was presented to Parliament in a garbled form. With this end in view politicians toured the rural districts of England and attempted to interest agricultural labourers in the road to Chitral. Before the fall of Sir Robert Peel's Government in 1835, Lord Heytesbury had been selected to succeed Bentinck as Governor-General of India. One of the first acts of the Melbourne Ministry, of which Palmerston was the Foreign Secretary, was to cancel this appointment on the grounds that Heytesbury, while ambassador at St Petersburg, had been too great an admirer of the Czar Nicholas. For many years after Auckland no British Government dared risk a repetition of the fiasco of the First Afghan War. Fear reigned supreme and paved the way for a ready acceptance of the Lawrence policy of masterly inactivity. This was the state of affairs until the 'seventies, when waves of Russophobia once more began to disturb the face of the waters. In 1874, the Liberals fell from power; Disraeli succeeded Gladstone as Prime Minister, and Lord Salisbury became Secretary of State for India. In order to counteract Russian influence, Salisbury proposed the establishment of British agencies at Herat and Kandahar. Lord Northbrook, the Viceroy, unable to agree to this proposal, resigned office early in 1876. The arrival of Lord Lytton was the signal for a more forward policy, and was followed within the short space of two years by the Second Afghan War. Before British troops had evacuated Afghanistan, Gladstone had become Prime Minister once more, and the Marquis of Hartington had succeeded Lord Cranbrook at the India Office. Disraeli's fall from power was followed by the resignation of Lord Lytton and the appointment of Lord Ripon, who went to India pledged to reverse the policy of his predecessor. The arguments for and against the retention of Kandahar have already been given in the chapter dealing with imperial strategy.

Fortunately, as far as Afghanistan was concerned, a policy was evolved which took the form of a compromise between the Lawrence and Forward Schools. It was evident that neither "masterly inactivity" nor "meddling interference" had proved successful. The one had been a shirking of our responsibilities, the other had led to advances which had bred suspicion in the minds both of the tribesmen and of the amir. Our occupation of Afghanistan from 1839 to 1842 and again from 1878 to 1880 had been merely a military occupation, effective only where it was backed by the presence of armed troops. Even the famous march of Lord Roberts from Kabul to Kandahar in August, 1880, would have been contested by the Afghan tribesmen had not Abdurrahman Khan himself made all possible arrangements with a view to assisting the march of the British forces.[1] In fact, one is led to the conclusion that Abdurrahman Khan turned out to be "a ram caught in the thicket". It was eventually decided to build up a strong, friendly and united Afghanistan as a bulwark against any aggression from the direction of Central Asia. It still behoves British statesmen, now that Afghanistan has become an independent state, to foster friendly relations between the two countries, for there can be nothing in common between Islam and Bolshevism.

Nevertheless, the defence of India from external aggression cannot be left entirely in the hands of diplomatists, especially when history proves that the Afghan alliance and even the stability of the Afghan state is, to say the least, an uncertain factor. While every effort should be made to foster friendly relations between India and Afghanistan, no effort should be spared in perfecting the defence of the north-west frontier. The essential function of any frontier is that of separation. But a good frontier, while serving this useful purpose, should

[1] F.O. 65, 1104. Kabul Diary week ending 8 August, 1880. This diary corroborates the claims made by Abdurrahman Khan in his *Autobiography*, I, 198.

at the same time constitute a line of resistance following as far as possible easily recognized natural features, and avoiding sharp salients and re-entrants. If possible, it should also be an ethnic line, and should not disturb existing boundaries, which although undemarcated are recognized as definite boundaries by the local inhabitants. In addition, it should avoid breaking existing lines of communication. There can be no doubt that the perfect frontier, which satisfies all these requirements, does not exist upon India's north-western borders.

What then is the true frontier of India, and what is our best line of defence? The north-west frontier of India is not represented by any particular boundary line: it is a zone or belt of mountainous country of varying width, stretching for a distance of about 1200 miles from the Pamirs to the shores of the Arabian Sea. Except where it is traversed by the Khyber, Kurram, Tochi, Gomal, and Bolan passes, it presents an almost impenetrable barrier to any invading foe. North of the Khyber, from the Mohmand country to the almost inaccessible Pamirs, which the Chinese call the "half-way house to heaven", although numerous passes exist, they can be placed outside the pale of strategical considerations, for over many miles of this stupendous barrier the eagle alone can wing its solitary flight. South of the Bolan, from Nushki to the Koh-i-Malik Siah, Baluchistan is protected by dreary wastes and uncompromising stretches of desert. The vulnerable portion of the frontier, therefore, lies between Peshawar and Quetta. To protect this area, military strategists are almost unanimous in the opinion that it is necessary to hold both the eastern and western extremities of the five main mountain passes. But it is equally true that the immense sums, which have been spent in fortifying our only vulnerable land frontier, would have been spent in vain, if any foreign power were allowed to establish itself in the Persian Gulf. British predominance in the Gulf is essential for the safety of the Indian Empire. Were Russia, for example, allowed to build a naval base on the shores of the Gulf, and if by any chance the British ceased to be supreme on the high seas, it would not be necessary for Russia to invade India by way of Afghanistan: the north-west frontier would be outflanked. It is therefore to be hoped that British statesmen will always act in accordance with the policy laid down by Lord Lansdowne in 1903.

We should regard the establishment of a naval base, or of a fortified port, in the Persian Gulf by any other Power as a very grave menace to British interests, and we should certainly resist it with all the means at our disposal.[1]

Although the Indian frontier system is the most highly organized in the world, it is by no means perfect. Tremendous improvements could be effected both in its road and railway systems. For the maintenance of peace and for the purpose of defence good metalled roads, lateral and otherwise, are of paramount importance. Frontier warfare has been completely revolutionized since 1890, and the days when mule and camel tracks sufficed as lines of communication have passed away never to return. Modern conditions demand roads suitable for mechanical transport. So far as possible these roads should be doubled, one for heavy traffic, the other for mule and camel convoys, because innumerable delays occur when the only available road is blocked by long strings of camels driven by Indians with Oriental ideas of punctuality. The construction of these roads will facilitate the pursuit of raiding gangs, further the interests of commerce, and lead to increased mobility. On the other hand, it can be argued that they will need constant repair, and will be extremely vulnerable, especially where there are bridges and culverts. In the same way, not only should more railways be constructed, but the existing lines should be doubled. What is needed more than anything else is a double line from Lahore to Peshawar.

[1] *Parl. Debates*, Lords, 5 May, 1903.

The frontier problem is not solved, the book of frontier war is not closed, but the British could have found a solution long ago. They could have made a solitude and called it peace; they could have followed the example of the Germans in South-West Africa and indulged in a wholesale smashing of tribal rights; they could have adopted the methods of General Skobeleff in his campaigns against the Akhal Tekkes, and massacred the frontier tribesmen. Then it could have been truthfully said that the last vestiges of border turbulence had disappeared. But, on the whole, we have been merciful; and, it is only necessary to compare British methods with those of their predecessors, the Sikhs, to recognize how humane British policy has been, and to understand how much progress has been made in this tedious process of taming the wild caterans of *Yaghistan*. Under the Sikhs, the Hindu borderers held their village lands under a ghastly system, known as the "Tenure of Blood": as yearly rent they had to hand over a hundred Pathan heads. In the early years of British rule murders were daily occurrences in the Peshawar district. This is no longer the case. On the contrary, under the British, tribal rights and customs have been respected; no attempts have been made to tamper with the religious beliefs of the tribesmen; and every effort has been made to conciliate our trans-frontier neighbours. Considerable success has been experienced in establishing a stable government in certain parts of tribal territory, especially where the tribes live under hereditary chiefs, as is the case in Chitral, Dir, and Amb. But amongst democratic communities, sectional jealousies have frustrated our efforts. There have been periods when peace has reigned supreme, but the sinister effect of Afghan wars and Afghan intrigues has shattered the edifice that has been building for years. Were it not for Afghan and other political intrigues the local problem of tribal control would have been solved long ago. Even in spite of these intrigues the work of civilization has made steady progress, the growth of trade has tended to foster friendly relations with the tribes, and, where once all was desolate, rich crops are now gathered. One is therefore led to the conclusion that the hope of permanent peace on the frontier lies in the spread of civilization both in Afghanistan and on the Indian borderland; and in the removal of an aggressive Russia.

Appendix A

A SELECT BIBLIOGRAPHY

The history of the Indian borderland lies buried in Secret Border
Reports, Administration and Intelligence Reports, in the Records
and Public Correspondence of the Panjab Government, in Parliamentary Papers, Settlement Reports and Gazetteers. My indebtedness to these sources has been specifically acknowledged in
footnotes. Use has also been made of the Persian and Russian
records at the Public Record Office in so far as they throw light
upon the history of Afghanistan, the advance of Russia in Central
Asia, and the problem of imperial strategy.

I. RECORDS (Unpublished)

Public Record Office.

The proceedings of Russia in Central Asia and the history of
Anglo-Afghan relations from 1858 to 1885 will be found in the
series F.O. 65, volumes 867–79, 901–4, 926–30, 956–8, 989–92,
1028–34, 1060–71, 1097–1105, 1128–32, 1150–5, 1171–5, 1202–13,
1235–52.

Much detailed information concerning the Seistan and Kalat
arbitrations and the Perso-Afghan frontier between 1869 and
1878 will be found in the series F.O. 60, volumes 385–94, and 417.
Volumes 392–4 inclusive contain papers relating to the Seistan
boundary dispute and the Goldsmid award. F.O. 248, volumes 7,
9, 90, 91; F.O. 249, 11, 14; and F.O. 251, 35 deal with the early
Persian missions; the French menace of the early nineteenth
century; the importance of an expedition to the Persian Gulf as a
means of coercing Persia; the origin of the First Afghan War,
1839–42; and the correspondence between Burnes and the
Government of India, 1837–8.

India Office.

The chief sources for the history of the Indian frontier are the
Secret Border Reports in the Political Department to which I have
had access.

II. RECORDS (Published)

Aitchison, C. U. *Treaties, Engagements and Sanads*, vol. xi. 1909.
Baluchistan Agency Reports. (Published annually.)
Baluchistan Code. 1914.
British Documents on the Origins of the War, 1898–1914 (ed. Gooch and Temperley). Vol. i, 1927; vol. iv, 1929.

Government of India Reports:

Barrow, E. G. *Tirah and Afridi Question*. 1881.
Davies, R. H. *Report showing relations of British Government with Tribes on N.W.F. of the Punjab*, 1855–64. 1864.
Edwardes, H. B. *Notes on the Valley of Kuram, and its People*. 1857.
Hervey, Capt. *Report on District of Sibi*. 1879.
Mason, A. H. *Report on the Hindustani Fanatics*. 1895.
Military Intelligence Reports on Afghanistan. 1879–82.
Report of the North-West Frontier Enquiry Committee (Bray Report). 1924.
Report on Pamir Boundary Commission. 1897.
Report on Tochi Pass into Dawar Valley. 1879.
Reports on Afghanistan. 1879–82.
Reports and Correspondence (1868–69) *relating to measures for maintaining peace and security on the Sind, Punjab and Baluch Frontiers*. 1869.
Scott, G. B. *Report on the Tirah Country*. 1880.
—— *Report on the country of the Mohmands*. 1880.
Taylor, R. *Memo. on the Dera Ismail Khan District*. 1852.
Temple, R. C. *Report showing relations of British Government with Tribes on N.W.F. of the Punjab*, 1849–55. 1856.

Meyendorff, A. *Correspondence Diplomatique du Baron de Staal* (1884–1900). 2 vols. 1929.
Moral and Material Progress of India. (Published annually.)
North-West Frontier Province Administration Reports. (Published annually.)
Panjab Administration Reports, 1850–1900.
Panjab and North-West Frontier Code. 3 vols. 1928–9.

Panjab, Selections from Public Correspondence of:

Lumsden, H. B. *Report on Yusafzai District*, vol. i. 1853.
—— *Report on the Eastern Khuttuks*, vol. i. 1857.
Memo. on the Dera Ghazi Khan District, vol. iv. 1860.
Pollock, F. H. *The Teree Khuttuks*, vol. i. 1857.
Udny, R. *Report on the trans-border trade of Bannu District*, N.S. xviii. 1882.

Panjab, Selections from Records of:

Bruce, R. *Notes on the Dera Ghazi Khan District and Tribes*, No. ix. 1871.
Cavagnari, P. L. N. *Report on Syads of Tira*, No. xi. 1875.

Minchin, C. *Memo. on Beloch Tribes in Dera Ghazi Khan*, No. III. 1869.
Plowden, T. C. *Papers relating to state of affairs in Swat*, No. XIV. 1877.
Urmston, H. B. *Notes on the Bannu District*, No. I. 1869.
Warburton, R. *Report on certain Frontier Tribes*, No. XIV. 1877.

Parliamentary Papers:
Afghanistan: 1839, XL; 1840, XXXVII; 1843, XXXVII.
Sind: 1843, XXXIX; 1854, XLIX.
Burnes's correspondence: 1859, XXV, 7.
North-West Frontier: 1864, XLIII.
Kalat: 1873, L.
Central Asia: 1873, LXXV, C. 699; C. 704.
Kalat: 1877, LXIV, C. 1807; C. 1808.
North-West Frontier: 1878, LVIII, 46; C. 1898.
Central Asia: 1878, LXXX, C. 2164.
Afghanistan: 1878–9, LVI.
Quetta and Central Asia: 1878–9, LXXVII.
Kandahar: 1880, LIII.
Central Asia: 1880, LXXVIII, C. 2470.
Afghanistan: 1881, LIII, C. 2457.
Kandahar and Khyber pass: 1881, LXX, C. 2776; 2811; 2852; 3090.
Central Asia: 1881, XCVIII, C. 2798; 2802; 2844; 3032.
Afghanistan: 1882, XLVIII, 118.
Central Asia: 1882, LXXX, C. 3136; 1884, LXXXVII, C. 3930.
Central Asia (Merv, Panjdeh, etc.): 1884–5, LXXXVII, C. 4387; 4388; 4389; 4418.
Central Asia (Afghan Boundary): 1887, LXIII, C. 5114; 5235.
——— : 1888, LXXVII, C. 5254; 5518.
Black Mountain: 1888, LXXVII, C. 5561.
Orakzai and Black Mountain: 1891, LIX, C. 6526.
Hunza-Nagar: 1892, LVIII, C. 6621.
Pamirs Agreement: 1895, CIX, C. 7643.
Chitral: 1895, LXXII, C. 7864; 1896, LX.
Bashgal Valley Boundary: 1896, LX, C. 8042.
Kafiristan: 1896, LXI, 262.
North-West Frontier: 1898, LXIII, C. 8713; 8714.
——— : 1901, XLIX, Cd. 496.
Mahsud-Waziri Operations: 1902, LXXI, Cd. 1177.
Afghanistan: 1905, LVII, Cd. 2534.
Anglo-Russian Convention: 1908, CXXV, Cd. 3750; 3753.
North-West Frontier: 1908, LXXIV, Cd. 4201.
Third Afghan War: 1919, XXXVII.

PELLY, LEWIS. *Views and Opinions of General John Jacob.* 1858.
Records of Scinde Irregular Horse. 2 vols. 1853–6.

III. SECONDARY WORKS

The books specially recommended are indicated by an asterisk.

ADYE, J. M. *Indian Frontier Policy.* 1897.
—— *Sitana: Mountain Campaign.* 1867.
AFGHAN WAR. *The Second. Official account.* 1908.
*AGHLAB, SYED MUHAMMAD HUSAIN. *Nairang-i-Afghan.* 1904.
AITCHISON, C. U. *Lord Lawrence.* 1916.
AITKEN, E. H. *Gazetteer of Sind.* 1907.
ALI, AMIR. "Afghanistan and its Ruler." *Nineteenth Century Magazine,* LXI. 1907.
ANDREW, W. P. *Our Scientific Frontier.* 1880.
—— *India and her Neighbours.* 1878.
ANONYMOUS. *Invasions of India from Central Asia.* 1879.
Anthropometric data from N.W. Borderland. 1909.
ARCHBOLD, W. A. J. "Afghanistan, Russia and Persia." *Cambridge History of India,* vol. v.
*ARGYLL, DUKE OF. *The Eastern Question,* vol. II. 1879.
BADEN-POWELL, B. H. *The Land Systems of British India,* vol. II. 1892.
*BALFOUR, B. *Lord Lytton's Indian Administration.* 1899.
BARRON, C. A. *Settlement Report of the Kohat District.* 1907.
BARROW, E. C. *The Peshawar Border of the Punjab.* 1884.
BARTLETT, E. A. *Shall England Keep India?* 1886.
BAXTER, W. E. *England and Russia in Asia.* 1885.
BELL, E. *The Oxus and the Indus.* 1874.
BELLEW, H. W. *Afghanistan and the Afghans.* 1879.
—— *An Inquiry into the Ethnography of Afghanistan.* 1891.
—— *General Report on Yusafzais.* 1864.
—— *North-West Frontier and Afghanistan.* 1879.
—— *The Races of Afghanistan.* 1880.
—— *Kafiristan and the Kafirs.* 1879.
—— *Political Mission to Afghanistan.* 1862.
—— "A new Afghan Question." *J.U.S.I.I.* vol. x, No. 47. 1880.
BEYNON, W. G. L. *With Kelly to Chitral.* 1896.
BIDDULPH, C. E. *Our Western Frontier of India.* 1879.
BIDDULPH, J. *Tribes of the Hindoo Koosh.* 1880.
BIRD, W. D. *Some Principles of Frontier Mountain Warfare.* 1909.
BLACK, C. E. D. *Geographical Notes on the Work of the Afghan Boundary Commission.* 1886.
BOLTON, H. N. *Settlement Report on the Dera Ismail Khan District.* 1907.
BOUILLANE, DE LACOSTE. *Autour de l'Afghanistan.* 1908.
BOULGER, D. C. *England and Russia in Central Asia.* 2 vols. 1879.
*—— *Central Asian Questions.* 1885.

BOULGER, D. C. "The Chances of Habibullah." *Contemporary Review*, vol. LXXX. 1901.

—— "A Russian Representative at Cabul." *Contemporary Review*, vol. LXXXIII. 1903.

—— "Our Relations with Afghanistan." *Contemporary Review*, vol. CXVI. 1919.

—— "The Waziri Object Lesson." *Contemporary Review*, vol. CXVII. 1920.

*BRAY, D. *Ethnographical Survey of Baluchistan.* 2 vols. 1913.

*—— *Life History of a Brahui.* 1913.

—— *Census of Baluchistan.* 1913.

*BRUCE, R. I. *The Forward Policy and its Results.* 1900.

BRYDGES, H. J. *Account of the Transactions of H.M.'s Mission to the Court of Persia in the years* 1807–11. 2 vols. 1834.

*BUCHAN, J. *Lord Minto.* 1925.

BUCKLE, G. E. *Life of Disraeli*, vols. V and VI. 1920.

BURNES, A. *Cabool.* 1842.

*BUTLER, W. *Life of Sir George Pomeroy Colley.* 1899.

CALLWELL, C. E. *Tirah.* 1911.

Causes of the Afghan War. 1879.

CHELMSFORD, LORD. "The Defence of India." *Asiatic Quarterly Review.* 1893.

CHIROL, V. *The Middle Eastern Question.* 1903.

*CHURCHILL, W. *The Story of the Malakand Field Force.* 1916.

COLLEN, E. H. H. *The Defence of India.* 1906.

—— "Our Position on the N.W.F. of India." *Empire Review.* 1901–2.

COLQUHOUN, A. R. *Russia against India.* 1900.

—— "Afghanistan: the key to India." *Asiatic Quarterly Review.* 1900.

COLVIN, A. "Indian Frontiers and Indian Finance." *Nineteenth Century Magazine.* 1895.

—— "The Problem beyond the Indian Frontier." *Nineteenth Century Magazine.* 1897.

COLYAR, DE H. A. *Candahar: our right to retain it.* 1881.

CONWAY, W. M. *Climbing and Exploration in the Karakorum Himalayas.* 1894.

CORY, A. *The Eastern Menace.* 1881.

COTTON, S. *Nine Years on the North-West Frontier of India* (1854–63). 1868.

CREALOCKE, H. H. *The Eastern Question and the Foreign Policy of Great Britain.* 1878.

*CURZON, G. N. *Russia in Central Asia.* 1889.

—— *A Recent Journey in Afghanistan.* 1895.

—— *The Pamirs and the Source of the Oxus.* 1896.

*—— *Speeches* (1898–1905). Ed. Sir Thomas Raleigh. 1906.

*—— *Frontiers.* 1907.

—— "The fluctuating frontier of Russia in Asia." *Nineteenth Century Magazine.* 1889.

DACOSTA, J. *A Scientific Frontier.* 1891.

*Dames, M. L. *The Baloch Race.* 1904.

*—— "The Barakzai Dynasty." *Numismatic Chronicle*, vol. VIII. 1888.

Dane, L. W. *Final Report and Settlement. Peshawar District.* 1898.

*Darmesteter, J. *Chants Populaires des Afghans.* 1888–90.

—— *À la frontière Afghane.* 1888.

Davies, C. C. "The Amir and the Frontier Tribesmen." *Army Quarterly.* April, 1926.

—— "Lord Curzon's Frontier Policy." *Army Quarterly.* January, 1927.

—— "An Imperial Problem." *Army Quarterly.* October, 1927.

—— "Coercive Measures on the Indian Borderland." *Army Quarterly.* April, 1928.

—— "British Relations with the Afridis of the Khyber and Tirah." *Army Quarterly.* January, 1932.

Davis, H. W. C. *The Great Game in Asia* (1800–44). 1918.

D. B. *Our Afghan Policy and the Occupation of Candahar.* 1880.

Deane, H. A. "Note on Udyana and Gandhara." *Journal Royal Asiatic Society.* 1896.

Dew, A. "Frontier Problems and Defence." *J.E.I.A.* 1924–5.

Diack, A. H. *Final Report on the Revision of Settlement. Dera Ghazi Khan District.* 1898.

Dictionary of Pathan Tribes on the N.W. Frontier. 1910.

Dilke, C. *Problems of Greater Britain.* 1890.

*Dodwell, H. H. "The Exclusion of the French." *Cambridge History of India*, vol. v.

Dorn, B. *History of the Afghans*, translated from the Persian of Neamet Ullah. 1829–36.

Drew, F. *Jumno and Kashmir Territories.* 1875.

Duke, J. *Recollections of the Kabul Campaign* (1879–80). 1883.

*Durand, A. G. A. *The Making of a Frontier.* 1899.

*Durand, H. M. *The First Afghan War and its Causes.* 1879.

—— "The Amir Abdur Rahman Khan." *P.C.A.S.* 1907.

Eastwick, W. J. *Lord Lytton and the Afghan War.* 1879.

*Edwardes, H. *A Year on the Punjab Frontier.* 2 vols. 1851.

—— *Memorials of Life and Letters of.* 2 vols. 1886.

Edwards, H. S. *Russian Projects Against India.* 1885.

Egerton, C. C. *Hill warfare on the N.W.F. of India.* 1899.

*Elphinstone, M. *An Account of the Kingdom of Caubul and its Dependencies.* 2 vols. 1839.

Elsmie, G. R. *Field-Marshal Sir Donald Stewart.* 1903.

—— *Thirty-five Years in the Punjab.* 1908.

Encyclopaedia of Islam, s.v. "Abd-al-Rahmān ('Abdu'r-Rahmān) Khan; Afghans."

Enriquez, C. M. D. *The Pathan Borderland.* 1910.

Farfan, A. J. T. "Mountain Artillery in Waziristan, 1919–20." *J.U.S.I.I.* January, 1921.

FEDOROV, M. P. "Russia and England in Asia." *Russia Review.* 1913.

FERRIER, J. P. *Caravan Journeys and Wanderings in Persia, Afghanistan, Turkistan, and Beloochistan, etc.* 1856.

—— *History of the Afghans.* 1858.

FITZMAURICE, E. *The Life of Granville George Leveson Gower.* 2 vols. 1905.

FORBES, A. *The Afghan Wars.* 1892.

FORREST, G. W. *Life of Sir N. Chamberlain.* 1909.

FORSYTH, T. D. *Report of a Mission to Yarkand in 1873.* 1875.

FOUCHER, M. *Sur la Frontière Indo-Afghane.* 1900.

—— *Notes sur la géographie ancienne du Gandhara.* 1902.

*FRASER, L. *India under Curzon and Afterwards.* 1911.

—— "Arms Traffic." *P.C.A.S.* 1911.

—— "Some Problems of the Persian Gulf." *P.C.A.S.* 1908.

FRERE, H. B. E. *Afghanistan and South Africa.* 1881.

FRONTIER AND OVERSEAS EXPEDITIONS FROM INDIA (*Confidential*):

Vol. I. Tribes North of Kabul River. 1907.

Vol. I. Supplement A. Operations Against the Mohmands. 1910.

Vol. II. Tribes between Kabul and Gomal Rivers. 1908.

Vol. II. Supplement A. Zakka Khel Afridis. 1908.

Vol. III. Baluchistan and the First Afghan War. 1910.

FURON, R. *L'Afghanistan.* 1926.

GARDANE, LE COMTE DE. *La Mission du Général Gardane en Perse.* 1865.

Gazetteers: Baluchistan, 6 vols., 1908: Bannu, 1884, 1907: Dera Ismail Khan, 1884: Hazara, 1884: Kohat, 1884: Kurram, 1908. *Imperial Gazetteer of India.* Provincial Series: Afghanistan, 1908: Baluchistan, 1908: North-West Frontier Province, 1908.

*GHANI, A. *Review of the Political Situation in Central Asia.* 1921.

GODFREY, S. H. "A Summer Exploration in the Panjkora Kohistan." *R.G.S.* XL. 1912.

GOLDSMID, F. J. *Eastern Persia: An Account of the Journeys of the Persian Boundary Commission.* 2 vols. 1876.

GRAY, J. A. *At the Court of the Ameer.* 1895.

GREEN, W. H. R. *The Retention of Candahar.* 1881.

—— "The Great Wall of India." *Nineteenth Century Magazine.* 1885.

GREY, OF FALLODON. *Twenty-Five Years* (1892–1916). 2 vols. 1925.

GRIERSON, G. A. *Linguistic Survey of India,* vols. I, VIII, X. 1921.

—— "Pisaca." *J.R.A.S.* 1905.

—— "On the Languages spoken beyond the N.W.F. of India." *J.R.A.S.* 1900.

GRIFFIN, L. "Chitral and Frontier Policy." *Nineteenth Century Magazine.* June, 1895.

—— "The Late Amir and his Successor." *Fortnightly Review.* 1901.

*HAMILTON, A. *Afghanistan.* 1906.

—— *Problems of the Middle East.* 1909.

*Hamley, E. B. *The Strategical Conditions of our Indian N.W.F.* 1878.
Hanna, H. B. *Indian Problems.* 3 vols. 1895–6.
*—— *The Second Afghan War.* 3 vols. 1899–1910.
Hansard. Chitral Debate. 3 September, 1895.
—— Balfour, A. J. Speech on the Defences of India. 11 May, 1905.
—— *Zakka Khel Expedition.* 26 February, 1908.
—— *India's Frontier Communications.* 31 May, 1921.
—— *North-West Frontier.* 3 May, 1923.
Harlan, J. *A Memoir of India and Afghanistan.* 1842.
Harley, Lieutenant. "The Defence of Fort Chitral." *Fortnightly Review.* July, 1895.
Hastings, E. G. G. *Settlement Report Peshawar District.* 1878.
Hellwald, F. von. *The Russians in Central Asia.* 1874.
Hensman, H. *The Afghan War* (1879–80). 1881.
Hills, J. *The Bombay Field Force* (1880). 1900.
*Holdich, T. H. *The Indian Borderland* (1880–1900). 1901.
—— *The Gates of India.* 1910.
—— "Swatis and Afridis." *Journal Anthropological Instit.* 1899.
—— "The Arabs of our Indian Frontier." *Journal Anthropological Instit.* 1899.
—— "Connection between Kafirs and the ancient Nysaeans of Swat." *R.G.S.* vol. vii. 1896.
—— *The North-West Frontier Survey.* 1882.
—— "Afghan Claim to Descent from Israel." *Nineteenth Century Magazine.* 1919.
—— "The Influence of Bolshevism in Afghanistan." *New Europe.* 1919.
*Holmes, T. Rice. *Sir Charles Napier.* 1925.
Hoskins, H. L. *British Routes to India.* 1928.
Hughes, A. W. *A Gazetteer of the Province of Sind.* 1876.
—— *The Country of Balochistan, its Geography, Topography, Ethnology, and History.* 1877.
*Hughes-Buller, R. *Census Report, Baluchistan.* 1901.
Hunter, W. W. *Indian Musalmans.* 1872.
Hutchinson, H. D. *The Campaign in Tirah.* 1898.
*Ibbetson, D. *Punjab Ethnography.* 1916.
"Imperial Strategy" (Military Correspondent of *The Times*). 1906.
"India and Afghanistan." A reprint from *The Times* of letters to the Editor and official correspondence. 1878.
**Indian Frontier Organization.* 1920.
*Indian Officer. *Russia's March Towards India.* 2 vols. 1894.
*Innes, J. J. M. *Life and Times of Sir J. Browne.* 1905.
James, H. R. *Settlement Report, Peshawar.* 1865.
James, L. *The Indian Frontier War.* 1898.
Jerningham, H. E. H. *Russia's Warnings.* 1885.

JOYCE, T. A. "Notes on the Physical Anthropology of Chinese Turkestan and the Pamirs." *Journal Anthropological Instit.* vol. XLII.

KALIPRASANNA, DE. *Life of Sir Louis Cavagnari.* 1885.

*KAYE, J. W. *History of the War in Afghanistan.* 2 vols. 1851; 3 vols. 1878.

KEPPEL, A. J. W. *Gun-running and the Indian N.W.F.* 1911.

*KHAN, SULTAN MAHOMED. *The Life of Abdur Rahman.* 2 vols. 1900.

—— *The Constitution and Laws of Afghanistan.* 1900.

KNIGHT, E. F. *Where Three Empires Meet.* 1893.

KRAUSSE, A. *Russia in Asia.* 1899.

LAL, MOHAN. *Life of Amir Dost Mohammed Khan.* 2 vols. 1846.

LANSDELL, H. *Russian Central Asia.* 2 vols. 1885.

—— *Through Central Asia.* 1887.

LATIMER, C. *Census N.W.F. Province.* 1912.

*LEE-WARNER, W. *The Life of the Marquis of Dalhousie.* 2 vols. 1904.

—— "India and Afghanistan (1815–69)." *Camb. Modern History*, vol. XI.

LEIGH, H. P. P. *Settlement Report of Barak Tappa of the Teri Tahsil Kohat.* 1889.

LEITNER, G. W. *Results of Tour in Dardistan, Kashmir, Little Tibet, Ladak, etc.* 1868–73.

—— *On the sciences of language and ethnography, with general reference to the language and customs of the people of Hunza.* 1890.

—— *Dardistan in 1895.* 1895.

LORIMER, J. G. *Grammar and Vocabulary of Waziri-Pashto*, with Appendix on Waziri Characteristics. 1902.

LOW, C. R. *Sir Frederick Roberts.* 1883.

LUMSDEN, H. B. *The Mission to Kandahar.* 1860.

LUMSDEN, P. S. *Lumsden of the Guides.* 1897.

LUSHINGTON, H. *A Great Country's little Wars.* 1844.

*LYALL, A. *The Life of the Marquis of Dufferin and Ava.* 2 vols. 1905.

LYONS, I. G. *Afghanistan the Buffer State.* 1910.

McFALL, C. *With the Zhob Field Force* (1890). 1895.

MACGREGOR, C. M. *Central Asia. Afghanistan.* 1871.

—— *Central Asia.* North-West Frontier. 1873.

—— *Central Asia.* Belochistan. 1875.

—— *Wanderings in Baluchistan.* 1882.

—— *The Defence of India.* 1884.

MACGREGOR, LADY. *Life and Opinions of Sir C. M. Macgregor.* 2 vols. 1888.

MACMUNN, G. "The North-Western Frontier of India To-Day." *Journal Royal Artillery Institute.* 1924.

—— *Afghanistan from Darius to Amanullah.* 1929.

MALLESON, G. B. *History of Afghanistan.* 1879.

—— *Herat: The Granary and Garden of Central Asia.* 1880.

—— *Russo-Afghan Question.* 1885.

MARTEN, J. T. *Census of India*, vol. I, part I. 1921.

MARTENS, M. F. *La Russie et l'Angleterre dans l'Asie Centrale.* 1879.
*MARTINEAU, J. *Life of Sir Bartle Frere,* vol. I. 1895.
MARVIN, C. *The Russian Advance towards India.* 1882.
—— *The Russians at the Gates of Herat.* 1885.
*MASON, A. H. *Expedition against Isazai clans on Hazara Border.* 1894.
*—— *Report on the Hindustani Fanatics.* 1895.
MASSON, C. *Travels in Balochistan, Afghanistan and the Punjab.* 4 vols.
    1842.
MERK, W. R. H. "Afghanistan." *P.C.A.S.* 1913.
MICHELL, J. AND R. *The Russians in Central Asia.* 1865.
MILES, C. W. *The Zakka Khel and Mohmand Expeditions.* 1909.
MILLS, H. W. *The Pathan Revolt in North-West India.* 1898.
—— *The Tirah Campaign.* 1898.
*MORIARTY, G. P. "India from 1833–49." *Cambridge History of Foreign
    Policy,* vol. II.
MUHAMMAD, GHULAM. "Festivals and Folk-Lore of Gilgit." *Asiatic
    Society,* vol. I, No. 7.
NAPIER, W. *Administration of Scinde.* 1851.
NEVILL, H. L. *Campaigns on N.W.F.* (1849–1908). 1912.
NEWTON, LORD. *Lord Lansdowne.* 1929.
NORMAN, H. *All the Russias.* 1902.
NORTHBROOK, EARL OF. *Brief Account of Recent Transactions in Afghanistan.*
    1880.
NOYCE, F. *England, India and Afghanistan.* 1902.
O'DWYER, M. *India As I Knew It* (1885–1925). 1925.
*OLIVER, E. E. *Across the Border or Pathan and Biloch.* 1890.
Operations in Waziristan, 1919–20. 1921.
ORR, G. "Waziristan in 1921." *United Services Magazine.* 1922.
*PAGET, W. H. AND MASON, A. H. *Record of Expeditions against the N.W.F.
    Tribes since the annexation of the Punjab.* 1885.
PARRY, E. G. *Reynell Taylor. A Biography.* 1888.
PATRIOT, SIKH. "The North-West Frontier." *Asiatic Quarterly Review.*
    1898.
PEARSE, H. "Former Campaigns Against the Afridi." *United Services
    Magazine.* 1897–8.
PENNELL, T. L. *Among the Wild Tribes of the Afghan Frontier.* 1909.
—— "Tribes on our N.W. Frontier." *Asiatic Quarterly Review,* vol. XXX.
    1910.
*PLOWDEN, T. C. *Kalid-i-Afghani.* 1875.
*POPOWSKI, J. *The Rival Powers in Central Asia.* 1893.
POTTINGER, H. *Travels in Beloochistan and Scinde.* 1816.
*PRIESTLEY, H. *Hayat-i-Afghani.* 1874.
*RAVERTY, H. G. *Ethnographical Notes on Afghanistan.* 1880–3.
*—— "The independent Afghan or Pathan Tribes." *Asiatic Quarterly
    Review,* vol. VIII. 1893–4.

*RAVERTY, H. G. "Afghan Wazirs and their Country." *Asiatic Quarterly Review.* January, 1895.

RAWLINSON, G. *Memoirs of Sir H. C. Rawlinson.* 1898.

*RAWLINSON, H. *England and Russia in the East.* 1875.

—— "The Afghan Crisis." *Nineteenth Century Magazine.* 1877.

—— "The Results of the Afghan War." *Nineteenth Century Magazine.* 1879.

—— "The Situation in Afghanistan." *Nineteenth Century Magazine.* 1879.

REES, J. D. *Russia, India and Persian Gulf.* 1903.

REPINGTON, COLONEL. *Policy and Arms.* 1924.

*RISLEY, H. *The People of India.* 1915.

*ROBERTS, F. S. *Forty-One Years in India.* 2 vols. 1891.

*ROBERTSON, G. *The Kafirs of the Hindu-Kush.* 1896.

*—— *Chitral.* 1898.

ROBERTSON, W. R. *Official Account of the Chitral Expedition.* 1898.

ROBINSON, G. *David Urquhart.* 1920.

ROMANOVSKI, M. *Notes on the Central Asiatic Question.* 1870.

*RONALDSHAY, EARL OF. *The Life of Lord Curzon,* vol. II. 1928.

*ROSE, H. A. *Glossary of Tribes and Castes of Punjab and North-West Frontier Province.* 3 vols. 1911.

*ROSE, J. H. *The Development of the European Nations,* chs. XIII–XIV. 1914.

ROUIRE. *La Rivalité Anglo-Russe au XIXᵉ siècle en Asie.* 1908.

—— "Les Anglais et l'Afghanistan." *Revue des deux mondes.* March, 1906.

ROUTH, G. M. "Waziristan in 1921." *J.U.S.I.I.* January, 1922.

SAUSMAREZ, C. DE. "Notes on the Bazar Valley Expedition." *Royal Artillery Journal,* vol. XXXV.

SHADBOLT, S. H. *The Afghan Campaigns* (1878–80). 2 vols. 1882.

*SHADWELL, L. J. *Lockhart's Advance Through Tirah.* 1898.

—— *North-West Frontier Warfare.* 1902.

*SHAND, A. I. *General John Jacob.* 1900.

SIMOND, C. *Les Russes aux portes de l'Inde.* 1885.

SINGH, LEHNA. *Census, North-West Frontier Province.* 1922.

SKRINE, F. H. AND ROSS, E. D. *The Heart of Asia.* 1899.

SLESSOR, A. K. *Tirah.* 1900.

—— "Why the Afridis Rose." *United Services Magazine.* 1899–1900.

SMITH, R. BOSWORTH. *Life of Lord Lawrence.* 2 vols. 1885.

STEIN, A. *Report of Archaeological Tour with the Buner Field Force.* 1898.

—— *Report of Archaeological Survey Work in N.W.F. Province.* 1905.

*—— *Serindia,* vol. I. 1921.

—— *On Alexander's Track to the Indus.* 1929.

STUMM, H. *Russia in Central Asia.* 1885.

SYKES, P. *Sir Mortimer Durand.* 1926.

TATE, G. P. *The Frontiers of Baluchistan.* 1909.

—— *The Kingdom of Afghanistan.* 1911.

TEMPLE, R. C. *Men and Events of My Time in India.* 1882.
—— "The Afghans and Mainotes." *J.U.S.I.I.* 1880.
THOMSON, H. C. *The Chitral Campaign.* 1895.
THORBURN, S. S. *Bannu or Our Afghan Frontier.* 1876.
—— *Settlement Report, Bannu.* 1879.
—— *Asiatic Neighbours.* 1894.
*THORNTON, T. H. *Sir Robert Sandeman.* 1895.
TOYNBEE, A. J. *Survey of International Affairs: The Islamic World since the Peace Settlement,* vol. I. 1927.
TRINKLER, E. *Through the Heart of Afghanistan.* 1928.
TROTTER, L. J. *The Earl of Auckland.* 1893.
—— *Life of John Nicholson.* 1897.
TUCKER, H. *Settlement Report of Dera Ismail Khan.* 1872–9.
—— *Settlement Report, Kohat.* 1884.
TUPPER, C. L. *Treatise on Punjab Customary Law,* vol. II. 1881.
UJFALVY, M. "Mémoire sur les Huns blancs." *L'Anthropologie,* vol. IX. 1898.
VAMBÉRY, A. *Central Asia and the Anglo-Russian Frontier Question.* 1874.
—— *The Coming Struggle for India.* 1885.
—— *Western Culture in Eastern Lands.* 1906.
VIGNE, G. T. *Visit to Ghuzni, Kabul and Afghanistan.* 1840.
VYSE, G. W. *Southern Afghanistan and the N.W.F. of India.* 1881.
WALKER, P. F. *Afghanistan.* 2 vols. 1885.
WALLACE, D. M. *N.W. Frontier of India.* September, 1897. MSS. Mackenzie Wallace Collection. Cambridge.
*WARBURTON, R. *Eighteen Years in the Khyber* (1879–98). 1900.
*WATSON, H. D. *Hazara Gazetteer.* 1907.
*WATTEVILLE, H. G. DE. *Waziristan,* 1919–20. 1925.
*WHEELER, S. *The Ameer Abdur Rahman.* 1895.
WHITE-KING, L. "History and Coinage of the Barakzai Dynasty of Afghanistan." *Numismatic Chronicle.* 1896.
WOLF, L. *Life of Lord Ripon.* 2 vols. 1921.
WOOD, J. *Journey to the Source of the River Oxus.* 1872.
*WYLLIE, J. W. S. *Essays on the External Policy of India.* 1875.
*WYLLY, H. C. *From the Black Mountain to Waziristan.* 1912.
YATE, A. C. *England and Russia Face to Face in Asia.* 1887.
—— "The Visit to India of Amir Habibullah Khan." *Asiatic Quarterly Review.* 1907.
*YATE, C. E. *Northern Afghanistan.* 1888.
—— "Baluchistan." *P.C.A.S.* 1906.
YAVORSKI, J. L. *The Russian Mission to Kabul.* 1885.
YOUNG, K. *Scinde in the 'Forties.* 1912.
YOUNGHUSBAND, F. E. *The Relief of Chitral.* 1895.
YOUNGHUSBAND, G. J. "The Permanent Pacification of the Indian Frontier." *Nineteenth Century Magazine.* 1898.

Appendix B

FRONTIER EXPEDITIONS, 1849–90

Year	Tribe	Commander	Troops employed	British casualties
1849	Baizais	Lt.-Col. Bradshaw	2300	51
1850	Kohat pass Afridis	Brig. Sir Colin Campbell	3200	94
1851	Miranzai tribes	Capt. J. Coke	2500	5
1851–2	Mohmands	Brig. Sir Colin Campbell	1597	9
1852	„	„	600	10
„	Ranizais	„	3270	40
„	Utman Khels		2200	18
1852–3	Darwesh Khel Waziris	Major J. Nicholson	1500	28
1853	Hassanzais	Lt.-Col. Mackeson	3800	18
1853	Hindustani Fanatics		2000	Nil
„	Shiranis	Brig. J. S. Hodgson	2795	Nil
1854	Adam Khel Afridis	Col. S. B. Boileau	1740	39
1855	Mohmands	Col. S. J. Cotton	1782	17
1855	Aka Khel Afridis	Lt.-Col. J. H. Craigie	1500	34
„	Miranzai tribes	Brig. N. B. Chamberlain	3766	15
„	Rabia Khel Orakzais		2457	15
1856	Turis	„	4896	8
1857	Yusafzais	Major J. L. Vaughan	3015	40
1859	Khudu Khels and Hindustani Fanatics	Major-Gen. Sir S. J. Cotton	4877	35
1859–60	Kabul Khel Waziris	Brig.-Gen. Sir N. B. Chamberlain	5372	20
1860	Mahsuds	„	6796	361
1863	Hindustani Fanatics	„ (later Major-Gen. J. Garvok)	9000	908
1864	Mohmands	Col. A. Macdonell	1801	19
1868	Bizoti Orakzais	Major L. B. Jones	970	55
„	Black Mountain Tribes	Major-Gen. A. T. Wilde	12,544	98
1869	Bizoti Orakzais	Lt.-Col. C. P. Keyes	2080	36

Appendix B (*continued*)

Year	Tribe	Commander	Troops employed	British casualties
1872	Dawaris	Brig.-Gen. C. P. Keyes	1826	6
1877	Jowaki Afridis	Col. D. Mocatta	1750	11
1877–8	,,	Brig.-Gens. C. P. Keyes and C. C. G. Ross	7400	61
1878	Utman Khels	Capt. W. Battye	280	8
,,	Ranizais	Major R. Campbell	860	Nil
,,	Utman Khels	Lt.-Col. F. H. Jenkins	875	1
,,	Zakka Khel Afridis	Lt.-Col. F. F. Maude	2500	11
,,	Powindahs, Sulaiman Khels, and others	Col. H. F. M. Boisragon	640	13
1879	Zakka Khel Afridis	Lt.-Col. F. F. Maude	3750	18
,,	Mohmands	Capt. O'M. Creagh and Major J. R. Dyce	600	24
,,	Zaimukhts	Brig.-Gen. J. A. Tytler	3226	5
1880	Mohmands	Brig.-Gen. J. Doran and Col. T. W. R. Boisragon	2300	5
,,	Bhittannis	Lt.-Col. P. C. Rynd	721	5
1881	Kabul Khel Waziris	Brig.-Gen. J. H. H. Gordon	800	Nil
1881	Mahsuds	Brig.-Gen. T. G. Kennedy	8531	32
1887	Bunerwals	Col. Broome	460	5
1888	Black Mountain tribes	Brig.-Gen. J. McQueen	9416	82

Appendix D

AN EXAMPLE OF TRIBAL ORGANIZATION
The Orakzai Tribe

Clans	Sections	Factions	Sect
Ismailzai	Rabia Khel	Samil	Sunni
	Akhel	Gar	,,
	Mamazai	Samil	,,
	Khadizai	,,	,,
	Isa Khel	,,	,,
	Sada Khel	,,	,,
Massuzai	Landaizai	½ Gar	,,
	Khwaja Khel	½ Samil	,,
	Alizai	,,	,,
Lashkarzai	Alisherzai	Samil	,,
	Mamuzai	Gar	,,
Daulatzai	Firoz Khel	Samil	,,
	Bizoti	,,	,,
	Utman Khel	,,	,,
Muhammad Khel	Bar Muhammad Khel	Gar	Shiah
	Abdul Aziz Khel	,,	,,
	Mani Khel	,,	,,
	Sipaya	,,	,,
Sturi Khel or Alizai	Bara Sturi Khel	,,	½ Shiah, ½ Sunni
	Tirah Sturi Khel	,,	,,
Hamsaya Clans	Ali Khel	,,	,,
	Mala Khel	Samil	Sunni
	Mishti	,,	,,
	Sheikhan	,,	,,

Appendix E

GLOSSARY

Afghan be iman, the faithless Afghan
arbab, middleman
badal, revenge
badmash, scoundrel
bania, Hindu shopkeeper, merchant
bar, hill
begar, forced labour on roads (*corvée*)
bhang, intoxicating drink
chalweshtis, Mahsud tribal police
chaprassi, messenger
charra folk, Powindahs seeking employment in the Derajat
chauk, platform near village mosque
daftar, share
daman, skirt of the hills (plain)
dartoche, carpenters
dasht-i-amwat, the desert of death
Derajat, Dera Ismail Khan
do-ab, between two rivers
doms, musicians
durbar, reception
fakir, priest; without status
fateha, prayers for the dead
feringhi, foreigner. It has a prejudicial significance
gur, crude, native sugar
hamsaya, vassal, protected
hujra, guest-house
ilaka, district
inam, reward
jast, headman
jehad, holy war
jezail, matchlock
jezailchis, tribal levies armed with jezails

jirga, council of tribal elders
jizya, poll-tax on non-Muslims
kach, stretch of alluvial land
kafila, caravan
kafir, unbeliever
Kafiristan, land of unbelievers
kanungo, land-revenue official
khasanne, see *vesh*
khel, clan
kichan, dirty
kirris, Powindah encampments
kohistan, mountainous country
kotal, pass
kulale, potters
kuz, plain, lower
lakh, 100,000
lashkar, large tribal force
malik, headman
mawajib, subsidy
Mehtar, ruler of Chitral
melmastia, open-handed hospitality
Muharram, Muhammadan festival in commemoration of the martyrdom of Hussain, the grandson of the Prophet
mullah, priest
naib, deputy
nanawatai, right of asylum
nullah, river-bed
Pakhtana, the Pakhtu-speakers
Pakhtunwali, Pathan code of honour
panchayat, council of "five", council of Elders, heads of families, formerly the managing body in every "landlord" (joint) village:

now applied to any body of arbitrators

pardah, curtain, veil

patwari, village official who surveys, keeps the accounts and records

raghza, plateau overlooking a valley

rahzan, war-leader of the Marri Baluch

Raj, Power

Sarkar, Government

Sipah Salar, Commander-in-Chief

sirdar, chief

spin, white

tahsil, sub-collectorate of a district

tahsildar, in charge of a *tahsil*

takht, throne

tangi, defile

tappa, division of tribal land

taqqiâh, Shiah doctrine of concealment of real religious convictions to avoid persecution

tezi dogs, hounds

thums, rulers of Hunza and Nagar

tiakhor, personal servants

tirni, grazing dues

tor, black

tumandar, headman or chief

Turizuna, Turi customary law

ulus, body of Mahsud tribe

Ur Jast, head of Kafir tribal council

vesh, periodical redistribution of land. See *khasanne*

yaghistan, land of the unruly

zai, son of

zamin, land

zan, woman

zar, gold

Appendix F

ISLAM AND TOLERATION

This is a subject of great difficulty, for the practice has varied with individual rulers and at different times. There is a passage in the Koran which clearly enjoins toleration; that a person should not be persecuted for his opinions. The policy of the Tartar conquerors, Chengiz Khan and Timur, was one of extreme political intolerance but one of religious toleration. This was followed by the Turks both in Europe and Asia. The Turk regarded a Muhammadan as a superior person to anyone who was not a follower of the Prophet. A Mussulman was entitled to serve in the army and could rise to any office in the state, except that of Sultan. In pursuance of this policy, during their conquests in Europe, the inhabitants were left in enjoyment of local government and religious toleration, but were as a rule excluded from posts in the army and state.[1] The massacre and oppression of Christians was due not primarily to a desire to attack their faith, but to punish political conspiracy; and, in fact, the Armenians, Greeks and others had usually been involved in some kind of political conspiracy with external Christian powers. This policy was pursued fairly systematically by the Turks.

The application of a similar policy in India appears to have varied very much with the personal characters of the rulers. Akbar, for example, was an advocate of toleration. According to the Jesuit Fathers, who resided for many years at his court, the one exception to his policy of *sulh-i-kul* (universal toleration) was his treatment of Muhammadans, who appear to have been subjected to petty persecution. Aurangzeb, on the other hand, was extremely bigoted and wholly intolerant. Akbar's policy it will be seen was a great deal more enlightened than that pursued normally by the Turks.

The Turkish position, and one apparently most in accordance with the Koran, is half-way between these two extremes. It may be compared roughly with the position inaugurated by the

[1] Temperley, H. W. V., *History of Serbia*, 1919, pp. 110–11.

Toleration Act of 1689 in England. Islam is recognized as a sort of state religion, and other faiths are tolerated and their holders allowed civil rights and private worship. They are, however, denied political privileges and prevented from serving in the army.

The Afghan rulers seem to have been generally intolerant, and, in the case of the inhabitants of Kafiristan, have forcibly converted them to the Muhammadan faith. On the other hand, colonies of Sikhs, the members of which are allowed to worship in their own way, are to be found in Afghanistan. Nevertheless all Hindus residing in Abdurrahman's dominions were forced to pay the *jizya* (poll-tax on non-Muslims).[1] The proclamation of a *jehad* has been used by Afghan amirs against unbelievers, that is, against non-Muhammadan powers, such as the English and Sikhs, but it is not inconsistent with the theory of limited toleration which appears to be prescribed by the Koran. The theory seems to be there laid down that Islam is justified in waging war against a power which politically supports an alien faith. It should also be remembered that until comparatively recent times most of these powers, and particularly the Christians, declined to tolerate Muhammadanism within their boundaries. At the end of the fifteenth century, for example, the persecution of the Moors and Jews by the Spaniards caused large numbers to leave the country. Thus, in these cases, the *jehad* appears to have been intended to be proclaimed against a persecuting power. But, of course, there have been many occasions when this power has been abused.

[1] F.O. 65, 1252. Report of British Agent at Kabul, 11 September, 1885.

INDEX

Abdali, 44

Abdurrahman Khan (Amir of Afghanistan), 14, 17, 94, 100, 156 ff.; attends the conference of Zimma, 137, 157; receives letter from Lord Minto (II), 148; attitude towards the Durand Agreement, 151, 159 ff.; accession of, 156; granted annual subsidy by the Marquis of Ripon, 157; policy in Kurram, 159; letter to Lord Lansdowne, 160–1; *Autobiography* quoted, 160–1, 165, 184; policy in Kafiristan, 163; responsibility for 1897 risings, 164–5; death of, 165; visits India, 168; attitude towards Russia, 170

Abdurrahman Khels, 91

Aborigines' Protection Society, 163

Adamzadas, 58

Adda Mullah, 92, 139, 150

Administrative boundary, 3, 68, 144, 175; as a line of defence, 6; not an ethnic line, 57, 66, 111

Adye, Sir John, objects to retention of Kandahar, 11; objects to retention of Chitral garrison, 88

Afghanistan, First Afghan War, 2, 8, 136, 149, 155, 182, 183, 184; Second Afghan War, 2, 3, 10, 24, 31, 106, 123, 137, 156, 158, 161, 174, 182, 183, 184; Third Afghan War, 162; danger from Russia, 2, 7, 153–5; base for conquest of India, 7, 153; as a buffer state, 17, 153, 172–3; inhabitants of, 44; asylum for outlaws, 72; anti-British intrigues of its rulers, 87, 93–4, 139, 141, 144–5, 153, 158 ff., 180, 187; history of, 153–73; reopening of Anglo-Afghan negotiations after 1842, 155–6, 158; under Abdurrahman Khan, 156 ff.; delimitation and demarcation of its boundaries, 157–62; and the Anglo-Russian Convention, 168–73

Afghans, origin of, 42–3; Hebraic descent theory, 42–3; meaning of term, 43–4

Afridis, 30, 35, 48, 92, 100, 127, 179; Adam Khel, 25; origin of, 39; bloodfeuds of, 49–50; distribution and characteristics of, 62–3; take part in the 1897 risings, 94–6, 175, 177; British relations with, 135–49

Afzal-ul-mulk, 83

Agha Khan, 59

Agror, 76

Ahmad Shah Durrani, 37

Ahmadzai, 65

Aitchison, Sir Charles, 104 n., 106

Ajab Khan, 181

Aka Khels, 127

Akazais, 76, 77, 79

Akhal Tekkes, 187

Akhels, 74, 76

Akora, 66

Akozais, 60

Alachi, 146

Aladad Khan, 136

Albanians, 42

Alexander the Great, 36

Ali Khel, 76

Ali Masjid, 135, 136

Alizai, 65, 118, 123, 130 n.

Allai, 61, 78

Aman-ul-mulk, 80, 83, 86

Amb, 187

Ambela, 27–8, 76, 175

Amir-ul-mulk, 84

Anambar, 72 n.

Annam, 100

Anti-Slavery Society, 163

Aparytae, 62

Appozai, 72, 73

Arabs, 42

Arbabzadas, 58

Armenians, 42

Aryans, 37

Asmar, 83

Astor, 58